ROYAL HISTORICAL SOCIETY
STUDIES IN HISTORY
SERIES
No. 13

LINLITHGOW AND INDIA

A Study of British Policy and the Political Impasse
in India, 1936-1943

Already published in this series

Copies obtainable on order from
Swift Printers, 1-7 Albion Place, Britton Street, London EC1M 5RE

LINLITHGOW AND INDIA

A Study of British Policy and the Political
Impasse in India, 1936-43

Gowher Rizvi

LONDON
ROYAL HISTORICAL SOCIETY
1978

ISBN 0 901050 49 0

The Society records its gratitude to the following, whose generosity made possible the initiation of this series: The British Academy; The Pilgrim Trust; The Twenty-Seven Foundation; The United States Embassy's Bicentennial funds; The Wolfson Trust; several private donors.

Printed in England
by Swift Printers Ltd
London, E.C.1.

For
Abboo and Amma,
who are no more

CONTENTS

ACKNOWLEDGEMENTS

Like any author writing his first book, I am indebted to many people. Two persons to whom I owe most, and in more ways than words can express, are Sir Edgar Williams and Dr A.F. Madden - they have been my friends, tutors, guides and benefactors. This work is as much theirs as mine.

I would also like to record my special gratitude to Dr I.J. Catanach, Mr J.P. Cooper and Dr T. Raychaudhuri for teaching me much that I did not know; to Professor R.J. Moore for quickening my interest in Linlithgow and from whose works I have drawn heavily; to Margherita and Pietro Barolo and to my brothers and sisters for their kindness and encouragement; and to Lady Williams under whose hospitable roof this book took final shape.

Without the help of friends and teachers this work could scarcely have been completed. I owe grateful thanks to Dr W.C. Beaver, Dr R. Bingle, Dr A.M. Chowdhury, Professor J. Gallagher, Dr K. Hossain, Dr M. Kabir, Dr K.M. Mohsin, Dr G. Krishna, Professor W.D. McIntyre, Professor W.H. Morris-Jones, Dr G. Pandey, Mr W. Rahman, Dr S. Sarkar, Mr I.M. Stephens, Mr R.J. Stooke, Mr D. Thomson and Sir Kenneth Wheare.

I must also thank Anna Barnett, Marieke Clarke and Julian Tonks for help with proof reading and index; and Barbara Bellerby for assistance with typing.

Many have contributed to the making of this book. The Rhodes Trust, by electing me to a scholarship, made possible the research for my D.Phil. thesis; the University of Canterbury in New Zealand appointed me to a Research Fellowship which enabled me to rewrite the book in its present form; and the ever generous assistance of the Beit Administrators and Rhodes Trustees helped me to complete my work.

And finally, I owe a profound debt of gratitude to my wife, Agnese, for her support, understanding and loving care during the many months when this book was under preparation.

G.R.
Rhodes House, Oxford
2 August 1978

ABBREVIATIONS

IAR	*Indian Annual Register* (Calcutta, 1936)

India Office Library (IOL)

Eur. D.596	*Erskine Papers:* Papers of John Francis Ashley, Lord Erskine (1895-1953) as Governor of Madras, 1934-40.
Eur. D.609	*Zetland Papers:* Papers of Lawrence John Lumley Dundas, second Marquess of Zetland (1876-1961) as Secretary of State for India, 1935-40.
Eur. E.240	*Templewood Papers:* Papers of Samuel John Gurney Hoare, 1st Viscount Templewood (1880-1959) as Secretary of State for India, 1931-5.
Eur. E.251	*Hallett Collection:* Papers of Sir Maurice Garnier Hallett (1883-1969) as Governor of Bihar, 1937-9 and of the United Provinces, 1939-45.
Eur. E.278	*Reid Papers:* Papers of Sir Robert Neil Reid (1883-1964) as Member of the Executive Council of Bengal, 1934-37; acting Governor of Bengal, 1938 and 1939; Governor of Assam, 1937-42.
Eur. F.97	*Brabourne Papers:* Papers of Michael Herbert Rudolph Knatchbull, 5th Baron Brabourne (1895-1939), as Governor of Bombay, 1933-7, Governor of Bengal, 1937-9, and Acting Viceroy and Governor-General of India, June to October 1938.
Eur. F.115	*Haig Papers:* Papers of Sir Harry Graham Haig (1881-1956) as the Home Member of the Executive Council of the Governor-General of India, 1932-4; and the Governor of the United Provinces, 1934-9.
Eur. F.125	*Linlithgow Papers:* Papers of Victor Alexander John Hope, second Marquess of Linlithgow (1887-1952) as the Viceroy and Governor-General of India, 1936-43:

India Office Records (IOR)

L/E/9	Economic and Overseas Department Collections.
L/I/1	Information Department Files.
L/PO	Private Office Papers.

x

1

INTRODUCTION

On 6 August 1935 the following announcement was issued from 10 Downing Street:

> The King has been pleased to approve the appointment of the Most Hon. the Marquess of Linlithgow . . . to be the Viceroy and Governor General of India in succession to the Right Hon. the Earl of Willingdon.[1]

The announcement caused little surprise. To many members of the British ruling classes Linlithgow seemed an ideal choice; for some, his previous experience even produced an element of inevitability in the appointment. Yet this impression was altogether false. Sheer chance played no small a role in Linlithgow's selection for the premier proconsulship in the British empire.

Linlithgow had, indeed, acquired a profound and specialized knowledge of India's political and constitutional problems. By presiding in 1933-4 over the long-drawn-out deliberations of the Joint Parliamentary Select Committee on Indian Constitutional Reforms, he acquired the experience which many felt had established his claim to the 'gaddi'. Yet this role had arisen quite unexpectedly. Originally Lord Peel, a former Secretary of State for India, had been selected to preside over that Committee, but could not take the chair owing to an attack of phlebitis a few hours before the opening of the meeting. The government of the day would have been fair game for the 'diehards' amongst the Conservatives, who were bent upon discrediting the proceedings, if it had had nobody to propose to the chair. On the spur of the moment, Sir Samuel Hoare, the Secretary of State for India, had decided in favour of Linlithgow, a choice no doubt influenced by Linlithgow's record as chairman of the Royal Commission on Agriculture in India between 1926 and 1928. Musing on 'the unexpected workings of chance', Sir Samuel wrote:

> If Peel had not been immobilized by phlebitis, Linlithgow would not have been chairman, and if Linlithgow had not been chairman, he would have been given no opportunity to exhibit the qualities that subsequently made Baldwin recommend him for the Viceroyalty.[2]

Although Linlithgow was apparently the favourite choice, Lord

1 *The Times,* 7 Aug. 1935.
2 Viscount Templewood, *Nine Troubled Years* (London, 1954), pp. 89-90.

Zetland and Sir John Anderson (later Viscount Waverley) both coveted the position. There is reason to believe that Sir John was seriously considered, but there was no doubt in Anderson's own mind that the 'gaddi' would go to Linlithgow, 'the distinguished Marquess' — as indeed it did.[1]

When Baldwin became Prime Minister in June 1935, he narrowed the choice to two men, Linlithgow and Zetland, and selected the man he knew better. Baldwin was Linlithgow's political patron and had first launched him on a political career. In 1922 he had appointed Linlithgow a Civil Lord of the Admiralty, and when the first Labour Government was formed in 1924, he made him deputy chairman of the Conservative and Unionist Party organization. Linlithgow was subsequently offered the chairmanship of the party in 1926 but declined as he was then engaged in the inquiry into Indian Agriculture. Baldwin now offered his protégé first pick of accepting either the Viceregal Lodge or the India Office. Linlithgow chose to be Viceroy, fired as he was with the ambition to see the implementation of the 1935 Act; his father had launched the federation in Australia, and now he had an opportunity to preside over the same process in India.

The new Viceroy was forty-nine. Victor Alexander John Hope, as he was christened, was born at Hopetoun on 24 September 1887. He was the eldest son of the seventh Earl of Hopetoun, afterwards the first Marquess of Linlithgow and the first Governor General of Australia. He succeeded as the second Marquess in 1908 at the age of 21. During the first world war Linlithgow, an active territorial, saw action on the western front. He was mentioned in despatches and got the OBE. His connection with India began through an interest in agriculture. In 1924 he refused the governorship of Madras, but his involvement in India and imperial affairs remained keen;[2] he first made direct contact with India as chairman of the Royal Commission on Agriculture in India from 1926 to 1928. For this he was well qualified by his background. The Hopetoun laird, one of the bigger land-owners of Scotland, had in 1923 served as chairman of a departmental committee on the Distribution of Prices of Agricultural Produce, and a year later of the Meat Advisory Committee of the Board of Trade. He now brought his agricultural experience to bear on the Indian inquiry. The result was a masterly survey which for many years remained the main source of information and guidance on the

---

1 J.M. Wheeler-Bennett, *John Anderson, Viscount Waverley* (London, 1962), p. 165.
2 From 1924 to 1931 Linlithgow was the president of the Navy League.

lives of eighty per cent of the Indian population,[1] a report which sought ways of bettering the peasants' standard of living. Later, as Viceroy, Linlithgow had the opportunity to extend the scope and usefulness of the Imperial Council of Agricultural Research which was set up on the recommendation of the Commission.

After the publication of the White Paper on Indian Reforms in March 1933,[2] based on the work of the three sessions of the Round Table Conference (RTC), a Joint Select Committee of both Houses of Parliament met under the chairmanship of Linlithgow, and produced the monumental report[3] upon which the Government of India Act was based. In the debate on the India Bill of 1934, in the Lords, Linlithgow showed himself to be an informed and convinced exponent of the federal scheme, notably its financial aspect, and made a great impression both by his grasp of broad details and by his dour faith in the 1935 Act.

To those who knew Linlithgow intimately, the hallmarks of his character were reliability, industry and 'conscientious thoroughness'. It was not always easy to fathom him, and only those near enough to him could get a real insight in his character. To his colleagues in Whitehall, Zetland and R.A. Butler, he was 'wise, cautious Hopie', and 'an honest but rigorous man'. Lord Wavell, the Commander-in-Chief of the Indian army (and later Linlithgow's successor as Viceroy) had 'the greatest admiration for Linlithgow' as 'a wise, strong man and very human really'. But others who could not penetrate his natural shyness and 'cold exterior' obtained a somewhat different impression. Ian Stephens, the young Liberal editor of the Calcutta *Statesman,* could not initially find 'rapport with . . .[this] cold, cautious, self-assured aristocrat in fact a Tory'. He found Linlithgow 'outwardly . . . an inscrutable, rather unpleasant figure: stiff, unsmiling; physically very large . . . and in some indefinable way uncouth'. But as Stephens saw more of Linlithgow, he was able to discover the 'pleasing personal glimpses' and admitted that Linlithgow was 'perhaps an over criticized man'. Jawaharlal Nehru, never a good judge of human character, was perhaps unfairly critical: 'Heavy of body and slow of mind, solid as a rock and with almost a rock's lack of awareness'. At the same time he admitted Linlithgow's 'integrity and honesty of purpose'.

Linlithgow's lack of social graces and his large and, as a result of an attack of polio, somewhat forbidding countenance were disadvantageous.

1 Cmd. 3132 (1928). *Report of the Royal Commission on Agriculture in India.*
2 Cmd. 4268 (1933). *Proposals for Indian Constitutional Reform.*
3 *Joint Committee on Indian Constitutional Reform (Session 1933-4): Report.* 2 vols. (HMSO, 1934).

Although Lord Halifax's comment that Linlithgow 'did not really get on human terms with anybody' is unjustified, it must be acknowledged that Linlithgow had little 'gift for establishing personal relationship'. He was, it ought to be mentioned at the outset, a rather oldfashioned British aristocrat, with a public school boy's sense of duty, but lacking in 'political imagination' and 'sensitiveness'. But what he lacked in imagination, he made up in reliability: if he was cautious in movement, he 'planted his feet firmly'.[1]

Linlithgow's Viceroyalty, the longest since Dalhousie's (1848-56), covered a period of special significance. 'No Viceroy has ever been appointed,' wrote *The Times*, 'at a moment at which it is at once so critical and so hopeful'.[2] Few people had any illusions as to the weight of the burden the new Viceroy would have to bear. India stood at the turning point on the road to self-government. The new Viceroy would be the key to the implementation of the Government of India Act which had received the royal assent on 4 August, two days before Linlithgow's appointment. It fell to him to introduce provincial autonomy; to launch the all-India federation; to superintend the separation of Burma from India; and to be the first Crown Representative especially charged with re-shaping the relationship with the Indian states.

In all these matters Linlithgow pressed ahead, but after the outbreak of war in September 1939 he put aside the constitutional questions and devoted himself wholeheartedly to organising India to play her full part in the war. 'The test of his every action,' writes Sir Cyril Philips, 'was the survival of Britain and the empire.'[3]

This book will not explore Linlithgow's achievements in defence and military organization; it may be, however, that his ultimate claim to fame lies there. The Committee of Imperial Defence was still

[1] These impressions of Linlithgow in the order quoted come from Wheeler-Bennett, *John Anderson, Viscount Waverley*, p. 162; Zetland to Willingdon, 22 Nov. 1936, cited in R.J. Moore, 'British Policy and the Indian Problem, 1936-40', in C.H. Philips (ed.), *The Partition of India*, p. 80; Lord Butler, *The Art of the Possible* (London, 1971), p. 50; Sir Penderel Moon (ed.), *Wavell. The Viceroy's Journal* (Oxford, 1973), p. 34; Ian Stephens, *Monsoon Morning* (London, 1966), pp. 78, 194; Jawaharlal Nehru, *The Discovery of India* (Bombay, reprint, 1969), p. 437; Halifax to Templewood, 13 July 1953, cited in Moore, 'The Making of India's Paper Federation, 1927-35', *Partition of India*, p. 55; Philip Woodruff (pseud. Philip Mason), *The Men Who Ruled India: The Guardians* (London, reprint, 1971), ii, 272; B.N. Pandey, *The Break-Up of British India* (London, 1969), p. 157; H.V. Hodson, *The Great Divide* (London, 1967), p. 110.

[2] *The Times*, 8 Aug. 1935.

[3] C.H. Philips and D.M. Wainwright (eds), *The Partition of India, Policies and Perspectives 1935-47* (London, 1970), p.17.

harbouring fears of attack by Russia through the north-western passes; the dangers to the north-east from Japan were ignored. Linlithgow refused to be mesmerized by the traditional fear of the Russians: he was more worried about the defence of Burma and Singapore and apprehensive of a Japanese invasion. At the very outset of his term, in 1936, he tried to impress upon the defence authorities the importance of India's north-eastern frontier and the case for an overland reinforcement route to Burma in an emergency. His forebodings about the defence of Singapore were even more prophetic: 'I believe', he said, 'that our guns in Singapore are facing the wrong way'. But his efforts to persuade the military leaders to change their strategy failed.[1] In 1942 the Allies paid a heavy price for their negligence.

Similarly, in the administrative field, Linlithgow took a closer interest than any Viceroy since Curzon (1898-1905) in every aspect of internal administration: village development, the problem of district administration, recruitment to the Indian Civil Service, archaeology, the improvement of the imperial capital, education, and so forth. He also took measures to stimulate industrial development and production.

This study is concerned with the political and constitutional developments of Linlithgow's Viceroyalty — whatever else may be said, an important aspect of proconsulship — and it is to the background of these developments that we must now turn.

Linlithgow arrived in an India which had for fifteen years been experimenting with a degree of self-government in the provinces. The 1914-18 war had shaken the belief in the stability and permanence of the British *Raj,* and vague expectations of impending changes had encouraged the latent forces of disorder. The demand for constitutional reform was voiced not only by the Indians. Many British, too, were sympathetic to the aspirations of Indian nationalists. The loyal support which many Indians had given during the war demanded some friendly response, and a war in defence of freedom and democracy could hardly be reconciled with Britain's autocratic rule in India. Already in 1909, despite the protestations of their sponsors, the introduction of the Morley-Minto reforms had sown the seeds of parliamentary institutions in India. Further advance towards self-government was called for. Accordingly in August 1917 it was declared that the aim of British policy in India was 'the gradual development of self-governing

---

[1] The above paragraph is largely based on Lord Glendevon's account of his father. See *The Viceroy at Bay: Lord Linlithgow in India, 1936-43* (London, 1971), pp. 26-8, 93-4, 184-5, 201-2, and 243-4.

institutions with a view to progressive realization of responsible government in India as an integral part of the British Empire'.[1]

In contrast to the earlier practice in the case of the older dominions, the British Government had decided to make an explicit declaration of its intentions in India, in order to allay the nationalist misgivings about the ultimate objective of British rule in India. It was the beginning of a policy which Britain may claim to have followed (despite the 'Rowlatt' back-sliding) up to the eventual transfer of power. Prior to the declaration of August 1917, it had not entered into the calculations of many British officials that the creation of a self-governing India would necessarily mean the cessation of British sovereignty in India. Accordingly the nationalistic aspirations of the Indian National Congress, the largest political party in India with a mass following which cut across the religious and regional barrier, had come to be seen as a threat to the permanence of British rule, but a serious danger only in so far as they were likely to be adopted by the whole population. The aloofness of many of the Moslems from any outward association with these aspirations had consequently been viewed with some sympathy.[2] The position, however, was altered with Montagu's declaration in which for the first time official recognition was given to responsible government in India as the goal of British policy. With recognition thus given to the impermanence of British rule, it gradually became clear that Britain would have nothing to gain, at least in the long run, if she attempted to prevent those nationalistic aspirations from being adopted by the whole population. In order to make the task of withdrawal easier, the natural policy for the British would seem to sustain unity and not encourage disunity.

Two years after Montagu's declaration the Government of India Act of 1919 remodelled the central legislature, giving greater weight to the principles of election and representation. In the provinces it introduced diarchy: the principle of ministerial responsibility. Certain departments of the government were entrusted to Indian ministers who were responsible to the provincial legislatures.[3]

The proposals fell short of the demands of the nationalists. Congress, while admitting that the reforms represented 'an advance in some directions', declared them to be 'disappointing and unsatisfactory'. Even if on their intrinsic merits the reforms might have been accepted, a split developed between Congress and the government.

1 Cmd. 9109 (1918). *Report on Indian Constitutional Reforms.*

2 Mss. Eur. F.125/9/19 (Linlithgow's Collection), Zetland to Linlithgow, 9 May 1940. IOL.

3 Cmd. 9109, pp. 134-7.

Three events in 1919 and 1920 stirred Indian political opinion deeply: first, the adoption of the Rowlatt bill extending the war time controls on seditious activities; second, the 'Jalianwalabagh massacre', where several hundred Indians were killed and over a thousand injured in the course of soldiers' firing to disperse a political gathering; and third, the announcement of the Treaty of Sèvres, which threatened to dismember the Ottoman Empire — an action which many Indian Moslems considered to be an attack on their religion, since the Turkish Sultan was also regarded as the Caliph of Islam.

It was in this situation that Mohandas Karamchand Gandhi proposed a campaign of 'non-violent non-cooperation' against the British Government. The result was the opening of a new chapter in the history of Indian nationalism. The Congress, under Gandhi's influence, was soon transformed from a loosely organized body of limited membership into a mass movement whose organization spread downwards to the villages. After 1920, the lowest level Congress association elected the delegates to the next highest, and so on to the level of the Provincial Congress Committee (PCC). Theoretically, the Congress was a democratic organization with clear links between the leaders and members in the villages. But this was not so in practice, for, if the principal aim of independence was to be pursued, the supreme executive body of the Congress - the All India Congress Committee (AICC) - needed to have sufficient authority to overrule sectional interests. Congress organization therefore included distinct channels by which that authority could send its instructions to the lowest level.

The Congress represented a broad national front; it was not a tightly organized party. It united under its umbrella articulate lawyers, wealthy traders, and illiterate peasants, western educated élites, orthodox Hindus and nationalist Moslems. Broadly speaking there were two main divisions: 'moderates' or 'Gandhi-ites' and 'modernists' or 'extremists'. These words are not precise, for they suggest that 'Gandhism' was something conservative, which it was not. But it certainly differed from the radicalism of the West, and an uncertain religious and metaphysical tinge about it did not fit in with the scientific spirit. The so-called 'modernists' were a motley group: socialists of various kinds who talked of science and progress. They also included the Communists.

In trying to analyse the various elements in the Congress, the dominant position of Gandhi must always be remembered. His relationship with the Congress is difficult to define in conventional terms. There were periods when he withdrew from active leadership, or even from formal membership. Yet for nearly three decades he remained its undisputed leader, its 'permanent super-president'.

All Indians, however, were not united in their support for Congress policies. The Congress, which had the clearly defined objective of winning India's independence, had no such clear-cut programme for achieving its goal. More particularly, it had no plan for combatting the suspicions of the Indian Moslems, who constituted about twenty-three per cent of India's population. Although there is no denying that, despite differences in religion, the two main communities, Hindus and Moslems, had lived for centuries in a harmony that was broken only infrequently, the Congress did not adopt measures to allay the dormant prejudices of the Moslems, prejudices upon which the Moslem League (ML) subsequently played with disastrous effects. The reforms of 1909, by requiring communities to vote separately according to their faiths, had poisoned the atmosphere with communalism and encouraged the formation of political parties on religious lines, thus undercutting the support of a secular party like the Congress. Montagu and Chelmsford (and later the Simon Commission) had recognized the evils of this system; nevertheless, the Montagu-Chelmsford reforms of 1919, and later Ramsay McDonald's Communal Award,[1] gave it further extension.

The government tried to justify separate electorates on the grounds that Moslems (like certain other groups) were not only a minority but also a politically backward community, lagging behind the Hindus in education, wealth, political organization and leadership. In order to bring them up to the level of Hindu development, the British felt obliged to arrange for separate electorates in the hope that in course of time their necessity would disappear. The nationalists, however, suspected that separate electorates were intended to strengthen the British hold over India: the growth of communalism would weaken nationalism.

The Congress leaders appeared to be divided about how to combat communalism. Nehru believed that a concentration on economic issues would undercut the communal leaders whom he regarded as 'relics of feudalism'. But Gandhi, who had a dominant voice in the formulation of Congress policies, sought to fight communalism, not by eliminating religion from politics, but by framing a political programme based on religious unity; an example was his alignment of the Congress

---

1 The Communal Award, announced in April 1932, gave separate electorates and reserved seats for Muslims, Europeans, Sikhs, Indian Christians and the Anglo-Indians, and weightage to the minorities. See Cmd. 4147 (1932). *East India (Constitutional Reforms): Communal Decision.*

with the Khilafat movement (a protest against the impending overthrow of the Ottoman Caliphate after the first world war). But thanks to the leanings towards Hindu revivalism found among many of the lesser Congress leaders, the Congress failed to convince the Moslems of its secular ideal. Mere assurances of religious toleration or cultural freedom could not allay the Moslems' suspicion of what had essentially become a political problem. It was not an easy task for the Congress to win over Moslem leaders who realized that, politically, they had more to gain by relying on the British than by compromising with the Congress. In the early 1920s the Moslem League was temporarily over-shadowed by the Khilafat Committee. For years it remained a tiny élitist clique.

The congress was also opposed by a section of the Hindus. Elements within the Hindu orthodoxy had formed the Hindu Mahasabha and resisted the Congress on the grounds that it unduly favoured Moslems. A section of the Scheduled Castes, led by Dr B.R. Ambedkar, dissatisfied with their treatment by the Congress, had also formed their own organization. The more radical groups, such as the Communists, attacked the Congress policies as weak and vacillating. Conversely, the National Liberal Federation, the members of which had broken away from the Congress when it had started non-cooperation, criticized the policy of civil disobedience for obstructing peaceful progress towards the development of self-governing institutions.

The Princes, who ruled over some 562 States that covered nearly two-fifths of the area of India and contained roughly one quarter of the population, were no less antagonistic to the Congress. Constitutional advance in the 'British' Indian provinces underlined the contrast between the two Indias: Indian India and British India. The Congress claimed that a self-governing British India would inherit the Paramount Power's supremacy over the states; whereas the Princes hoped that the Paramount Power would grant them full internal autonomy and allow them to negotiate future arrangements with the British Indian politicians. The princes' vision resembled that of the Moslems - sovereign states and provinces should agree to arrangements for some sort of federation.

The 1919 Act provided that its working would be reviewed after ten years. The appointment of a statutory commission was therefore not due until 1929. But the Conservative government advanced the date to forestall the possible appointment of a commission by a Labour Government after the 1929 election.[1] The announcement

---

1 S. Gopal, *The Viceroyalty of Lord Irwin, 1926-31* (Oxford, 1957), p. 19.

of the commission's exclusively British membership evoked protests from almost all the political parties in India. Since the commission was to be drawn from the British parliament, Indians could technically not be included. And even if they had been, it would have been difficult to find the right men without making the commission extremely large. Nevertheless, as a protest, all the major Indian parties agreed to draft their own constitution for India. A committee was appointed under the chairmanship of Motilal Nehru which submitted its report in August 1928. It was a genuine attempt to reach the greatest measure of agreement on the political issues and at the same time face the Hindu-Moslem problem squarely.

The appointment of an all-British commission proved to be a tactical error. Lord Irwin, the Viceroy, realized the necessity of making some gesture to dispel the distrust of British intentions and secure Congress's cooperation. The Labour Government which came to office at this juncture approved Irwin's scheme, which was twofold: first, he proposed that members of the British parliament and representatives of British India and the Indian States should meet in a conference to discuss the Simon report and consider proposals for constitutional advance before those were placed before Parliament; second, he announced that 'the natural issue' of India's constitutional progress was the attainment of dominion status.[1]

The Congress decided to boycott the proposed Round Table Conference because of Irwin's refusal to guarantee beforehand that the purpose of the conference was 'to frame a scheme of a Dominion constitution for India',[2] and instead launched a civil disobedience movement. The British Government, however, went ahead with its plan, and the first conference was held in London from November 1930 to January 1931. It appeared to be a considerable success. The idea of a self-governing federal India was mooted, and the princes agreed to join it. The British Government conceded provincial autonomy and the gradual introduction of responsible government at the centre. Two more conferences followed. Congress had abstained from the first conference, but Gandhi was prevailed upon to attend the second as the sole spokesman of the Congress. His presence complicated rather than clarified the proceedings. Gandhi was adamant that as spokesman for Congress, the only truly national Indian body, he could fairly claim to represent all groups and parties, including the Indian states. The others, however, refused to admit this claim.

1 Sir Maurice Gwyer and A. Appadorai, *Speeches and Documents on the Indian Constitution 1921-47* (Oxford, 1957), i, 228-9.
2 *The Times,* 4 Nov. 1929.

Moreover, in Britain the Labour Government had been replaced by the National Government. Labour's policy of conciliating the Congress was checked after the 1931 election by an overwhelming Conservative majority. The National Government found itself making concessions not so much to the Labour members as to the resurgent 'diehards' on the Conservative right.

In March 1933, the British Government's proposals, resulting from the three sessions of the Round Table Conference, were published in a White Paper; and in April a Joint Select Committee of Parliament was appointed to consider the future constitution of India. The committee was authorized to call into consultation delegates from British India and the states. The Congress did not participate in the discussions. The Select Committee submitted its report in October 1934. On 12 December, a motion that a bill based on the report be submitted to Parliament was carried in the Commons; and on 19 December, the Government of India Bill was introduced. After a stormy debate, lasting in the Commons for forty-three and in the Lords for thirteen days, the Bill was passed, and received the royal assent on 4 August 1935.

The federal aspects of the 1935 Act did not come into operation immediately. The federation could be established only when a sufficient number of rulers of states (representing not less than half the aggregate population of the states and entitled to not less than half the seats allocated to the states in the federal legislature) had signified their desire to accede.[1] Accession of a state to the federation could be effected by an Instrument of Accession executed by its ruler; and with respect to a federated state, the federal authorities could exercise such functions as might be vested in them by or under the Act 'by virtue of his Instrument of Accession, but subject always to the terms thereof'.[2] Once an Instrument of Accession had been executed by the ruler on behalf of 'himself, his heirs and successors', and accepted by the Crown, it permanently and irrevocably limited the ruler's sovereignty to the extent to which he had acceded to the federation. Though accession was to be voluntary, the rulers were expected to agree to the first forty-seven of the fifty-nine items of the federal legislative list, and the terms of accession were to be as uniform as possible for all the states.[3] A ruler might, by a supplementary Instrument of Accession, executed by him and accepted by the Crown, agree to an extension of the functions of federal authorities in relation

1 *Government of India Act, 1935* (Delhi, 1936), Section 5(2).

2 1935 Act, Section 6(1).

3 V.P. Menon, *The Story of the Integration of the Indian States* (London, 1956), p. 35.

to his state.[1] The Instrument of Accession, once accepted, was to be conclusive 'to the extent of Federal authority, both legislative and executive, in relation to that State',[2] and for the purposes of determining federal jurisdiction due judicial notice thereof was to be taken by the Federal Court.[3]

The place of the provinces in the federation was clearly defined in the Act. The reason for treating the provinces and the states differently was explained in the Joint Select Committee's report: '. . . the Indian States are wholly different in status and character from the provinces of British India, and they are not prepared to federate on the same terms as it is proposed to apply to the Provinces'.[4]

Here was an obvious anomaly: a federation composed of disparate constituent units in which the power and authority of the central government would differ from one constituent unit to another. Thus, in the British Indian sphere of the proposed federation, the whole field of legislative activity was mapped out by the Act between the federal legislature in British India and the provinces of British India, and residual powers were to be vested either in the federal legislature or the provincial legislatures at the discretion of the Governor General; on the other hand, in the case of the states, the federal powers alone were enumerated and the residuary powers remained with the states. Even so, the states were not required to accede to all matters specified in the federal list; their acceptance of the various entries in this list could be made subject to such limitations as might be specified in the Instruments of Accession. Unlike the provinces, they were also to have concurrent jurisdiction over specified matters in the federal list, subject to the overriding power of the federal legislature.

In the executive field too, the authority of the federation, in its application to the states, was to be correspondingly circumscribed. The executive authority of the federation was to be further limited by the rulers' reservation of the executive powers in their Instrument of Accessions, for which authority was found in Section 8 (1) (c) (ii) of the Act. List 1 in the Seventh Schedule of the Act contained several matters with regard to which it was not expected that any of the states would federate, for which reason those subjects would be a federal concern in the British Indian provinces. This implied the

1 1935 Act. Section 6(3).

2 J.P. Eddy and F.H. Lawton, *India's New Constitution: A Survey of the Government of India Act, 1935* (London, 1938), p. 32.

3 1935 Act, Sections 204 and 207.

4 *Report of Joint Committee on Indian Constitutional Reforms, 1933-34* (henceforth *JSC Report*) (HMSO, 1934), para. 29.

introduction into the Act of a theory of division of powers in the federal sphere itself. Such an arrangement was contrary to the division of judicial, executive and legislative powers found in other federal constitutions.

In the fiscal field also, there was no uniformity between the states and the provinces. The states were required to accede on a limited number of items such as customs and excise duties, corporation and salt taxes. Even here there was a concession to the demands made by the states that they should contribute to the federal finances by indirect taxation only, which enabled the states to pay an appropriate contribution in lieu of such taxes as corporation tax. The unevenness of financial burdens was inevitable in a scheme where some of the federating units retained control over federal subjects such as armed forces or railways.

Similar limitations applied in the judicial sphere. The jurisdiction of the federal court was extremely restricted. The internal constitution of the states was of no concern to the framers of the 1935 Act. The Instruments of Accession were to guarantee the sovereignty and the rights of the rulers, and the Act excluded from its purview the 'rights and obligations of the Crown in relation to the States'. In fact, despite the provision in the Act authorizing the Governor General to issue directions to the rulers for the enforcement of the federal obligations of the states, it was thought that paramountcy would provide the ultimate sanction for the enforcement of the federal authority in the states. The scheme of 1935 thus lacked many of the essential elements of a federal constitution.

The 1935 Act forms our starting point. The Act sought to maintain the unity of India by federating the multitude of princely states together with the eleven British Indian provinces and by granting responsible self-government to the latter.

The primary aim of this work is to examine the complexities of the constitutional impasse and seek to explain why the attempts at solution failed - the various constraints and obstacles which prevented the political parties from accepting the several offers made by the British Government; conversely, it attempts to explain why the British authorities could not accept all the demands of the Indians. The aim is to provide a documented and analytical account of both the imperial policy and nationalist politics during the Viceroyalty of Linlithgow. This work is not, however, an account of Linlithgow's Viceroyalty.[1]

[1] An account of Linlithgow's viceroyalty is recorded in Glendevon, *The Viceroy at Bay, passim.*

Consequently certain areas of his Viceroyalty, such as administrative and fiscal measures, health, education, agriculture, the separation of Burma from India, or the famine which marred his last year in India - important in themselves but without direct relevance to the main theme - have either been excluded or touched on only briefly. Nor does the study claim to be a comprehensive survey of Indian politics during the period under review. Modern Indian historiography is expanding rapidly, and any attempt to cover the politics of all parts of India might appear rash. Following the lead given by the Cambridge South Asian school, scholars are tending to concentrate on smaller areas - localities, districts and provinces. 'Historians have switched their attention from Imperial fiats to Indian facts, from rambling generalization on the Raj to the concreteness of local studies, from large imprecision to minute exactitude'.[1]

Nevertheless an overall perspective of Indian history can be obtained only at the all-India level, the world of Council Chambers and the all-India Working Committees. The Indian leaders, at the national level at least, had to operate mainly within the constitutional frameworks created by the British. This was true whether they were pressing for further concessions or working in the government. It is for this reason that attention has been focused on Linlithgow. He was the central figure: a supreme liaison officer between the imperial government and the Indians. An understanding of his policy is essential in any analysis of the changing style and content of Indian politics, since the British-imposed constitutional arrangements determined the options of the Indian politicians. Most modern British-Indian historians, in concentrating on an analysis of social changes and political developments, emphasize the limitations imposed by the rulers on political developments, but ignore the forces constraining those rulers. As Dr Judith Brown has pointed out: 'There are studies of Indian politicians struggling with the constraints imposed on them by their society and their rulers, but not of Viceroys and civil servants racking their brains in the early hours'.[2]

This book is intended to contribute to the larger debate on British policy touching the devolution of power in India. The actual transfer of power in 1947 was only a minor part of the full story of the

---

1 Anil Seal, 'Imperialism and Nationalism in India' in J. Gallagher, G. Johnson and A. Seal (eds.), *Locality Province and Nation. Essays on Indian Politics 1870-1940* (Cambridge, 1973), p. 2.

2 Judith M. Brown, 'Imperial Façade: Some Constraints upon and Contradictions in the British Position in India, 1919-35', *Transactions of the Royal Historical Society,* 5th series, vol. 26 (London, 1976), pp. 35-52, see especially pp. 35-6.

demise of the British *Raj*. A study of the period 1936-43 should enable us to see in perspective the events leading to India's independence and the decision to partition the country. It was during this period that attempts were made to implement the carefully drawn 1935 Act which was to fulfil the British political dream of a united and responsibly ruled India. If it had been fully implemented and a responsible government had been established at the centre before the outbreak of the war, the story of the transfer of power in India might have been different. Independence would have perhaps come no later than it did, but partition might have been avoided.

It was during the decisive years, 1936-43, when the British Government was preoccupied with the war, that the Moslem League gained strength, turned against the 1935 Act and committed itself to 'Pakistan'. It will be shown that the failure to solve the war-time constitutional impasse, coupled with Congress's opposition to an all-India federation and its failure to disarm Moslem suspicions, led to the demand for and final emergence of 'Pakistan'. This study will also examine the various obstacles to a swifter transfer of power and the shattering impact of the war on Indian politics.

India's transition from empire to dominion has been the subject of much historical writing but scholars seem to have concentrated their attention mainly on two periods: first, the period from the mutiny in 1857 to the foundation of the Moslem League in 1906; and second, the period after 1942 when Moslem separatism had established a firm foothold. The final phase of the transfer of power (1945-7) has already been covered in detail. Thus we have the excellent, though not entirely unbiased or objective, works of A. Campbell-Johnson, *Mission with Mountbatten* (1951); E.W.R. Lumby, *The Transfer of Power in India* (1954); V.P. Menon, *The Transfer of Power in India* (1957); L. Mosley, *The Last Days of the British Raj* (1961); Sir Penderel Moon, *Divide and Quit* (1961); I. Stephens, *Pakistan* (1963); H. Tinker, *Experiment with Freedom: India and Pakistan* (1967); H.V. Hodson, *The Great Divide* (1967); and Sir Penderell Moon (ed.), *Wavell: The Viceroy's Journal* (1973). Apart from the fact that these works have primarily concentrated on the concluding years of the *Raj*, they suffer from two defects. The authors of most of them have been in some way intimately connected with the events of the period and their interpretation of those events have naturally tended to vary with their preconceptions and past experiences, which, though useful, tends to result in the defence of entrenched positions with passion and is thus not always objective. In addition they either deliberately refrained from detailed references to the sources, or did not have access to government records or various private papers. A book of essays, *The Partition of India. Policies and Perspective 1935-47* (1970) edited by Sir Cyril Philips has attempted to cover the period of Linlithgow's Viceroyalty and contains two detailed studies by Professor Moore. More recently we have R.J. Moore's, *The Crisis of Indian Unity, 1917-40* (1974) and B.R. Tomlinson's, *The Indian National Congress and the Raj, 1929-1942* (1976). Both these are scholarly additions to literature, but the former, despite its title, effectively ends in 1935, and the latter ignores the Moslem League politics, crucial to any understanding of the transfer of power in India.

In the chapters which follow I not only attempt to cover the crucial period 1936-43, but also endeavour to throw some new light on events by using documents hitherto untapped. This was made possible under the new thirty years' rule which came into operation on 1 January 1968, when the India Office records, all departmental files and collections for the period, together with the papers of Linlithgow, the relevant Secretaries of State for India, and others prominently connected with British rule in India became available to students. This book has drawn heavily on the 'private' papers of Linlithgow and Zetland. Lord Curzon had noted that it was in the private correspondence between the Viceroy and Secretary of State that the real history of the régime was to be found. Linlithgow's own experience led him to endorse that judgement:

> It is only in that correspondence that one can record with entire frankness for the Secretary of State the daily ups and downs of the situation here; the clashes of personalities, the emergence of new figures; and the signs of dangers ahead.[1]

Unfortunately access to the private papers of Churchill and Amery, which might have deepened our insight into the problem, has proved impossible.

---

[1]   P.N.S. Mansergh (ed.), *Constitutional Relations between Britain and India, The Transfer of Power, 1942-7*, iv, ix.

2

ELECTION AND PROVINCIAL AUTONOMY: DOMINANCE OF THE CONGRESS.

Lord Linlithgow had arrived in India with a firm determination to implement the new constitution. But he was also anxious, so far as possible, to make the scheme acceptable to all parties. He urged the Indians to 'give these Reforms a fair and reasonable trial . . . and work the constitution in a spirit of tolerance and cooperation, for the honour and good of their motherland'.[1]

After years of investigation and deliberation, the British Government had prepared a constitution which the main political parties had either rejected or acquiesced in only reluctantly. Some parties had hoped to destroy the new constitution and replace it with a new instrument framed by a properly elected constituent assembly; and others, at best, were willing to work the scheme 'for what it is worth'. It was to Linlithgow's credit that he was able not only to persuade the various political parties to participate in the government, but also to demonstrate that the constitution, despite some drawbacks, was capable of being worked.

The British Government announced that the Government of India Act of 1935 would come into force on 1 April 1937. The federal part of the scheme was kept in abeyance as it depended on the fulfilment of the precondition that a sufficient number of Indian States should accede to the proposed federation. Nevertheless it was decided that the implementation of the provincial part of the constitution should go ahead.

Provincial autonomy could not, however, begin to function until a general election to fill the seats in the provincial legislatures had been held. Indian politics were in some confusion. Paradoxically most of the important parties had expressed dissatisfaction with the constitution, and yet all of them eventually resolved to work it at least to the extent of participating in the elections.

The new constitution had not given the 'complete independence' demanded by the Congress. It was not immediately known whether the Congress would reject the constitution completely and revert to non-cooperation, or whether it would participate in the coming

---

1 The Viceroy's address to the Indian Legislatures, 21 Sept. 1936. *IAR* ii, 100; see also V.B. Kulkarni, *India and Pakistan* (Bombay, 1973), pp. 311-12.

elections and use the new constitution as a means to gain its overall aims: the achievement of a *Purna Swaraj* or complete independence. The initial impulse was to have nothing to do with it, but on this question the Congress was by no means united among itself. Officially, it had opposed the new constitution from its inception in 1933-4. The British Government's White Paper of 1934 outlining the essentials of the proposed constitution[1] was condemned by the Congress Working Committee (CWC), which declared that the 'only satisfactory alternative to the White Paper is a Constitution drawn up by a Constituent Assembly elected on the basis of an adult franchise'.[2]

Once the Act had been given the royal assent, however, there was little that the Congress could do to alter its format. The Lucknow session of the Congress held in April 1936 approved the decision to contest the elections, but this did not mean that the Congress had agreed to work the constitution. In an obvious reference to the Viceroy's appeal for cooperation, Jawaharlal Nehru retorted:

> We go to the Legislatures not to cooperate with the apparatus of British imperialism, but to combat the Act and to seek to end it.[3]

The attitude of the Congress towards the constitution was one of militant hostility, and it was in this mood that its members entered upon the election campaign. In April 1936, the Congress Working Committee appointed a parliamentary sub-committee, with Sardar Vallabhbhai Patel as president, to organize the election campaign. But the unity of the party was threatened by internal conflict. There were sharp differences between the socialistic programmes of Nehru and those of the more conservative leaders such as Patel and Rajendra Prasad. Gandhi was afraid that Nehru's radical political and social philisophy, unfolded at this juncture,[4] might precipitate a premature cleavage in the nationalist ranks and thereby jeopardize the Congress's prospects in the forthcoming elections.[5] At the same time Gandhi realized that Nehru was the only leader who could bridge the growing gap between 'Socialism' and 'Gandhism'. As the accepted leader of the Congress 'left wing'[6] Nehru enjoyed the confidence of the radicals; and

---

1 *Proposals for Indian Constitutional Reform*, Cmd. 4268 (HMSO, 1934).

2 *The Indian National Congress, Resolutions 1934-36* (AICC, Allahabad), pp. 19-20.

3 Sir Maurice Gwyer and A. Appadorai (eds.), *Speeches and Documents on the Indian Constitution 1921-47* (London, 1957), p. 386; see also J. Nehru, *India and the World* (London, 1936) pp. 91-2.

4 J. Nehru, *Eighteen Months in India* (Allahabad, 1938), pp. 28-40.

5 A. Singh, 'Is Gandhi's Life Work Ruined?', *Asia* (Oct, 1936), p.627.

6 R. Coupland, *Indian Politics 1936-42* (Oxford, 1943), p. 11.

as Gandhi's favourite he was also acceptable to the 'moderates' in the Congress. He was thus ideally fitted to the task of reconciling the two groups. But more than anything else Gandhi was aware that, apart from himself, Nehru was the only other leader who had a mass appeal and could gather votes. Thus in an astute move Gandhi secured Nehru's re-election to the Congress Presidency.[1]

The Congress, owing to its initial hesitation over its attitude towards the new constitution, had failed to make elaborate preparations in advance. Unlike some other parties and candidates, the Congress had not taken any interest in the enrolment of voters or in the delimitation of the constituencies. At a very late stage an effort was made, particularly in Madras and Bombay, to enrol voters, but with limited success. But the Congress made amends for all these omissions and handicaps by making a direct appeal to the masses, voters and nonvoters alike.[2]

As the date of the election drew nearer, the Congress leaders worked in unity. In August 1936 the All-India Congress Committee (AICC) adopted an election manifesto which repeated that the purpose of sending Congressmen to the legislatures would be, as Nehru had said earlier, 'not to cooperate in any way with the Act, but to combat it and seek an end of it'. The decision with regard to accepting office was postponed, but the manifesto went on to state that, whatever the decision might be on this question, the object in view remained the same — getting the Act repealed. At the same time the manifesto declared (a little illogically) in favour of reforms in the economic, industrial and social fields — promising, for instance, reforms of the system of land tenure and revenue and immediate relief to the smaller peasantry by an exemption from or a substantial reduction of agricultural rent and revenue.[3]

The Congress had a considerable advantage over its opponents. It was the only organized all-India political party, and its parliamentary wing, the *Swaraj* party, was experienced in electioneering and had built up elaborate electoral machinery throughout the country. The Congress had an army of electioneering agents in the towns and villages. Subhas Chandra Bose has described how the party workers in 1920 were organized:

1 S. Gopal, *Jawaharlal Nehru: A Biography* (London, 1975), p. 200; see also H Mukherjee, *The Gentle Colossus — A Study of Jawaharlal Nehru* (Calcutta, 1964), pp. 74-5.

2 K.M. Ashraf, 'The Congress and the Elections', *Contemporary India*, 1st quarter, pp. 146-7.

3 Full text of the manifesto in *IAR*, 1936, ii, 188-91.

> Students responded to the appeal in large numbers ... It was these student-workers who carried the message of Congress to all the corners of the country, who collected funds, enlisted members, held meetings and demonstrations, preached temperance, established arbitration boards, taught spinning and weaving and encouraged the revival of home industries. Without them all the influence of Mahatma Gandhi would not have carried very far.[1]

Most of these student-workers were still available seventeen years later, and their numbers had been augmented to many thousands by the recruitment of enthusiastic young people who welcomed the prominence that politics gave them. They cost very little, having few needs and asking for no more than bare subsistence; and they were now organized and trained by the master hand of Gandhi. It required a herculean effort to organize campaigns, to explain to the newly enfranchized masses, mostly illiterate, the meaning of the ballot boxes, and to select prospective candidates for the Congress election tickets. As proof of their claim to represent a particular constituency, hopeful candidates would refer to their long services in the party as organizers or financiers, but above all to their jail records. To choose one person from several applicants was not an easy task. Luckily for the Congress, Patel as the chief organizer achieved the seemingly impossible with amazing ease.[2]

The Congress placed primary importance on winning the elections. The Congress parliamentary board glossed over any ideological controversies and laid down only three conditions to guide the selection of candidates: that they should have signed the Congress pledge, that they could finance their campaign, and that they had a good chance of winning.[3] In giving party nominations there was no insistence on habitual wearing of *khaddar,* hitherto an essential Gandhian prerequisite. Nor was the nomination limited to those who had been members of the Congress for a prescribed period — indeed many of the Congress nominees had joined the Congress merely in order to get a Congress ticket. In Madras, for example, the Justice Party had suffered from the natural reaction against its long period of office and also from a lack of able leadership. There is little doubt that a number of political aspirants, realizing the weakness of other parties, had jumped on to the Congress bandwagon in order to get an easy run in the election.[4]

---

1 S.C. Bose, *The Indian Struggle* (London, reprint, 1964), p.52.

2 D. V. Tahmankar, *Sardar Patel* (London, 1970) pp. 143-4.

3 Rajendra Prasad, *Autobiography* (Bombay, 1957), p. 427.

4 Dr C. J. Baker gives an interesting account of sudden 'conversions' throughout 1936. *The Politics of South India 1920-37* (Cambridge, 1976), pp. 297-9.

The only Moslem party with some claims to an all-India organization was the All-India Moslem League (AIML).[1] The League, however, could be described as an all-India body only by courtesy: prior to the 1936-7 elections it was in a dormant condition. Muhammad Ali Jinnah, its permanent president, had stayed on in Britain after the second Round Table Conference, and during his absence abroad the party had existed on paper only.[2] During the 1930s the League was neither so communal nor so militant as it was to be in later days: it was an organization of Moslems to protect what were considered to be their special interests, and was not yet committed to the partition of the country on a communal basis. Economically it had little to offer in the way of constructive ideas and had done little for the improvement of the standards of workers and peasants. It was essentially an upper and middle-class organization, wanting an all-India leadership. Its lack of success in becoming a dynamic organization was largely due to the fact that its leadership had been dominated by 'careerists' — professional politicians who felt no particular dedication to their cause. Convenience rather than conviction governed their politics.[3]

The League was dominated by landlords and titled gentry.[4] Its Secretary was Liaquat Ali Khan, a Nawabzada and a Landlord from the United Provinces (UP), while Nawab Ismail Khan, another landlord, was president of the UP *Moslem League*. The Nawab of Mamdot was president of the Punjab *Moslem League*. There were also a sprinkling of knights in the party: Sir Muhammad Saadullah, Sir Khwaja Nazimuddin and Sir Abdoola Haroon were the provincial presidents of the ML in Assam, Bengal and Sind. Landlords represented the largest single group in the ML Council. Out of a total membership of 503, there were as many as 163 big landlords. The Punjab contributed the largest share of 51, followed by the UP and Bengal. Proportionately, Sind's share was the highest in that, of its 25 members, in the Council 15 were landlords.

Jinnah, returning to India from self-imposed exile in Britain in 1935, had immediately set about trying to revitalize the League. At its annual session of April 1936 (the first since that of November 1933), the

1   For a discussion on Moslem politics during this period see Z.H. Zaidi, 'Aspects of the Development of Moslem League Policy, 1937-47', in C. H. Philips and D. Wainwright (eds.), *The Partition of India, Policies and Perspectives 1935-47*, (London, 1970), pp. 247-75. This paper is extremely informative but biassed in a Moslem League direction.

2   K. B. Sayeed, *Pakistan: The Formative Phase* (London, new edition 1968), p. 81.

3   Choudhry Khaluquzzaman, *Pathway to Pakistan* (Lahore, 1961), pp. 137-9.

4   Humayun Kabir, *Muslim Politics 1905-42* (Calcutta, 1942), p. 25; Khaliquzzaman, *Pathway to Pakistan*, p. 137.

Moslem League condemned the federal scheme of the 1935 Act as 'most reactionary, retrograde, injurious and fatal' and 'totally unacceptable', but nevertheless decided to utilize the provincial part of the Act 'for what it is worth'.[1] Jinnah was authorized, like the Congress, to form a central election board for organizing the League's election campaign.[2] With few provincial and district branches, and limited financial and publicity resources,[3] the League gathered itself to go into the elections for the first time on an all-India basis.

The Moslem League election board published an election manifesto which declared that the League stood for 'full responsible government for India'. The social and political objectives outlined in the manifesto were very similar to those of the Congress.[4] Most historians, however, in trying to point out the similarities in these manifestos,[5] have failed to notice the marked conflict between them. In general, the election manifestoes of most parties bore a striking resemblance to that of the Congress, but in detail the Congress manifesto with its socialistic bias stood apart from the rest, the most elementary difference being the League's opposition to any attempt to expropriate private property: it would not interfere with the landed interests, while the Congress was committed to sweeping land reforms. It is essential to bear this in mind, because it was largely because of this difference of approach between the Congress and the League that the rift between the two parties widened. Another striking difference was the League's pledge to 'protect and promote the Urdu language and script', the insinuation being that the Congress was trying to make Hindi the national language of India. The merits of the arguments will be examined later on;[6] here we need only note that the Hindi-Urdu controversy was one of the main factors contributing to bad feelings between the two parties. Similarly the Lucknow Pact of 1916 was hailed as 'one of the greatest beacon lights in the constitutional history of India' and a 'signal proof of the identity of purpose, earnestness and cooperation between the two sections of the people of India'.[7] Again this could be interpreted

---

1   Resolution of the AIML, 11-12 April 1936, Gwyer and Appadorai, *Speeches and Documents*, i, 384-5.

2   R. Coupland, *Indian Politics 1936-42*, p. 13.

3   *Star of India*, (Calcutta) was the solitary English daily of the ML.

4   Text of the Manifesto in *IAR*, 1936, ii, 299-301.

5   Tara Chand, *History of the Freedom Movement in India*, (Delhi, 1972), IV, pp. 224-5 Chaudri Muhammad Ali, *The Emergence of Pakistan* (New York, 1967), p. 27; Coupland, *Indian Politics, 1936-42* pp.11-16; Abul Kalam Azad, *India Wins Freedom*, (Calcutta, 1959), pp. 160-1; Khaliquzzaman, *Pathway to Pakistan*, pp. 156-7.

6   See chapter 5 below.

7   *IAR*, 1936, i, 299.

as meaning that the League solemnly stood by separate electorates, which was one of the central pillars on which the Lucknow Pact was based.

Nevertheless the Moslem League did not openly oppose the Congress: Indeed some of the members of the League continued to be members of the Congress, and Jinnah's election speeches stressed compromise and mutual accommodation between the two parties.[1]

The real opposition to the Congress came from the landed aristocracy who during the era of the Montagu-Chelmsford Reforms had entered the Councils and as subsidiary partners had collaborated with the British in running the government. The big landowners were afraid of the growing radicalism in the Congress and had in some provinces organized themselves into local parties. In the United Provinces they formed the National Agriculturalist Party (NAP) under the leadership of the Nawab of Chhatari. In the Punjab, the landowners had organized themselves into the Unionist Party under the leadership of Sir Sikander Hyat Khan and Sir Chotu Ram. In Madras the Justice Party was reactivated; in Bombay and the Central Provinces Independent Workers' Parties were formed; and in Orissa there appeared the Advanced Party.[2] The purpose of most of these parties was to protect the interest of the landed class by keeping the Congress out of power. The landed aristocracy did not depend for electioneering on popular propaganda, public meetings, speeches and processions. Their mainstay was official support and pressure on the peasant tenants.

There is evidence to suggest that behind the scenes some government officials were supporting the electoral efforts of non-Congress parties, as they had done in the 1934 elections.[3] There were, for example, the activities of the officials of the Court of Wards in the UP.[4] Sir Henry Craik, the Home Member of the Viceroy's Executive Council, claimed that the Court of Wards was a non-official institution. This was not strictly correct. The chairman and the secretary of the Court were government officials; and so were most of the managers of the Estates. *Sarvokars* and *Ziladars* were appointed by the District Magistrate. In the District Board elections these officials of the Court

1   See *Star of India*, 29 July and 24 Aug, 1936.

2   S. M. Ikram, *Modern Muslim India and the Birth of Pakistan* (Lahore, 1965), pp. 252-60; V. V. Balubushevick and A. M. Dyakov, *A Contemporary History of India* (Delhi, 1964), p. 302.

3   G. Pandey, *The Indian National Congress and Political Mobilization in the UP, 1926-1934*, (Oxford, D. Phil. thesis, 1975), p. 200.

4   L/P&J/7/1126, Secretary, Court of Wards to District Officers of UP, 9 July 1936, IOR.

of Wards acted as polling officers. Moreover, the polling booths were usually 'situated within the *Zamindari* and in their [the polling officers'] presence the illiterate tenants found it impossible to vote against a candidate they [the polling officers] were supporting'.[1]

Nor were these instances of official sympathy towards non-Congress parties confined to the lower officials. As early as 1934, Lord Erskine, governor of Madras, assured Sir Samuel Hoare, then Secretary of State for India, that the Congress victory in the elections to the Central Legislature 'may be a blessing in disguise as they will teach the Justicites [i.e. the Justice Party] the importance of good organization', and he hopefully asserted that 'the present contests are no guide at all to the future results in the next provincial elections'.[2] Erskine had tried to rally the non-Congress elements under the banner of the Justice Party in order to put up a united front against the Congress. 'I hope to be able to compose some at least of these quarrels [between the land-lords] in the next few months and then if they will pull together I see no reason why, with the new provincial electorate, they should not be returned again'.[3] Erskine's efforts seem to have been successful. In August he was able to write with satisfaction that the Justice Party had 'woken up' and 'if they can maintain this activity till the first elections under the new Act they should stand quite a good chance of being returned again'.[4]

The governor of the United Provinces, Sir Harry Haig, is also reported to have taken an active part in organizing the National Agriculturalist Party, the party of the landholders. When Linlithgow learnt of it, he was appalled at such indiscreet interference in the elections. Haig, he complained, 'had associated himself throughout the pre-election period (and not always entirely discreetly) with the efforts — or want of them! — of the landlord party in the UP to get them together on a programme and conduct its propaganda'.[5]

The attempt of government officials to encourage the non-Congress

1 *Ibid.* Government of UP to Government of India, Home Department, 29 Oct. 1936. IOR.

2 Mss. Eur. D.596/12 (Erskine Papers), Erskine to Hoare, 23 Nov. 1934. IOL.

3 Mss. Eur. D.596/12, Erskine to Zetland, 5 June 1935. IOL.

4 *Ibid.,* 12 Aug. 1935.

5 Mss. Eur. F.125/161 (Linlithgow Collection), Linlithgow to Zetland, 17 Mar. 1937. IOL. In the same letter Linlithgow revealed that Haig's conduct was nothing new, his predecessor had followed a similar policy; 'I rather think Haig in some measure inherited this tendency to act as party organizer to the landlord party from Hailey; as Hailey . . . inherited it from Harcourt Butler. The great landed proprietors of Oudh have seemed to be a valuable shield against the spread westward of subversive tendencies from Bengal through Bihar'. *Ibid;* see also Khaliquzzaman, *Pathway to Pakistan,* pp. 152-3.

parties was not entirely due to their hostility to the Congress. It was at least partly owing to an underestimation of the Congress's strength among the masses, voters and non-voters alike. Many of the officials had expected that the results of the 1936 elections would be a re-run of the earlier election to the Central Legislature in 1934 in which the Congress had won only about fifty per cent of the general seats. They therefore looked to the provincial parties — the Unionist Party in the Punjab, the Justice Party in Madras, the National Agriculturalist Party in the United Provinces, and the Marathas in Bombay — to stand up against the Congress. Although there seems to have been little doubt in official thinking that the Congress might emerge as the largest single party in several provinces, it was hoped that Congress would have to depend on the various provincial parties in order to form ministries. This was completely mistaken.

The elections to the provincial legislatures under the new constitution were held throughout British India in the winter of 1936-7. The electorate had been greatly enlarged to thirty million men and women. Some 15·5 million or over fifty-four per cent of the voters went to the polls.[1] Voting was assisted by the use of symbols, and in some places with coloured voting boxes, a system which gave advantage to organized parties as against independent and small groups.

Contrary to the expectations of many, when the results were announced the Congress emerged as the majority party in five provinces and was the largest single party in two others. It had won 711 out of 808 general seats.[2] Table 1 gives the position of the Congress in the provincial assemblies.

Of the 38 seats reserved for 'labour', the Congress won 18; of the 37 allotted to landowners and 56 to 'commerce', the Congress obtained four and three respectively.

The Congress showing in the Moslem constituencies was extremely poor. In the 489 Moslem seats the Congress could only muster 58 candidates, winning 26 of which 19 were in the North West Frontier Province (NWFP) alone. Nehru attributed this to the physical limitations of his organization.[3] This was only partly true. Another reason was that, generally speaking, the Congress policy had small appeal for the

1   Balushevik and Dyakov, *Contemporary History of India*, p. 314.

2   The triumph of Congress was even more impressive than these figures indicate, for in the provinces the seats reserved for special interests, and thus not ordinarily open to be contested on the Congress ticket, totalled nearly half of the total strength of the assemblies. The total number of seats in the provincial lower houses was 1585.

3   Kulkarni, *India and Pakistan*, p. 308.

Moslem masses, who were not prepared to leave their security to an uncertain future in the hands of a party which had done very little to win their confidence.[1]

Table 1

PROVINCES	TOTAL NO OF SEATS	SEATS WON BY THE CONGRESS	PERCENTAGE OF TOTAL
Madras	215	159	74
Bihar	152	95	65
Central Provinces and Berar	112	70	62·5
UP	228	133	59
Orissa	60	36	60
Bombay	175	86	49
NWFP	50	19	38
Assam	108	33	30·5
Bengal	250	60	22
Punjab	175	18	10·5
Sind	60	7	11·5

Yet if the Congress polled poorly in Moslem constituencies the Moslem League did not fare nearly as well in those constituencies as it had hoped. Out of 489 Moslem seats, the League captured only 105. Only 4·8 per cent of the Moslems who went to the polls voted for it.[2] It won a substantial number of seats in the Hindu majority provinces of the United Provinces and Bombay, but in the Moslem majority provinces it did not create much of an impression. It failed to secure a single seat in Bihar, Orissa and the NWFP, the latter a predominantly Moslem province. Its performances in the Punjab and Sind, both Moslem majority provinces, were equally dismal, its gain being a single seat in the former and none in the latter. In Bengal the League won only 37 out of 119 Moslem seats. Its performance in Bombay and UP where it won 20 out of 39 and 27 out of 64 Moslem seats respectively were impressive.[3] In the Province of Madras, out of 28 Moslem seats, the League secured 11. These are significant figures which show that in 1937 the League was not a vital force in Indian

1 Z. H. Zaidi, 'Aspects of the Development of the Muslim League Policy, 1937-47', Philips and Wainwright (eds.), *Partition of India,* p. 263.

2 The total number of Moslem votes cast was 7,319,445 and of these only 321,772 were for the Moslem League.

3 Khaliquzzaman's claim that the ML won 29 seats in the UP seems incorrect. Cf. Khaliquzzaman, *Pathway to Pakistan,* p. 186; *Command Paper* 5589 of 1937.

politics. Comparatively speaking, the League won a substantial number of seats in the Hindu majority provinces, but in the Moslem majority provinces it did not create any impression. Table 2 shows the position of the Moslem League in the provincial assemblies.[1]

Table 2

PROVINCE	TOTAL MOSLEM SEATS	SEATS WON BY LEAGUE	PERCENTAGE OF MOSLEM SEATS
Madras	28	11	39
Bombay	39	20	51
Bengal	119	37	31
UP	64	27	42
Punjab	86	1	1·1
Assam	34	9	26·4
NWFP	36	–	–
Orissa	4	–	–
Sind	36	–	–
Bihar	39	–	–
CP	14	–	–

The poor showing by the ML was neither surprising nor unexpected. The League was essentially an urban-based political party and had little or no contact with the masses in 1937. It has been pointed out by Khaliquzzaman that from its birth in 1906 the League's activities were 'always' confined to 'indoor political shows'. He further writes: 'Even its annual sessions were held either in well decorated pandals [stages] or in big halls where a few honourable invitees were allowed by special cards. Mass public meetings were unknown'.[2] In 1937, the year which marked the beginning of the 'parting of the ways' between the Congress and the League, it was claimed by some Congressmen that the Congress had more Moslem members on its rolls than its Moslem rival. It is also perhaps true that Gandhi and Nehru were better known to the Moslem masses than was Jinnah.[3]

1 For these figures see *Returns Showing the Results of Elections in India, 1937,* Command Paper No. 5589. In arriving at precise figures regarding the Moslem League gains in the provincial elections, only those seats have been included which were won by the League candidates. Those won by Independents with Moslem League leanings have been excluded. This has been done because if Independents with League leanings were included in the League total, then the League candidates with Congress leanings in a province like the UP would have to be excluded from the League total.

2 Khaliquzzaman, *Pathway to Pakistan,* p. 137.

3 *The Pioneer* (Lucknow), 26 Sept. 1937.

The results of the elections were astonishing, far exceeding the expectations of the Congressmen themselves and upsetting the calculations of the officials. The surprise of government was well exemplified in the forecasts of Sir Hyde Gowan, the Governor of the Central Provinces. Here the Congress had claimed that it would win 65 out of 112 seats. On 17 December 1936 Gowan had called this 'an incredible boast'. On 4 February 1937 he forecast that they would win 35 seats. By February his estimate was up to 60. On 7 March Gowan reported that the Congress had won 70 seats.[1]

In their estimates, the officials had reckoned without the name of the 'Mahatma', the organizing ability of Azad and Patel, and the army of Congress volunteers backed by financial support from industrial magnates of Bombay and Ahmedabad. It must not be forgotten that for many of the electors the issue was not between rival parties attempting to obtain a majority in the provincial legislatures, but between a supposed candidate of the government and his flesh and blood opponent, the Congress. The electors were mainly illiterate. The town workers were told that work would be lessened and wages increased. The agriculturalists, the mass of the electorate, were promised rent-free land, the liquidation of debts and higher prices for their produce. All this would come if the people voted for the Congress candidate, who was also the nominee of the 'Mahatma'. No device was too extravagant. A Congress worker would heap dry grass at his meeting and light it with fire. 'As this grass burns and disappears, so will your debt disappear'.[2] It is on record that many of the ballot boxes of the Congress candidates were filled not only with votes but also with petitions to Gandhi, as though the ballot box was a sort of postal delivery to the 'Mahatma'.[3]

But these factors alone do not explain the numerous Congress victories. The party's general programme was more positive and constructive than those of its opponents. In agricultural constituencies, where it had been specially successful, it had put forward an extensive programme of rural reforms. The Congress had won its victories on issues which appealed to millions of voters and to many more who had no votes. On the other hand, its opponents were divided and failed to put up a united front. The landed proprietors had not yet

1 J. Glendevon, *The Viceroy at Bay. Lord Linlithgow in India, 1936-1943* (London, 1971), p. 49.

2 Mss. Eng. Hist. C.627, *The Proposed Dominion* by Sir Louis Stuart. Bodleian Library.

3 Lord Erskine, 'Madras and the New Constitution', *Asiatic Review,* (January 1941), p. 21.

learnt that they would have to rely for political organization upon their own efforts and not upon official machinery.

Another factor of no less importance in accounting for the Congress success was Nehru's ability to carry the Congress message to the masses. Professor Brecher sums up Nehru's contribution thus:

> Like an arrow he shot through the country, carrying the Congress message to remote hamlets in the hills and on the plains. He covered some 50,000 miles, using every conceivable means of transport ... All told, about 100,000 persons attended his meetings and millions more lined the route to catch a glimpse of the Congress crown prince.[1]

Nehru's approach to the electors was ideological in the main, with very few references to individual candidates. The Congress election manifesto was explained in simple terms, and a few core themes were stated *ad infinitum:* 'Fight for India's freedom; build the Congress into a mighty army of the Indian people; organize to remove poverty, unemployment and social and cultural degradation'. 'Let every voter, man or woman, do his or her duty to the country and vote for the Congress', was his constant theme. 'Thus we shall write in millions of hands our flaming resolve to be free'.[2] The technique of hammering on a few key objectives was successful in carrying the message effectively to the Indian countryside.

Sir Harry Haig has suggested another explanation for the Congress victory: the sense of change awakened in the villages. The government, which had in the past Agitation opposed the Congress with the weight of its authority, now stood inactive. It was too much to expect that the villager would understand the constitutional necessity for this attitude. 'He felt that the British Raj was weakening, that the Congress was coming, and, as so often happens, threw himself definitely on what seemed to be the winning side'.[3]

The electorate had given the Congress its confidence in ample measure, and the Congressmen were naturally jubilant.[4] The successful operation of the new constitution would largely depend on the Congress's attitude; it was in a position to assume ministerial responsibilities in seven provinces. Therefore as soon as the election results were known, the question of whether or not the Congress would accept

---

1   M. Brecher, *Nehru: A Political Biography* (London 1959), pp. 227-8.

2   D. G. Tendulkar, *Mahatma: Life of Mohandas Karamchand Gandhi* (Bombay, 1951-4), iv, 165.

3   Harry Haig, 'The United Province and the New Constitution', *The Asiatic Review,* (1940), xxxvi, 425.

4   Tara Chand, *History of the Freedom Movement,* iv, 226-9.

office came to a head. The Congress, while it had contested the elections, was still undecided about the acceptance of office, but a decision could no longer be delayed since the British Government had announced its intention of inaugurating the provincial part of the constitution on 1 April 1937.

There were two options open to the Congress in the wake of its electoral victory. The first was to work the constitution and press for such modifications, within the four corners of the Act, as would commend themselves to progressive Indian opinion. This was the policy adopted by the Indian Liberal Party. In doing so the Liberals were acting logically because they were committed to a policy of striving for independence constitutionally. But could the Congress take the same view? The answer, it seemed at first, had to be no. The Congress had long given up its belief in constitutionalism and had embraced direct action by a mass movement as its policy. 'Direct action' and 'constitutionalism' were incompatible. The Congress could not honestly profess its faith in the former if it agreed to accept office. Refusal by the Congress to accept office would have been a natural policy: it would have forced the governors to carry on the administration by the exercise of their emergency powers which were given them under the new Act.

Throughout India a wave of speculation followed the election results. Opinion within the Congress was divided and naturally coloured by local successes or failures. 'The attraction of the Congress in [Madras] ', Dr C.J. Baker confirms, 'depended very much on its potential for capturing the new positions of power that were becoming available'.[1] Congress failure was followed, predictably by strong opposition to the constitution, as, for example, in Bengal and the Punjab, two provinces where the Congress could not have any hope of forming ministries.[2] In provinces such as Bihar, Bombay, Central Provinces and Madras, the views of the delegates tended to reflect a desire to assume office.[3] The UP, the home province of Nehru, despite a Congress majority in the provincial legislature, decided against an acceptance of office.[4]

The All India Congress Committee was thus faced with the problem of placating Congressmen throughout India. But opinion within the Congress Working Committee was itself divided. Gandhi and the

---

1 Baker, *Politics of South India 1920-37* pp. 294-5.

2 *Pioneer*, 19 Feb. 1937.

3 *Leader*, 20 Feb. 1937.

4 A. W. Rixon, 'The Office Acceptance Issue and the United Provinces Congress: February-July 1937', (M.A. thesis, University of Sussex, 1968), pp. 27-8.

'moderates', who seemed to be in effective control of the party, maintained that by accepting ministerial responsibilities the Congress could improve its position in the fight against the new constitution. They argued with some truth that, if the Congress declined to accept office, it would surrender the advantage to the government, or to the parties opposed to the Congress. Many Congressmen believed that, despite its many inadequacies, the constitution could be used to serve the masses. Dr K.M. Munshi, the Congress leader from Bombay, clearly saw such possibilities:

> I had little doubt that, if the Act were worked properly, the transition to full fledged Dominion Status for the whole of India would have been easy, with the executives in the provinces being made responsible to their respective legislature.[1]

Moreover many other, basically 'moderate', men within the Congress were keen to take office: the lure of power is always sweet, and some were genuinely anxious to implement the social and agrarian reforms promised in the election manifesto which, they knew, bore more closely on the lives of the ordinary people than the struggle for constitutional changes and independence.[2] Those who were in favour of accepting office began to press Gandhi to support their effort.[3]

The Madras Congress in particular was anxious to form a ministry and began to flood the AICC with copies of resolutions passed by the various Congress gatherings urging the Congress to accept office.[4] S. Satyamurti had been campaigning for a 'return to a Council strategy' ever since it had been abandoned in 1929; and C. Rajagopalachari, leader of the Congress party in Madras, had stated: 'My own view is that . . . as much benefit should be wrung out of the Councils as possible for strengthening the prestige and position of the Congress'.[5]

But despite their desire to accept office, many Congressmen were genuinely apprehensive and their minds were torn by alternating hopes and fears. They were suspicious of the honesty of British intentions and believed that 'special powers' might be used to keep real power in the hands of the British governors. Allied with this suspicion was the fear that members of the Indian Civil Service might try to obstruct the Congress reform programmes.[6]

1   K. H. Munshi, *Pilgrimage to Freedom* (Bombay, 1967), i, 41-2.
2   Rixon, 'The Office Acceptance Issue', p. 18.
3   Munshi, *Pilgrimage,* p. 43.
4   Baker, *Politics of South India,* p. 314.
5   Rajagopalachari to R. Prasad, n.d., cited in Baker, *Politics of South India,* p. 294.
6   P. J. Griffiths, *The British Impact on India* (London, 1952), p. 337.

Nehru and the left wing group were strongly opposed to taking office, on the grounds that to participate in a British-controlled administration would be a fatal compromise of the Congress position and a betrayal of the nationalist movement. They believed that the Congress would have to bear the odium of forming a government under the constitution without securing real relief for the people; and that the Congress would go the way of the 'moderate parties' by ceasing to be a revolutionary organization.[1] They distrusted the moderate group's cautious 'constitutionalism', and were afraid that, once in office, the ministers would tend to cooperate with the conservative industrial and landlord interests, and would become increasingly hostile towards nationalist agitation. Involvement in reformist activity would mean relegating the freedom struggle to the background. The initiative would thus pass from the masses, and the activities of the Congress would be confined to the limited sphere of the council chambers.[2] Nehru maintained that the whole policy would be inconsistent with the declared policy of entering the legislature only to destroy the constitution. 'To accept office and ministry is to negative our rejection of it and to stand self-condemned'.[3]

A 'National Convention' of the Congress was held at Delhi in March, after the election results had been declared, in order to decide the issue. Nehru urged that the Congress should refuse to accept office, force the Governors to form minority ministries, defeat such ministries by a vote of no confidence (thereby forcing an impasse which would oblige the Governors to resort to 'Section 93')[4] and thus demonstrate the failure of the constitution. Many of the delegates, however, apparently anxious to assume ministerial offices and press ahead with 'constructive work', were little impressed by these somewhat dubious arguments. Thus the Convention at once revealed a sharp division of opinion between the 'moderates' and the 'left wing'. Even amongst the 'moderates' who were willing to accept office, opinion varied regarding the approach to be taken. One section wanted to enter office

---

[1] See Nehru's speeches at Lucknow and Faizpur, *IAR.*, 1936, i, 271-74 and *Ibid.*, ii, 226-28; for the attitude of the Congress Socialist Party (CSP) — the left wing group of the Congress — see S. C. Bose, *The Indian Struggle 1920-42* (London, reprint, 1964), pp. 328-9; H. V. Hodson, *The Great Divide, Britain-India-Pakistan* (London, 1968), pp. 63-4.

[2] Jawaharlal Nehru, *The Unity of India* (London, 1941), p. 60.

[3] *Statesman,* (Calcutta), 16 April 1936.

[4] Section 93 of the 1935 Act provided that if the Governor of a province were satisfied that a situation had arisen in which government could not be 'carried on in accordance with the provisions of the Act', he might, by Proclamation, 'assume to himself all or any of the powers vested in or exercisable by any Provincial body or authority'.

provided an assurance was given by the Governors that they would not use their 'special powers'. The second group held that, since it was believed that the Governors would not wish the Congress ministries to remain in office for a long time, the initial attempt of the Congress ministries should be directed towards ameliorative measures, and that as their work developed conflict with the executive should be precipitated. [1] Both groups, however, were unanimous that the Congress ministries should not cooperate with the Governors but rather attempt to override them, and that, should any Governor invoke his 'special powers' against a ministry, it should resign.

On 18 March, after prolonged discussion, the moderates, backed by Gandhi were able to carry a resolution permitting the acceptance of office. The resolution, however, contained a rider; office would be accepted only if the governors gave an assurance that they would not use their 'special powers' or set aside the advice of the ministers in regard to 'constitutional activities'.[2] This 'conditional clause' was an astute Gandhian device for patching up the differences within the Congress and presenting a united front against the government: the permission to accept office was given to pacify the moderates and the condition was imposed to placate the left wing.

The Congress claimed that by seeking such an assurance from each governor they hoped to develop a sort of 'cabinet convention' whereby the advice of the ministers would prevail in all matters including those which came under the governor's 'special responsibilities'.[3]

It has been said that the Congress leaders did not fully comprehend the working of parliamentary government.[4] Those Indians who were acquainted with the course of British constitutional history ought perhaps to have been able to argue that, as the working of parliamentary government became better understood and operated without friction, the power of the Viceroy acting 'at his discretion' or in his 'individual judgement' would in effect be exercised on the advice of ministers, in spite of the words of the Act which placed them outside the ministerial

---

1 *Statesman,* 4 March 1937.

2 Gwyer and Appodorai, *Speeches and Documents,* i, 392-3; *Statesman,* 18 March 1937.

3 Section 52 (corresponding to Section 12) of the Government of India Act of 1935 laid down that the executive powers of the governors were of three kinds: the first included those to be exercised in the governor's sole discretion; second were those in which the governor was to exercise individual judgement; and third were those in which the governor was required to act upon the advice of the ministers.

4 R. Coupland, *Britain and India 1600-1941* (London, 1948), pp. 83-4.

sphere. The constitution by which Britain is governed, we have always been told, flows not from a legal document, but from a series of conventions in the development of the actual working of the constitution. But this was India, not Great Britain, and the situation was still to some extent a 'colonial' one. In any case, in 1937, Congressmen, even if they understood their British Constitutional history, were too impatient to wait. They wanted full responsibility immediately.

The Congress leaders in the provinces met their respective governors and asked for an assurance which they could make public 'that in regard to constitutional activities of his ministries His Excellency will not use his special powers of interference or set aside the advice of the Cabinet'.[1] There was considerable ambiguity about the phrase 'in regard to their constitutional activities'. The Congress resolution, it will be noted, had the appearance to all intents of leaving it to the judgement of each prospective chief minister to decide whether he could regard the assurances he might be able to obtain from his provincial governor as satisfactory.

In official circles the resolution was interpreted to mean that the Congress might be prepared to accept office. It was also widely assumed in the press and elsewhere that the formula had been so designed as to enable the Congress leaders to satisfy themselves as to the attitude of the governors without requiring from them specific assurances which they could not give. It seemed fairly certain that the Congress would form ministries.[2] Towards the end of March, however, a complete change occurred. The Congress leaders, acting upon instructions from the Congress Working Committee declined to accept office unless they received a specific assurance that the governors would not use their 'special powers'. Many Congressmen were themselves bewildered. The governors were being asked to give an assurance which could not possibly be given without a violation of the constitution. The governors therefore informed the Congress representatives that they could not concede their demands. The negotiations came to an end.[3]

Nevertheless, the reluctance of the Congress party to accept office perturbed Linlithgow who had come to India with the object of implementing the new constitution. The resounding success of the Congress at the polls had confirmed his earlier impression that a policy of repression would not work: the successful implementation of the

---

[1] L/PO/57, Memorandum by Zetland, 'Provincial Ministries in India', 31 March 1938. IOR.

[2] Mss. Eur. F.125/15/92. telegram from Linlithgow to Zetland, 18 March 1937. IOL.

[3] *Ibid.*

1935 Act would largely depend, at least in the short term, on the co-operation of the Congress.[1] His thinking was very similar to that of the 'elder statesman' of Indian officialdom, Lord Meston. 'No indigenous government', wrote Meston, once the election results were known, 'can ever hope to function unless it succeeds in harnessing the energies and enthusiasm of the Congress to the administrative machine'.[2] Linlithgow was therefore reluctant to allow the governors to proclaim Section 93 without first exhausting all efforts to win over the co-operation of the Congress. He hoped that the lure of power and the attractions of 'constructive' work would prove too strong to resist, and that the 'provincial outlook' of the Congress members would make it difficult for the Congress 'high command' to hold their party together on a policy of negation. Furthermore, even if the 'high command' gained a temporary success in that direction, it would still have to reckon with the electors who had been liberally fed on the promises of benefits to come; in the next elections the Congress could well find itself at a disadvantage against any party with a constructive programme of its own.[3] Linlithgow therefore stressed in private letters to the governors that, rather than take any precipitate action, they should make every effort to secure the cooperation of the Congress: 'We should at no stage lay ourselves open to any suggestion that we have failed to give the utmost possible help in working or trying to work the parliamentary system'.[4]

The provincial governors were temporarily able to overcome the difficulty created by the Congress's refusal to accept office by forming minority ministries from among the non-Congress elements,[5] and by postponing the summoning of the legislatures.[6] In the non-Congress provinces, namely, Bengal the Punjab, Sind and Assam, there was no difficulty in forming such ministries. In Bengal, Fazlul-Huq formed a coalition government based mainly on his Krishak Proja (Peasant-Tenant) Party, Independent Moslems, the Moslem League and the representatives of the scheduled castes. In addition, he had the support of 25 Europeans. In the Punjab the Unionist Party, representing the rural interests of all three communities — Moslems, Hindus and Sikhs — and led by Sikander Hyat, formed a ministry. Non-Congress ministries

---

1 Glendevon, *The Viceroy at Bay,* p. 51.

2 Lord Meston, 'India's Decision', *Fortnightly Review,* Jan.-June 1937, p.415.

3 Mss. Eur. F.125/4/12, Linlithgow to Zetland, 5 March 1937. IOL.

4 Glendevon, *The Viceroy at Bay,* p. 51.

5 *Statesman,* 1 April 1937.

6 Under Section 63(3) of the 1935 Act, the governor was under no obligation to summon the legislature for six months after the commencement of the provincial part of the Act.

were also formed in Assam and Sind, but politics in those provinces remained highly complex and unstable throughout the period of provincial self-government.

The formation of caretaker ministries in the Congress provinces afforded only temporary respite. It was evident that, as soon as the legislatures met, the *ad interim* minority ministries would be defeated by a vote of no confidence. As it would have been impossible for the governors to form alternative non-Congress ministries in Congress provinces, such a vote might have led to the abrogation of the constitution or at best the taking over of the administration of the province under the governor's direct rule. Therefore the efforts to persuade the Congress to accept office had to be continued if the new constitution were to have a chance of being implemented successfully.

The stand taken by Linlithgow was admittedly constitutionally correct. Beyond a general offer of goodwill and cooperation, it is difficult to see how the Viceroy (or the governors) could, within the limits of the constitution, concede the Congress's demand for an assurance.[1] But it appears that Linlithgow's attitude might have been influenced by considerations other than legal and constitutional technicalities.

There had always been a lurking suspicion among the officials about the motives of the Congress, and they now suspected something sinister behind the demand for an assurance. Linlithgow began to assert in his letters to the Secretary of State that the Congress was attempting to consolidate its position in order to overthrow British rule through a 'revolution'. 'We have ample proof', wrote Linlithgow, 'that the ultimate purpose of Nehru and Gandhi is to make for the overthrow of the government by organization of agrarian mischief on a grand scale'. He went on to add: 'Our best hope of avoiding a direct clash is the potency of provincial autonomy to destroy the effectiveness of Congress as an all-India instrument of revolution'.[2]

Although Linlithgow's correspondence with the India Office is replete with hostility to the Congress and more particularly to its leaders, it should nevertheless be noted that as a practical statesman he remained at this stage aware of the short term necessity of enlisting the cooperation of the Congress. Linlithgow saw that the election results had not only demonstrated the massive popular support enjoyed by the

---

[1] G. D. Birla, *In the Shadow of the Mahatma* (Bombay, 1953), p. 207.

[2] Mss. Eur. F.125/4/12. Linlithgow to Zetland, 5 March 1937, IOL; see also Mss. Eur. F.125/16/69 telegram from Linlithgow to Zetland, 4 March 1937; Glendevon, *The Viceroy at Bay*, p. 53.

Congress, but had also removed from the political scene many of the alternative parties and individuals who might have been of assistance to the British government. But the Congress, Linlithgow observed, despite its apparent strength as an all-India political party, was vulnerable in the provinces. Except in Madras, there were no outstanding Congress leaders at the provincial levels. The Provincial Congress Committees (PCC) were usually manned by comparatively inexperienced men who took their instructions from the All India Congress Committee. These provincial leaders could, no doubt, face their respective governors with a set formula provided by the Congress Working Committee for their use, but the moment there came any question of negotiation with the governors they would tend to be either too weak or too rigid.[1] Linlithgow therefore endeavoured to weaken the control of the CWC over the provincial bodies. By encouraging the parochial tendencies, Linlithgow hoped that the PCCs would be able to pursue a policy independent of the CWC, which might make them more amenable to official manipulation.[2]

It seems that Linlithgow might have obtained this idea from Erskine. Erskine, who had close contact with the Madras Congress leaders, had reported to Linlithgow, shortly after the election results were in, that the members of the Congress party in the Madras legislature were not a cohesive group; indeed many of them had formerly been members of the Justice and Liberal parties. These men had no particular loyalty to the Congress and would be 'quite furious' if they were not allowed to accept ministerships. They were essentially careerists, and Erskine was confident that, by offering offices and patronage, some members of the Congress could be persuaded to collaborate with the government in the assembly. He hopefully told Linlithgow:

> ... if they are given three months or so in which to intrigue amongst themselves, a sufficient number of them may break away from the Congress and support a ministry in order to avoid being dissolved.[3]

Rajagopalachari had visited Erskine a fortnight before the polls and told him that Congress would accept office. Similarly in June 1936 Erskine had reported to Delhi that Satyamurti, another prominent Congress leader, was 'cooing like a dove' and that Madras leaders were 'panting for office'.[4]

---

1   Mss. Eur. F.125/4/12, Note by Linlithgow, 12 March 1937. IOL.

2   Mss. Eur. F.125/4/12, Linlithgow to Zetland, 19 March 1937. IOL; also see Glendevon, *The Viceroy at Bay*, p. 45.

3   Mss. Eur. D.596/18, Erskine to Linlithgow, 10 March 1937.

4   See Mss. Eur. D.596/18 letters from Erskine to Linlithgow dated 3 Feb. 1937 and 14 June 1936.

Zetland shared Erskine's view: he too believed that a 'break through' might be possible at the provincial level. He told the British Cabinet that the deadlock could only be possibly ended by the 'right wing' of the Congress breaking away from the 'tyranny of the caucus'. 'And it occurs to me that in Madras where some at least of those returned on the Congress ticket are in name only [sic]'.[1] He argued that, since many Congressmen were anxious to accept office, it might be possible for the Viceroy to induce those with such ideas to accept office by separate agreements with the governors concerned. If such a tendency could be started, he believed, Congress unity would collapse. 'I attach importance', wrote Zetland, 'to negotiations being entered into wherever possible between the governors and the leading Congressmen in the provinces'.[2] Zetland thus hoped to bypass the national leaders, particularly Nehru, and concentrate British attention on the newly elected Congress leaders in the provinces. It was a sound piece of strategy which would seriously test Congress solidarity and the strength of the control of the All India Congress Committee over the provincial groups. Zetland and Erskine were unduly optimistic.

Linlithgow attempted to transfer the initiative from the centre to the provinces by insisting that discussion should take place between the governors and the Congress leaders in the provinces. But the efforts to tempt away some Congressmen by lure of office did not succeed. It seems that Gandhi, too, had been aware of this weakness in the Congress's provincial leadership. And in consequence he was, as Linlithgow soon discovered, 'most anxious that means should be found to cause the venue of touch[3] to be shifted from the Province to the Centre, between the Viceroy and Gandhi'.[4] Congress was not always the disciplined, monolithic organization it claimed to be. But at the same time it was not the congeries of autonomous provincial parties which some officials fondly imagined it. It was managed by a powerful Working Committee of fourteen members, and so long as men like Gandhi, Nehru, Azad and Patel were in control, the government would continue to face tough bargaining at the centre.

The idea that Gandhi was manoeuvring to create an agrarian upheaval did less than justice to him. It is true that his faith in

---

[1] Mss. Eur. F.125/4/17, Zetland to Linlithgow, 3 May 1937; See also F.125/4/12, 12 April 1937. IOL.

[2] John L Dundas, *Essayez, the Memoirs of Lawrence, Second Marquess of Zetland* (henceforth *Essayez*) (London, 1956), p. 221.

[3] A rugby football phrase 'touch-in-goal' which denotes an area behind the opponents' goal-line where the ball must be 'grounded' or 'touched' in order to score a 'try'.

[4] L/PO/463, Linlithgow to Zetland, 13 March 1937. IOR.

the possibility of achieving India's freedom through constitutional processes had been shaken in 1920; after his release from prison in 1924 he had differences with C.R. Das and Motilal Nehru who were in favour of lifting the boycott of the Councils.[1] But ten years later, in 1934, Gandhi had encouraged the revival of the parliamentary wing of the Congress as he felt that work within the legislature was needed:

> The boycott of legislatures, let me tell you, is not an eternal principle like that of truth and non-violence. . . . The question is of strategy and I can only say what is much needed at a particular moment.[2]

The need of the moment was constructive work. Since the suspension of civil disobedience in 1934 Gandhi had been pre-occupied with activities which, though non-political, were nevertheless important — such as a clean water supply, a cheap nutritious diet, a sound educational system, and a healthy and self-sufficient economy for the Indian villages. Now that he was actually faced with a new constitution he wondered whether, with all its deficiencies, it could further this programme of village improvement. There was no reason why the Congress ministries in the provinces could not encourage village industries, reduce the burden on the peasantry, promote the use of homespun cloth, extend education and combat untouchability.

One further consideration seems to have influenced Gandhi. In the two previous decades he had launched two major civil disobedience campaigns. He had seen the country roused to a new political consciousness under their impact, but he had also seen that the spirit of non-violence had been slow in developing amongst the people. Violence seemed not only latent, but imminent, erupting unexpectedly; the atmosphere requisite for launching a *satyagraha* campaign was not easy to create. At the same time discontent in the country continued to grow. The new constitution had not given India the independence which the Congress had sought, but it had created an electorate of 30 millions. The constitution could be construed, Gandhi wrote, as an attempt, however feeble and limited, to replace the rule of the sword by the rule of the majority. 'If the Congress worked the new constitution to achieve its goal of independence', he suggested, 'it would avoid a bloody revolution and mass civil disobedience'.[3] Gandhi, then, asked the Congress to accept office. He was motivated by his

---

1 J. H. Broomfield, *Elite Conflict in a Plural Society. Twentieth Century Bengal* (Berkeley, 1968), pp. 227-35.

2 *Harijan,* 1 May 1937.

3 *Ibid.,* 17 July 1937.

desire to accomplish something constructive under the new constitution; he did not intend to lay a trap or instigate agrarian upheaval.[1]

In addition to the element of suspicion of Gandhi there were two other factors which promoted Linlithgow to refuse the assurances demanded by the Congress. Linlithgow was fearful that if he gave in to the Congress's demands the prestige of the Congress would rise to a 'most dangerous level'. The masses, by and large uninstructed in the conduct of the affairs of government, would construe such a move as a victory for the Congress over the British government. This was particularly true, Linlithgow perceived, of the Moslems who had hitherto not joined the Congress in large numbers. But if the impression got around that the Congress was strong enough to wrest concessions from the government, there would be a tendency on the part of the 'Muhammadans to drift towards Congress'. This Linlithgow wanted to prevent. The formation of the minority ministeries and the appointment of Moslem Chief ministers in Bihar and the United Provinces had offered considerable encouragement to the Moslems and given them confidence to stand up against the Congress. He wanted the Moslems to realize that, if they could unite and hold their own against the Congress, they would have greater chances of controlling the government and need not remain in opposition for ever even in Moslem minority provinces.[2] Furthermore, the Viceroy clearly believed that any deviation from the strict interpretation of the Statute would mean 'goodbye to the federation for good and all'. The Princes were at that moment engaged in scanning, with meticulous care, the Act and the draft Instrument of Accession. The Princes regarded the sanctity of the constitution, under which their position in the federation was to be safeguarded, as of 'cardinal importance'. Many of them were arguing that if they acceded to the federation, the words of the constitution would 'stand for them and their descendents as the charter of their rights'. Linlithgow pointed out that if the government allowed itself to be pressurized into amending the constitution, 'the princes would be in full flight'. And if that happened, the prospect of federation would be ruined for ever.[3] Linlithgow's fears, as we shall see, proved to be remarkably soundly based.[4]

A long public controversy ensued on the issue of 'assurances'. On 30 March Gandhi published a statement analysing the deadlock created by the Congress demand and said;

1 H. Mukherjee, *Gandhiji: A Study* (Bombay, 1960), p. 119.
2 Mss. Eur. F.125/4/21, Linlithgow to Zetland, 9 April 1937. IOL.
3 Mss. Eur. F.125/4/22, Linlithgow to Zetland, 16 April 1937. IOL.
4 See below chapter 3.

> My desire was not to lay down any impossible condition. On the contrary, I wanted to devise a constitution that could easily be accepted by the Governors. There was no intention whatsoever to lay down a condition whose acceptance would mean the slightest abrogation of the constitution.[1]

Gandhi argued that the purpose of accepting office was to strengthen the Congress and bring about beneficial reforms until such time as the Act could be replaced by a new constitution framed in accordance with the policies of the Congress. This object could not be secured unless there was an understanding between the governors and their ministers that they would not exercise the 'special powers' as long as the ministers acted within the limits of the constitution. The governors were vested with discretionary powers, but, Gandhi argued, there was nothing extra-constitutional in their saying that they would not exercise such powers against the ministers carrying on constitutional activities. A strong party, decisively backed by the electorate, could not be expected to put itself in the precarious position of being in dread of interference merely by the will of the governors. He reminded them that during the debate on the India Bill in 1934 it had been repeatedly stated by Sir Samuel Hoare that 'ordinarily the governors would not use their admittedly large powers of interference'.[2]

Gandhi's statement elicited little support in the India Office. Zetland described it as 'so astonishing' that it appeared to be explicable only on the assumption that either he had never read the Act, or the report of the Joint Select Committee, or that, if he had done so, he had completely forgotten them when he made his statement.[3]

This brought Lord Lothian, who had been closely concerned with the framing of the Act, into the debate. He asserted that the 'safeguards' would in practice be controlled by public opinion. The history of responsible government showed, he said, that a governor's decision to differ from his ministers depended on whether they could count on the support of the electorate in the event of 'dissolution'. If they could, 'the governor had usually decided not to provoke a constitutional crisis of which there is no solution save the suspension of the normal functioning of the constitution'.[4] Lothian's main point was that the Congress should rest assured that any difference of opinion between

---

1 Gwyer and Appodorai, (eds.). *Speeches and Documents,* i, 393-4.

2 *Ibid.*

3 House of Lords, *Parliamentary Debates,* 8 April 1937, vol. 104, cols, 875-85.

4 Letter to *The Times,* 6 April 1971. It appears that Lothian wrote the letter at the request of the India Office. See L/PO/57, Sir Findlater Stewart to Lord Lothian, 2 April 1937. IOR.

a Congress ministry and the governor, if it led to a collision, would in the last resort be referred to the provincial electorate. Therefore, when the Congress had a large majority and continued to enjoy the support of the voters, it did not need to worry much about the governor's 'special powers'. To students of politics, Lothian continued, it had seemed clear that 'special powers' would rarely, if ever, be used, for ministers would be unwilling to compel a governor to override them unless they were sure of public support. If they were overridden, ministers would presumably resign and force an election, at which, again presumably, they would retain, or increase, their majority, thus bringing about a deadlock with the British governor and the Indian electorate in open conflict.

Lothian's views harmonized with the democratic doctrines of the Congress. The basis of the Congress's demand was modified accordingly. It was now demanded that if the governor overruled his ministers, he must dismiss them.[1] If they retained the support of the majority in the legislature, this would mean a dissolution and fresh elections. The governor's right to dismiss ministers and dissolve the legislature 'when serious differences of opinion arise' was not questioned. But the Congress Working Committee still insisted that 'without specific assurances as required by the Congress, popular Ministries will be unable to function properly and without irritating interference'.[2]

Legal opinion in India and Britain began to range itself on opposite sides. Sir Tej Bahadur Sapru, for example, considered the Congress demand 'unreasonable';[3] while Professor Arthur Berriedale Keith criticized the British government for its failure to realize that responsible government was incompatible with such executive safeguards as over-riding powers vested in the governors and praised the Congress for their appreciation of this fact. He expressed regret that governors were not authorized to give a much more definite pledge than the frequently expressed desire of the government to see a wide measure of responsibility entrusted to the people of India.[4] Professor Keith apparently overlooked the effect of such a 'definite pledge' on the minorities for whom the safeguards were primarily intended.

As the controversy took a legal turn, Gandhi proposed that the

---

1 *IAR,* 1937, i, 258.

2 Gwyer and Appadorai (eds.). *Speeches and Documents,* i, 394-95; Tendulkar, *Mahatma,* iv, 184-5.

3 Tendulkar, *Mahatma,* iv, 181.

4 *The Scotsman,* 12 April 1937, quoted in L/PO/57, telegram from Zetland to Linlithgow, 14 April 1937. IOR.

matter should be referred to a legal tribunal for a decision. 'I want the right to prevail', he said. He claimed that the refusal to submit the whole question to a legal tribunal would raise a strong presumption that the British Government had no intention of dealing fairly with the majority party whose 'radical' programme they disliked. 'I would prefer', Gandhi said, 'an honourable deadlock to the dishonourable daily scenes between the Congress and the governors'.[2] Gandhi's demand was vague and he did not define the nature and the composition of the tribunal he proposed. The obvious difficulty in his suggestion was whether the arbitrators would also be asked to decide what activities of the ministers were 'constitutional activities'. If the arbitrators said that the governors could constitutionally give the assurance which the Congress had asked for, would not the minorities protest? Furthermore would not such an undertaking conflict with the basic principles of British-style constitutional democracy, namely, that neither the majority party nor the monarch or governor should be able to exercise arbitrary power without an appeal to the electorate? The key to the solution lay, as Lothian had pointed out, in the recognition of the fact that under a system of responsible government the ultimate control on an abuse of power rested with the electorate. Not surprisingly, since major questions remained unresolved, little notice was taken of Gandhi's suggestions.

At the same time Zetland reported that 'opinion' was building up in Britain to the effect that the Viceroy's inaction must end. It was generally felt that it was not enough for the government to have made the constitutional position clear; it should also endeavour to find means of giving the Congress an opportunity of reconsidering the situation which, in the absence of any move on the part of the government, it was not likely to do. A formula should be devised which would leave the constitutional position undisturbed and yet enable the Congress to accept office without losing face.[3]

Signs of anxiety were also visible in the British Cabinet. Linlithgow's policy of allowing the Congress to 'stew in its own juice' came in for severe criticism. Several members of the Cabinet, who spoke with authority on India, were in obvious disagreement with the Viceroy's view. Halifax (previously Lord Irwin) maintained that the Government of India was not attaching sufficient importance to the psychological aspects of the case; that a stonewalling policy over guarantees showed a

---

1   *The Times*, 14 April 1937.

2   Tendulkar, *Mahatma*, iv, 184.

3   L/PO/463, Zetland to Linlithgow, 22 April 1937. IOR.

lack of imagination and would get the Viceroy nowhere; and that while a strong case could be made out for such a policy, on purely logical grounds, the Government of India should show appreciation of the fact that human action, in India as elsewhere, was governed by sentiment rather than reason. Moreover, he feared that if, as a result of the Viceroy's policy Gandhi had eventually to climb down, he would be so bitter that he might devote his whole energy to a crusade among the masses aimed at the destruction of British rule.[1] The Chancellor of the Exchequer, Neville Chamberlain, was also emphatic on the necessity of reaching an agreement with the Congress. The government's hands, he pointed out, were sufficiently full with the troubled situation in the North West Frontier Province where troops were engaged in punitive action against the frontier tribesmen. It was undesirable, he said, to have trouble with the Congress and the North West Frontier Province simultaneously.[2] The dangers of a combination of civil disobedience and turmoil on the Frontier had been brought home to the government during Gandhi's 1929-30 campaign.[3] Zetland also expressed his fears that, if some initiative were not taken immediately, the Congress might issue a manifesto defining its position more rigidly; this would make further attempts to end the impasse difficult. He therefore suggested that Linlithgow should make a statement that the government would not use its powers in a legalistic way nor to halt reforms, but would adopt a sympathetic attitude to work the proposed reforms.[4]

There was some merit in Zetland's suggestion. Without a compromise on the use of the governors' safeguards, the Congress could be assured that the governors would not interfere with the implementation of their election manifesto in the social and economic field. This would also refute Gandhi's allegation that the British government had no intention of dealing fairly with the Congress whose radical programme they disliked.[5] But the Viceroy remained unconvinced. He maintained that it would be a mistake to yield to Congress pressure in the hope of finding a way out of the immediate difficulties. Any such concession, he claimed, would seriously shake the civil administration and demoralize the princes and the Moslems.[6] Linlithgow's assessment may

1 *Essayez*, pp. 220-1.

2 Conclusions — Cabinet Meetings, 20(37)3, CAB 23/88, PRO; See also Mss. Eur. F.125/4, Zetland to Linlithgow, 26 April 1937. IOL.

3 See S. Gopal, *The Viceroyalty of Lord Irwin 1926-31* (Oxford, 1957), pp. 54-88, especially pp. 67-70.

4 L/PO/463, Zetland to Linlithgow, 22 April 1937. IOR.

5 See above p.43

6 Mss. Eur. F.125/4/163. telegram from Linlithgow to Zetland, 23 April 1937. IOL.

have been realistic, but he could not see that options other than a total concession of the Congress demand were still open. Determined to bring in the Congress on his own terms and conditions, he ignored the fact that in so doing he would deprive the moderates of their grip on the Congress organization and provide a convenient pretext for further agitation by the extremists.

Nor was Linlithgow impressed by Halifax's suggestion of a conference with the Congress leaders at which, it was hoped, the latter would make their position clear and at which, as Sapru and some newspapers had been suggesting, the only way out of the impasse could be found.[1] Linlithgow, for two reasons, did not think it was feasible to work out a formula which attempted to define what a governor could or could not accept: first there would be the difficulty of interpretation; second a proposal, legislative or administrative, which might be harmless in ordinary times, might in altered circumstances appear so inadvisable as to warrant a governor exercising his special responsibility.[2] Besides, he suspected that his intervention would give Gandhi an opportunity to re-establish his position and enhance the prestige of the Congress by bargaining at the centre on provincial matters and thus open a sustained attack on the existence of the 'safeguards'. This he was determined to avoid.[3]

The stalemate remained unbroken. While the Government of India stood firm, the Congress Working Committee met at Allahabad towards the end of April and reiterated its position that without specific assurances as required by the Congress, the 'popular ministries [would] be unable to function properly and without irritating interference'.[4] The resolution showed clearly that the Congress attitude had not changed and that it would be unwilling to accept office without some sort of assurance, however vague. Having taken such a rigid stand, the Congress could not climb down without losing face.

Shortly afterwards the *Statesman,* in an article 'Indian Impasse Deplored — Unofficial Anxiety — Viceroy's Silence Unhelpful', severely criticized the Viceroy for his inaction. It claimed that many members of Parliament in Britain, extremely anxious about the deadlock in India, were critical of the government's handling of the situation

1 *Statesman,* 8 April 1937; for comments of the *Times of India* and *Pioneer* see Mss. Eur. F.125/4/21, Linlithgow to Zetland, 9 April 1937; Mss. Eur. F.125/4, Zetland to Linlithgow, 26 April 1937. IOL.

2 Mss. Eur. F.125/4/163, Linlithgow to Zetland, 23 April 1937. IOL.

3 *Ibid.*

4 Gwyer and Appadorai (eds.), *Speeches and Documents,* i, 394-95.

and more particularly of the Viceroy's prolonged silence. Parliamentary opinion, the article continued, was impatient of this attitude and held that unless the legislatures in the Congress provinces were summoned, the Government of India would incur some share of responsibility for the failure to solve the deadlock. Those anxious to give vitality to parliamentary institutions should not flout a demand for summoning the legislatures.[1]

The *Statesman* article coincided with a debate on India in the House of Lords. Lord Snell led the Labour opposition. The deadlock seemed to him due to a clash of temperaments rather than to substantial differences. He felt that the time had come for both sides to be asked to make another effort to reach a settlement. The British government should remove any misapprehension which might exist concerning its intentions. For instance, he went on, Gandhi had expressed his surprise that the government did not see his words as he himself saw them. Snell urged that the government should give an assurance that the reserved powers of the governors would not be used indiscriminately.[2]

In India, too, the situation was becoming critical. The Viceroy could not ignore the impact of Congress agitation among the peasants and factory workers. The Congress election campaign had already aroused political consciousness in the industrial and rural areas; the result was a wave of strikes and demonstrations. A strike of 60,000 Bengal-Nagpur railwaymen had ended in February in partial victory for the workers.[3] Following it more than 200,000 workers of the jute mills in Bengal had gone on strike and did not return to work until some of their demands had been conceded by the Fazlul Huq ministry.[4] The *Kissan Sabhas* (peasant organizations) also showed signs of restlessness. Linlithgow was alarmed. If the Congress could not be persuaded to accept office, the more extreme leaders might incite 'agrarian mischief' (the official phrase). On the Congress side, Erskine reported to Linlithgow, Rajagopalachari was arguing that if the Congress were forced to accept office without 'assurances' it would mean the passing of the initiative within the Congress to the extremists, whereas 'assurances' would strengthen the moderates.[5] Erskine's report

1 *Statesman*, 2 May 1937, cited in Mss. Eur. F.125/6/170, Linlithgow to Zetland, 23 May 1937. IOL.

2 *Parliamentary Debates*, House of Lords, fifth series, vol. 105, cols. 182-195, 6 May 1937.

3 *Indian Labour Journal*, 29 Feb. 1937.

4 P. Sitaramayya, *The History of the Indian National Congress*, (Bombay, 1947), ii, 51.

5 Mss. Eur. D.596, Erskine to Linlithgow, 11 June 1937. IOL.

strengthened Linlithgow's own anxiety to see the Congress controlled by the moderates. He therefore began to explore the possibilities of various initiatives that could be made from his end. These essentially were two. First, the governors could intensify their efforts to make contacts with the Congress leaders in the provinces, offer further explanations and repeat the assurances in general terms. Second, the Viceroy might himself make a statement on the issue.[1]

Although the fundamental objections of the Congress had been in no way weakened by recent events, it was apparent that some Congressmen were eager to take office. The earlier demands of the Congress regarding 'special powers' were modified, even if only slightly. Suggestions were now made by some Congressmen that the great need, more than the assurances, was for proof of British sincerity.[2] Towards the end of April, Gandhi expressed his anxiety that the Congress should take office. He shifted his grounds slightly and demanded that if the governor, using his special powers, decided to override the ministry, he should dismiss them and not leave them to resign.[3] This was a very subtle and astute move by Gandhi. He preferred dismissal because that would improve the chances of the Congress before the electorate. An illustration will make this clear. If for example, the *casus belli* between the governor and the ministry touched the 'peace and tranquility' of the province, the ministry could then go to the constituencies with the cry 'the ministry and liberty' *versus* 'the governor and the British empire'. It would be impossible for the governor to continue in the province if as a consequence of an appeal to the electorate a vote of confidence was obtained in a matter over which the ministry were in a conflict with the governor. Not surprisingly both the Viceroy and the Secretary of State rejected Gandhi's suggestion.

At the beginning of June Rajagopalachari had another interview with Erskine during which he explained that the question of dismissal of a ministry ought, in the Congress view, to arise only in a 'vital crisis'. Congress had to make this condition in order to assuage the extreme elements in the party. The British Government, he pointed out, did not realize that Gandhi was 'holding an olive branch'. Even if his demands were partially met, Gandhi could agree to the working of the constitution and would not countenance serious hostility. Here was the chance, Rajagopalachari wishfully claimed, to get rid of the civil disobedience mentality forever. Rajagopalachari may have gone some way towards

1 Glendevon, *The Viceroy at Bay*, p. 85.

2 *Ibid.*, p. 61.

3 Hindu, 22 April, 1937; see also CWC resolution of 29 April. *IAR*, 1937, i, 258.

convincing Erskine of Gandhi's sincerity. However, Zetland dismissed the hope of getting rid of the civil disobedience mentality as 'optimism run mad'. He suspected that Gandhi — 'Saintly old sinner and humbug'— was trying to trick both the government and the Congress in order to prevent a split in the Congress ranks. 'And to what end?', asked Zetland, going on to give the answer: 'I can see no other end than to have his forces united and, when he considers that the moment has arrived, for dropping the mask and launching a grand offensive against the British connections'.[1]

As the controversy continued there was a slight tempering of the Congress's interpretation of their original demand. The British Government also slowly changed their ground. The Viceroy was uneasy because the position of the *ad interim* ministries was becoming difficult. They were unpopular and had no sanction behind them except the will of the governor. As they could not face the legislatures, the legislatures were not summoned despite repeated demands from the elected members. Provincial autonomy seemed to be reduced to a farce. It was obvious that these conditions could not last much longer, as the legislatures would have to be summoned within six months and the budget placed before them. It was this deepening crisis which led to some change in the position of the British Government, a change which was accompanied by a hint from the Viceroy that, if the Congress persisted in their refusal to accept office the constitution would have to be suspended in provinces in which the Congress had a majority. The indication of a conciliatory attitude on the part of the British government was first revealed in a statement by the Prime Minister, Neville Chamberlain,

> I hope, (he told the House of Commons on 17 June) that I am justified in assuming that in every quarter of the House there is a desire that provincial self-government in India should work, and work well. I cannot believe that this is possible unless we in this House frankly recognise the new distribution of responsibilities.[2]

The stalemate was finally ended by the Viceroy on 22 June. After explaining why the governors could not give the assurances which the Congress had demanded, he said that the working of provincial autonomy since the election showed that the reality of power and responsibility had been transferred under the new constitution to the 'elected' ministries and expressed the wish that this transfer might be accepted without distrust. The experience of the last three months,

---

1 Glendevon, *The Viceroy at Bay*, p. 62.

2 *Parliamentary Debates*, House of Commons, 17 June 1937, vol. 325, cols. 552-7.

he said, had cleared up certain misconceptions about the position of the governors and the use of the safeguards. It was now understood that the governors were not partisans, that their experience and advice was at the disposal of any ministry which was willing to work the constitution, and that they would accept any such ministry's programme for the advancement of the province provided it did not run counter to the purposes which they were charged by their special responsibilities to ensure. Those responsibilities did not entitle a governor to intervene at random in the administration of the province. They had been restricted in scope to the narrowest possible limit. Within this narrow field the governors were anxious to leave nothing undone to avoid and to resolve such conflicts. As to the question of the dismissal or resignation of ministries, the Viceroy argued in favour of the latter as being more in accordance with constitutional precedent and with a ministry's self-respect. But he accepted the suggestion (in fact it had been Gandhi's) that 'it is only when the issue between a governor and his ministers constitutes a serious disagreement that any question of the severing of their partnership need arise'. It would have to be so major a question that the ministers would feel that their position had been 'hopelessly compromised' by the governor's rejection of their advice. The decision, therefore, would depend on the circumstances of each case and could not properly be determined *a priori* by binding rule.[1]

The Viceroy's statement was generally well received. Its tone was acknowledged to be beyond criticism, and, read along with the Prime Minister's statement a few days earlier, it removed many of the possible grounds of misunderstanding. Most of the Congress newspapers strongly advocated acceptance of office. Even the more militant groups acknowledged the Viceroy's conciliatory attitude. The Congress Working Committee met on 7 July and decided to come in. The resolution, however, maintained that office was to be accepted and utilized to further the Congress policy of combating the Act while simultaneously implementing the programmes contained in the election manifesto.[2]

The Congress accepted office with mixed feelings. Nehru was not happy with the decision, but he had no choice: the pressure from his colleagues and the rank and file was too strong. Faced with reality, he tried to rationalize the 'retreat': 'Acceptance of office does not mean by an iota acceptance of the slave Constitution. [!] It means a fight

1 Gwyer and Appadorai (eds.), *Speeches and Documents,* i, 395-96.
2 *Statesman,* 15 July 1937.

against the coming of the Federation by all means in our power; inside and outside the legislatures'.[1]

The Congress's decision to accept office was a personal triumph for Linlithgow but only in the strict constitutional sense: no constitutional ground had been surrendered. But his statement was born of a hard struggle with the British Cabinet, in which he came close to breaking with them.[2] While the Congress Working Committee was deliberating the Viceroy's statement, a state of near panic gripped the Cabinet. They feared that the Congress would refuse to accept office and that if that happened, the government would come under severe criticism. Zetland also felt that this was the turning point. If the decision was against co-operation, the left wing would carry the bulk of the Congress with them and the moderate leaders would lose control of the party. If the Congress agreed to cooperate, the gulf between Britain and nationalist India would be narrowed because the Congress would be absorbed in administration. Zetland therefore argued that when so much depended on the acceptance of office by the Congress it was not right to be rigid and legalistic. Linlithgow was taken aback at Zetland's apparent *volte face*. He could not agree to any arrangement which would entail a compromise in the constitution. He informed Zetland that if he was ordered to yield, he would tender his resignation. The necessity for this did not arise since the Congress decided to accept office.[3]

Within a few days of the resolution of the Congress Working Committee, interim ministries resigned and the leaders of the Congress in Bihar, Central Province, Bombay, Madras and the United Provinces were invited to form governments.[4]

The long debate and its outcome provided a somewhat curious spectacle. Did the Congress gain anything from the controversy? Did the government give way to its demands? Linlithgow accepted neither Lothian's view that a conflict between a governor and his minister should be resolved by an appeal to the electorate, nor that accepting the view that only a conflict on a major issue would justify an open breach implied that on other issues the 'safeguards' would not operate at all. On minor questions, as on others, it was not to be supposed that the ministers would try, as a matter of deliberate policy, to do what the safeguards had been designed to prevent. Differences of opinion on such questions would probably be due to misunderstanding and would

1   Jawaharlal Nehru, *Eighteen Months in India*, pp. 234-40; especially p. 235.
2   Hodson, *The Great Divide*, p. 65; Glendevon, *The Viceroy at Bay*, pp. 64-7.
3   Glendevon, *The Viceroy at Bay*, pp. 64-5.
4   *Statesman*, 22 July 1937.

have to be overcome by frank discussion. The efforts of the British authorities, from the Secretary of State down to the provincial governors, in bending and stretching the spirit of the new Act in order to secure the cooperation of men pledged to overthrow British rule, presented a strange paradox.

It may perhaps be argued, at least in retrospect, that the Congress's hesitancy to accept office displayed a certain lack of understanding. Even for a party pledged to wreck the constitution it was obviously *Realpolitik* to take advantage of any opportunity to improve its position. The only effective alternative was a total boycott of the parliamentary programme and concentration upon agitation and organizational work. The policy actually followed by the Congress combined the disadvantages of both alternatives without any of their advantages. It wasted time in attempting to wrest an assurance from the governors, but achieved little by the controversy. In spite of the elaborately courteous and diplomatic phraseology, the letter of the constitution remained intact. That Congress demands might have been made merely for public consumption is suggested by the fact that after several months of controversy the Congress assumed offices in the provinces under exactly the same constitution as that to which they had objected; and furthermore the Congress made that constitution work for over two years. Besides, it was the same Act which, with few modifications, was to form the basis of independent India's government till the promulgation of a new constitution in 1950. The question then arises why the Congress made such a fuss about an 'assurance'. Although there is no definite evidence for what was in their minds, but it may be suggested that its members were playing to the gallery. In order to ward off uninstructed criticism from the public, the Congress made a show of accepting office only after a hard bargain. Such tactics, it may be added, helped to raise the stock of the Congress as the implacable foe of the British.

Nevertheless, in its hesitation to accept office, the Congress missed the opportunity of capturing power in some of the 'non-Congress' provinces, where, by a coalition with other groups, it might have obtained a share in the government. In Bengal Fazlul Huq had pleaded in vain for such cooperation. Thus forced into the arms of Jinnah, Huq perhaps did more than anybody else in India to win support for the League among the masses of Bengal.[1] Similarly in the Punjab, the

---

1 In his unfinished Memoirs, the late H. S. Suhrawardy the principal organizer of the Moslem League in Bengal, wrote: 'The Krishak Proja Party won 21 seats against 32 [?37] captured by the Muslim League. To prevent Fazlul Huq from falling into the clutches of the Hindus, with whom he had started negotiations,

constant bickering of the Congress forced Sikander Hyat, a moderate and on the whole a non-communal politician, into tacit cooperation with the Moslem League. Another unfortunate effect of this controversy was the heightening of the anxieties of the minorities for whose benefit some of the safeguards had been devised.[1] As they watched the wrangling over the governors' powers, many Moslems came to believe that the Congress was out to establish 'Hindu Raj' and would throw away the minorities' constitutional safeguards.

But this is not to suggest that the result of the controversy was entirely negative. It had marshalled opinion against the 'special powers' and had brought out eminent constitutionalists in opposition to their indiscriminate use. It was clear that the governors would now be extremely careful in using them and would hesitate to use them for trivial matters. Moreover, as a result of the controversy the Congress emerged with a greater cohesion, and the authority of the Congress Working Committee over the Provincial Congress Committee was clearly demonstrated and established. Henceforth, the Viceroy, despite his dislike of doing so, would have to deal with the Congress at the central and not at the provincial level. The unanimity with which the various provincial Congress parties officially acted on this question was characteristic of their conduct throughout the period under review. They worked under the direction of the 'high command'. Congress has frequently been criticized for this practice, which was certainly at variance with democratic principle: the Congress' provincial governments were responsible not only to the legislators but also to the 'high command'. But the Congress could argue in justification that inasmuch as it was not possible for it to gain control of the central government, this unity of direction by the party machine was a necessary substitute, besides fulfilling the essential purpose of ensuring that the great objective of independence should neither be lost sight of nor compromised.

Nor would it be correct to say that the Congress' decision to accept office was determined by the constitutional discussions. The government certainly wanted the Congress to take office, but so did a good number of Congressmen. Coupled with this desire were other practical

the Muslim League party in its turn offered to support him for the Chief Ministership, in coalition with his party. His renewed contacts with the Muslim League led him to attend the crucial Lahore session of the All India Muslim League in 1940, where he was entrusted with the honour of moving the Pakistan Resolution'. H. S. Suhrawardy, *Political Memoirs*, (mss.) p. 39; see also A. S. M. Abdur Rab, *A. K. Fazlul Huq, Life and Achievements* (Barisal, 1966) p. 89. (Because of inaccuracies this work should be used with care).

1 Hodson, *The Great Divide*, pp. 65-6.

considerations which had influenced the Congress leaders in opting for office. It was clear that, whether or not the Congress accepted office, the non-Congress provinces were working the constitution and had shown to the masses that the Act could operate to their benefit. By successfully running the government, they had shown the electorate that many of the Congress complaints were without foundation. For the Congress now to demonstrate the unsuitability of the constitution in other provinces would only be interpreted as meaning that the Congress was unwilling and unable to work it and that it preferred talking about things to doing them. Rumours were also rife that the Congress was unwilling to accept office because it was afraid that it could not fulfil the large promises it had made during the elections. Such a situation would indeed give an important weapon to its opponents.[1] For three months the Congress had seen the Act in operation, it had seen the powers the Act gave to the ministers, and whatever its reasons for asking for assurances, it did not want to be prevented from using that power to carry out the programme — for some the socio-economic programme particularly — for which it had received the mandate of the electorate.

It is not possible to say precisely what impelled the Congress Working Committee to change its decision. It was not entirely in response to the Viceroy's statement: the speech was the occasion but not the cause. It seems possible that the Congress may have realized that persistence in the policy of obstruction required as a consequence non-cooperation in the villages, if the administration were to be brought to a standstill. Gandhi, who during this period had been working in the villages,[2] was in a good position to decide the prospects of success of a non-cooperation campaign. The campaign of 1930-1 had failed and in 1937 the country was not ready for another struggle. It may be conjectured that Gandhi may have convinced Nehru and the Congress Working Committee that the refusal to accept office was inadvisable, and that the Congress had more opportunities for preparing a successful non-cooperation campaign by taking office and organizing the party at village level and with the help of government patronage.

The first part of Linlithgow's mission, the inauguration of the provincial autonomy, had been successfully implemented. In spite of early protestations by the Congress that it accepted office in order to destroy the constitution from within, in practice there was hardly any indication of such intentions. The Congress ministries showed an

1   *Statesman,* 18 Feb. 1937.
2   Penderel Moon, *Gandhi and Modern India* (London, 1968), p. 183.

increasing awareness of their responsibility and a readiness to discharge it. We now turn to Linlithgow's second important task, the launching of the all-India federation.

3

THE INDIAN STATES AND ALL-INDIA POLITICS:
ATTEMPT AT FEDERATION

After some initial difficulties, Linlithgow had successfully inaugurated the provincial part of the constitution: elected ministries were functioning smoothly in all the eleven British Indian provinces. His main task now was to implement the federal scheme envisaged in the Act.

The idea of a federation of the British Indian provinces and Indian States originated in dramatic circumstances. It was mooted before the first Round Table Conference, on board the ship in which many of the Indian delegates travelled to London.[1] The princes had become concerned about their position *vis a vis* the Government of India in the aftermath of the Butler Report which had declared the sovereignty of the British Crown supreme in India, so that no ruler of an Indian State could justifiably claim to negotiate with the British Government on an equal footing. Its supremacy was not based solely upon treaties and engagements, but existed independently of them.[2] The princes therefore began to discuss the establishment of an all-India federation in which their states could participate fully and thus escape from the 'irritating interference' of the Political Department.[3] This had been mentioned as a possibility both in the Simon Report[4] and by the Government of India's despatch on the Commission's report which endorsed the ultimate object of an all-India federation.[5] Prior to that, as early as 1918, it had been suggested as an ultimate possibility by Lionel Curtis. Montagu and Chelmsford had expressed a vague notion that the only form of government suitable to British India and the states was

---

1 D.A. Low, 'Sir Tej Bahadur Sapru and the First Round Table Conference', in *Soundings in Modern South Asian History* (London, 1968), pp. 294-325.

2 *Report of the Indian States Committee, 1928-29* (Butler Report), *Cmd.* 3302, 1929, pp. 56-7

3 Lord Meston, 'India's Decision'. *Fortnightly Review* (Jan.-June 1937), p. 418; Sir Kenneth Fitze, *Twilight of the Maharajas* (London, 1956), p. 77; S. Gopal, *The Viceroyalty of Lord Irwin 1926-31* (Oxford, 1957), p. 124.

4 The Simon Commission stated that only a federal constitution was capable of combining 'elements of diverse internal constitution and of communities at very different stages of development and culture; and predicted the necessity of an all-India federation in the 'distant' future. *Report of the Indian Statutory commission*, Recommendations, ii, *(Cmd.* 3568-9, 1930), paras 24, 30.

5 *Government of India's Despatch on Proposals for Constitutional Reform, September 20, 1930 (Cmd.* 3700, 1930), para 16; Fitze, *Twilight of the Maharajas*, p. 27.

some sort of federation.[1] But no one had hitherto thought of federation as an immediate possibility.

The federal idea had taken firm root when the delegates to the Round Table Conference arrived in Britain. Not one of the 89 Indian delegates was prepared to accept the Simon plan of provincial autonomy without some immediate transfer of responsibility at the centre.[2]

On the first day of the conference, Sapru called for a federal system of government at the centre, and invited the rulers to agree to the creation of an all-India federation.[3] The rulers, he said, would furnish a stabilizing factor, and their adherence would enable the process of national unification to begin without delay. Sir Muhammad Shafi for one wing of the Moslem League, and Jinnah for the other, welcomed Sapru's proposal.[4]

The princes then publicly and unexpectedly announced their support for early federation.[5] The Maharaja of Bikaner identified himself and the princely order with the idea of an all-India federation. The Nawab of Bhopal went one step further and avowed: 'We can only federate with a self-governing and federal India'.[6] This general consensus of opinion virtually created a common Indian front.

These were decisions of great importance, leading, as they did, to Ramsay MacDonald's announcement: 'With a legislature constituted on the federal basis, His Majesty's Government will be prepared to recognize the principle of responsibility of the executive to the Legislature'.[7] The general tone of the speeches at the conclusion of the conference was harmonious and optimistic. The agreement on an all-India federation was hailed as a significant achievement.

The federal scheme, as we have noted earlier, could not come into operation until a sufficient number of rulers of the states had signified

[1]   *Report of Indian Constitutional Reforms* (Montagu - Chelmsford Report), Cmd. 9109, 1918, paras. 120, 300; L.F. Rushbrook Williams, 'The Eclipse of the Princes', *South Asian Review* (July, 1971), pp. 338-40.

[2]   Viscount Templewood, *Nine Troubled Years* (London, 1954), pp. 47-8.

[3]   Surprisingly enough, the idea of a federation had not appealed to Sapru before. He had joined with Motilal Nehru to draft the *Nehru Report* which recommended a unitary government. See *Report of the All Parties Conference, 1928* (Allahabad, 1928), Schedule 1.

[4]   *Indian Round Table Conference, Proceedings, 12 November 1930 - 19 January 1931* (HMSO: 1931), p. 29. (henceforth *RTC Proceedings*).

[5]   *Manchester Guardian,* 12 Nov. 1930.

[6]   *RTC Proceedings,* p. 37.

[7]   *RTC Proceedings,* pp. 505-6.

their accession to the federation. Linlithgow earnestly set about persuading the princes to do so.[1] As the chairman of the Joint Select Committee Linlithgow was confident that the provisions of the Act could be depended upon to ensure the retention of real power in British hands and would at the same time spare Parliament for some years the trouble and worry of framing a new constitution for India.[2] The federal scheme, as it finally emerged, postulated a responsible government with the Viceroy having overriding powers for the maintenance of law and order, defence, foreign affairs and relations with the Indian states; the control over the rest of the departments would be devolved on Indian ministers. It was apparent to Linlithgow that despite devolution of authority into Indian hands, the direction of policy could be retained by the British through a strict control of the army and the finances. Together with Sir Samuel Hoare, he believed that the federal scheme with the presence of the princely representatives provided greater stability at the centre. Linlithgow was a conservative, but not a 'diehard', and he saw the 1935 Act as an opportunity for advancing India towards self-government without immediately endangering British imperial interests.

However, the launching of the federation, as Linlithgow soon discovered to his chagrin, was not an easy task and was complicated by many conflicting pressures. Some of the governors and civil servants were not only sceptical about the scheme themselves, but were also labouring under the false impression that the British Government was not anxious to implement it.[3] On the other hand there was the unhelpful and indifferent attitude of the India Office, which for fear of a renewed attack by the diehards in Parliament was hesitant to make any determined move. In addition Linlithgow had to face the hostile opposition of the Congress and the Moslem League (though for different reasons), and had to overcome the fears of the princes who had gone back on their earlier promises.

At the close of the first Round Table Conference it was generally expected that the requisite number of princes would accede to the federation, and the federal part of the Act would be brought into operation within a relatively short period.[4] The initial enthusiasm of the princes for the federation, however, soon cooled.[5] It may be asked

1 R. Coupland, *India : A Re-statement* (London, 1945), p. 149.

2 J. Gallagher, G. Johnson, A. Seal (eds.), *Locality Province and Nation. Essays on Indian Politics 1870-1940* (Cambridge, 1976), p. 269.

3 Mss. Eur. F.125/3/10, Linlithgow to Zetland, 15 June 1936. IOL.

4 Coupland, *Indian Politics, 1936-42*, p. 2.

5 Coupland, *Re-statement*, pp. 142, 149.

why, after such enthusiasm at the Round Table Conference, the princes refused to associate themselves with an all-India federation on terms highly favourable to them. Two factors explain this change of attitude. First, the desire to federate disappeared fast when the princes became more fully aware of what was involved. Second, the Congress' agitation in the states after 1937 brought home to the princes the dangers of federating with the 'democratic' provinces.

Indian politics of the 1930s had suddenly awakened the princes to an unfamiliar India of civil disobedience, movement for *swaraj* and boycott; and they could fall back only upon an association with a more familiar British guardianship. On reflection they realized the practical implications of federation, A federal government must enjoy certain 'sovereign' powers at the expense of its constituent units. The princes were not coming into the federation in order to share in the governing of the British India alone, but of the whole of India, their own and each others' individual states; and they would have to give up some of their powers, just as the provinces would be doing. This was the obvious price which they would have to pay for their 'liberation' from the control of the Political Department.

In the interval between the Round Table Conference and the passing of the 1935 Act, however, many factors had changed to the disadvantage of the princes. There was widespread political awakening among the masses, partly due to the election campaign by the various parties. This awakening was not confined to the limits of the British India. Democratic aspirations had penetrated states which were once thought to be the bulwarks of absolutism. The Congress publicly condemned the autocratic nature of the states. A good deal of the glamour of paternal despotism had worn off. Even in the states with reputations for comparatively good administration – for example Mysore and Travancore – there had been much agitation for responsible government. This had led to repressive measures which in turn attracted much outside attention. Denunciation of princely rule and rejection of its claim to respect on historical or political grounds had been widespread in the pro-Congress press. Furthermore, the princes had learnt that many of their rights and privileges which they had expected to retain were not considered by the 'Paramount Power' to be sacrosanct under a federal constitution. These considerations largely accounted for the subdued enthusiasm with which the princes approached the question of federation. To these causes may be added the natural instinct of the princes to maintain the *status quo*. The princely order, by tradition and training, was conservative. The old type of rulers (as represented by the Maharaja of Jaipur) were disappearing; but even the younger generation was suspicious of change and averse to letting any outside authority intervene between themselves and their subjects. It was no light matter for them to abandon their 'divine right' in order to become constitutional rulers.[1]

Nevertheless, to many British statesmen the offer made by the princes to join in an all-India federation had seemed to be a promising solution to the Indian constitutional problem. Without the stabilizing weight of the princes in federal government, they believed it would be unsafe to introduce self-government in the provinces. This belief was clearly stated in the Joint Select Committee's report:

> To create autonomous units without any corresponding adaptation of the existing Central Legislature would be ... to give full play to the powerful centrifugal forces of Provincial autonomy without any attempt to counteract them and to ensure the continued unity of India.[2]

The report went on to say that the Army Budget could be jeopardized in a central government under a responsible ministry because the ministers would want to save money on defence in order to finance the 'nation building' departments. The declaration of the princes introduced a new factor.

> It is reasonable to expect [the Report claimed] that the presence in the Central Executive and Legislature of representatives of Princes who have always taken so keen an interest in all matters will be weighed and considered with a full appreciation of the issues at stake.[3]

This was also the reason which prompted the Conservative party to accept the proposal of an all-India federation with limited responsibility at the centre. Sir Samuel Hoare, the then Secretary of State for India, stressed that federation had been an important feature of the Simon Report and its acceptance by the princes had only brought the time closer. The Legislative Assembly of British India had been removed at a stroke, and it was now possible to 'rescue British India from the morass into which the doctrinaire liberalism of Montagu had plunged it'.[4]

Zetland, Secretary of State for India from 1935, was also of the opinion that the weight and influence of the princes could be used to keep the Congress away from complete control of the central government. He pointed out that the federal legislature would be so composed as to preclude the Congress from securing an absolute majority in either

1 Lord Meston, 'India's Decision', *Fortnightly Review* (Jan.-June 1937), p. 418.

2 *Report of Joint Committee on Indian Constitutional Reforms, 1933-4* (HMSO, 1934), para. 27.

3 *Ibid.,* para. 39.

4 Mss. Eur. E.240/52 (*Templewood Collection*), Memorandum by Hoare, 'Conservative Policy at the Round Table Conference', 12 Dec. 1930. IOL.

house 'unless they can capture substantial numbers of seats allotted either to the Muslim community or to the Indian States'.[1]

The variety of motives for which the British advocated the idea of federation makes it difficult to express any enthusiasm for the scheme. The units of which the federation was to be composed were too disparate to be joined suitably together; and it was obvious that on the British side the scheme was favoured because it provided an element of conservatism to act as an insurance against any extreme actions by the nationalists.[2] It was therefore not surprising that the states should be given such preferential treatment in the Federal Legislature. The idea was not only to secure their accession to the federation, but also to make their voice there a strong one.

The princes, however, had their own desiderata and were reluctant to enter the federation unless those were fulfilled. The Chamber of Princes had, as early as March 1933, put forward a number of demands: safeguard of their treaty rights, no interference in their internal affairs, the states to be required to join the federation collectively through a 'confederation'. A further conference of the rulers and the States' representatives was held in February 1935 when it was resolved that unless the Bill secured the vital interests of the States, 'the Bill and the Instrument of Accession cannot be regarded as acceptable to the Indian States'. Many of the objections raised to the Bill suggested that the princes, now that they were confronted with it, were not really willing to permit the federal authorities to exercise those minimal powers within their states which were essential in any federal system. A good example was their protest against the Governor General's being charged with a 'special responsibility' to prevent 'any grave menace to the peace or tranquillity of India or any part thereof' – a provision, they argued, that menaced their sovereign rights.[3]

Linlithgow was convinced, however, that it was in the best interest of the States that the federal scheme should be implemented quickly.[4] He emphatically pointed out that 'the interval between the initiation of provincial autonomy and the advent of Federal scheme cannot be in the nature of things a long one'.[5] Shortly afterwards the Viceroy decided to send special representatives to the important Indian states to 'assist' the

---

1 Mss. Eur. D.690/25B, Memorandum by Zetland, 9 Feb. 1939. IOL.

2 A.B. Keith, *A Constitutional History of India 1600-1935* (London, reprint, 1961), p. 474.

3 *Report of the Indian States Committee* (*Cmd.* 3302, 1928-29), p. 20.

4 Mss. Eur. F. 125/7/11, Note by C. Latimer, 20 Mar. 1939. IOL.

5 *Statesman*, 2 Aug. 1936.

princes in arriving at a decision on the federal issue.[1] Though Zetland viewed this procedure with a certain amount of misgiving,[2] he agreed in the end to Linlithgow's proposal. This was to be the last major diplomatic mission of the Political Department, but it was a mission with a difference:

> Our officer', wrote Sir Terrence Coen, 'toured not, as once, to Shah Shuja or to Ranjit Singh to acquaint them that the British were coming, but to Hyderabad, Mysore, Gwallior, Kashmir and the rest, saying that British were going.[3]

The result was obvious. Once the princes realized that British rule was on its last legs, they were no longer interested in complying with the wishes of the Viceroy. They were more concerned with the safeguarding of their 'sovereignty' when the British should relinquish power. Moreover, the emissaries were given no powers to 'coerce' the princes: their duty was simply to explain the Act and the draft Instrument of Accession. To explain, not persuade. They were in no sense plenipotentiaries.

Linlithgow commissioned Sir Courtenay Latimer, Sir Francis Wylie and A.C. Lothian. Each emissary would visit a group of states and discuss points of difficulty with the rulers and their ministers. In his letter to the princes, the Viceroy assured them that his own experience of the subject matter and of the discussion which culminated in the Act of 1935 had left him in no doubt about the difficulty which certain points could present to any one not closely associated with the preparation of the Act. The draft Instrument of Accession formed a balanced whole, and the Viceroy hoped that any difficulty which the rulers might experience with regard to the Act and the history of the federal scheme would be easily resolved with the assistance of the emissaries.[4]

The reports from the emissaries showed the value of Linlithgow's decision to send out this team. Wylie's report was particularly useful. He had been present at the discussions with the rulers of eleven states, none of which had apparently understood the practical aspects of the federation. The princes were under the impression that the federation would be much looser in nature than that which was actually embodied in the Act. The rulers made it clear that in their case the urge to unity was not

1 L/PO/463, telegram from Linlithgow to Zetland, 20 Aug. 1936. IOR.

2 Sir Conrad Corfield, 'Some Thoughts on British Policy and the Indian States, 1935-47', in C.H. Philips and P.M. Wainwright, (eds.) *Partition of India*, (London, 1970), pp. 527-8; A.C. Lothian *Kingdoms of Yesterday* (London, 1951), pp. 149-50.

3 Terence Creagh Coen, *The Indian Political Service; A Study in Indirect Rule* (London, 1971), p. 107.

4 L/PO/463, telegram from Linlithgow to Zetland, 20 Aug. 1936. IOR.

dominant, nor were they supplicants asking to come into the federation. The question which interested them was not whether the federation would enable them to contribute to the benefit of India as a whole, but whether their own position would be better and safer inside the federation than outside it. Wylie felt that he had managed to dispel many of their misconceptions and fears. There were, of course, some genuine problems for the states, but Wylie found that the princes were suggesting every limitation they could think of because they did not want to overlook any possibility which might occur to others. Wylie therefore suggested that the government should reassure them by a promise to give all the states equal terms so far as possible.

The mission, however, failed in its objective of expediting the federal negotiations. Most of the states clamoured for better terms and refused to accede unless those were granted. The concessions demanded varied from Hyderabad's request for a port at Masulipatnam to trivial demands like the addition of more guns to a ruler's salute. The envoys were able to achieve very little because they did not possess powers to negotiate. Moreover, the states had engaged a whole battery of lawyers who confused the minds of the princes by pointing out the various legal and constitutional loop-holes.[1] Linlithgow realized the necessity of giving the princes a firm lead in order to prevent the broad question of federation from being lost in detailed legal controversy.[2] He therefore urged Zetland to give the emissaries the authority to give rulings on certain questions put by the princes on the effects of accession to the federation without having to refer to the government.[3] Zetland restrained him. He thought that it would be a mistake to compress into one stage what had originally involved two. The emissaries might, he said, reach a point in their negotiations where more haste would result in less speed. The princes might feel that they were being rushed and take fright: let this particular series of visits remain exploratory.[4] Linlithgow surprisingly acquiesced.[5]

Soon after the receipt of the draft Instrument of Accession, a conference of the princes met in July 1936, and decided to prepare a

---

1   MSS. Eur. F.125/3/47, Wylie to Bertrand Glancy, 27 Nov. 1936. IOR.

2   Tara Chand, *History of Freedom Movement in India* (Delhi, 1961-72), iv, 258; Coen, *Indian Political Service,* p. 104.

3   Mss. Eur. F.125/15/103, telegram from Linlithgow to Zetland, 17 Sept 1936. IOL.

4   Mss. Eur. F.125/3/28, Zetland to Linlithgow, 26 Sept 1936; see also Mss. Eur. F.125/3/13, dated 28 June 1936.

5   See R.J. Moore, 'The Making of India's Paper Federation, 1927-35', C.H. Philips and M.D. Wainwright (eds.), *The Partition of India: Policies and Perspectives 1935-47* (London, 1970), p . 76.

questionnaire dealing with the various aspects of the federation. The data compiled from the replies were to be arranged in a tabular form which would help the rulers to make a comparison of their cases with those of others on any particular item[1] The princes were uniting for tough bargaining. It was apparent that they were in no mood to comply with the Viceroy's wishes and that they viewed their participation in the federation as a grave threat to their safety and 'sovereignty'. The rulers and their ministers again met in November 1938. Whilst reiterating their faith in the idea of federation, they declared that in the fast changing circumstances of the country it would be impossible for them to 'discharge their duties to the Crown, to their dynasties and their people' without the aid of specific safeguards. In January 1939, Linlithgow, whose patience had been severely taxed, decided to confront the rulers with a final offer and accordingly sent them a revised Instrument of Accession. The rulers were asked to decide within six months whether they were prepared to execute the Instrument of Accession or not.[2]

The reply came sooner than was expected. A committee of ministers of the Indian states under the presidency of Sir Akbar Hydari reported that the terms of the Instrument of Accession were unsatisfactory and demanded that the existing treaty rights should be guaranteed; protection should be afforded against subversive movements in the states; and federal officials should be excluded from the administration of the federal matters in the states. Questions affecting the fiscal arrangements were also raised, which will be discussed later.

The Hydari report, together with another report drafted by representatives of certain other states, came before a meeting of the princes in June 1939. The conference adopted a unanimous resolution which declared that 'the terms on the basis of which accession is offered are fundamentally unsatisfactory . . . and are therefore unacceptable'.[3] The conference also recorded its hope that the Government would not 'close the door on all-Indian Federation'.

The method adopted by the princes deserves notice. In the formal meetings the princes would not take a definite stand one way or the other — displaying a 'facing both ways resolution', as H.V. Hodson puts it — but subsequently they would approach the Political Department and plead for further concessions so that they could bring round the 'responsible section of rulers'. The Political Department would then get

---

1   *Statesman*, 27 Oct 1936.

2   Mss. Eur. D.609/25B, Memorandum by Zetland (Annexure 1), 27 July 1939. IOL.

3   *Ibid.*

busy in an effort to accommodate the demands, and there was thus a merry-go-round of demands and concessions.

It was surprising that at this late stage the princes should still show distrust of the scheme which, from their point of view, was unlikely to be bettered in the future. Nor was it easy to understand a decision which aimed at retaining the existing 'sovereignty' of the states almost unaltered, particularly in view of the constitutional changes in British India where substantial power had been transferred from British hands to 'elected' Indian ministers. Indeed the decision of the princes appeared to run counter not only to the scheme of federation, but also to the whole trend of political development in India. It was of vital importance that the princes should have a voice in the federal legislature and the executive; the existing irresponsible centre would constitute a weakness in the administrative structure which would ultimately effect the states even more than the provinces. The princes could not view with satisfaction a position in which all central matters would be dealt with by a legislature and by a ministry drawn exclusively from British India, and containing elements hostile to the existence of the states in their existing form.

The decision of the princes to reject the revised Instrument of Accession would have created a constitutional crisis had it been based on the same objections to the federation as were raised by the main political parties. This would have thrown the whole question of the future government of India into the melting pot.

The policy of gentle persuasion had failed. Linlithgow, in fact, would have preferred to exert pressure on the princes to jostle them into making up their minds quickly.[1] But Zetland did not approve of such a course as he felt helpless in the face of the 'diehard' opponents in Britain who, as we shall see later, 'were applying all the pressure they could muster to dissuade the princes from acceptance'.[2] Linlithgow therefore had little choice but to continue to plead with the princes to withdraw their opposition to the federal scheme. In the course of a speech to the Chamber of Princes just before the outbreak of the War in August 1939 Linlithgow assured the rulers that he would not have commended the federation to them if he had not been personally satisfied that it effectively secured their future safety. 'The offer', he declared, 'embodies the safeguards which His Majesty's Government regards as appropriate and sufficient for that purpose.' The princely

---

1   Mss. Eur. F.125/4/47, Zetland to Linlithgow, 19 Apr 1937. IOL.
2   J. Glendevon, *The Viceroy at Bay* (London, 1971), p. 129.

order, with one-third of the seats in the lower house and two-fifths in the upper, would have an influential voice in the federal legislature. 'This has always seemed to be a bloc which, if the Princely Order are wise, and hold together, no political party can afford to ignore.'[1] However, it was clear that despite Linlithgow's coaxing, the chances of the princes' acceding to the federation were remote. In view of the persistent obstinacy of the princes, Linlithgow extended the date for returning replies to the Instrument of Accession to 1 September 1939. He was hopeful that during the interval he would be able to secure the accession of some important states which would possibly influence others to view the proposals more favourably.[2]

Apart from difficulties in individual cases, there was one aspect of the scheme preventing the accession of the states which was common to the princes as a whole. The princes were unwilling to forego certain sources of revenues, such as the excise duties, which the constitution had assigned to the federation. The princes had hoped, as we noted earlier, that the participation of the states in the federation would improve their financial position, because the states would presumably have a share in determining the fiscal policy of India and thereby would be able to further their own interests to some extent. The findings of the Davidson Committee[3] seemed to indicate, however, that the subjects of the states would, under certain conditions, become liable to direct taxation levied by the federal government, and that some of the sources of revenue at the disposal of state administrations might be tapped by the federation. The states would also be deprived of their right to levy the salt and match excises. It thus seemed probable that the taxable capacity of the peoples of the states would in time be greatly diminished by the prior claims of federal taxation, and that the states would not secure a compensating share in the customs revenues of India. Instead of improving the economic resources of the states, as the princes had hoped, the scheme appeared likely to diminish them.

Linlithgow realized that if federation meant an immediate sacrifice of revenue it would have no attraction for the states. He therefore urged that in regard to financial matters the *status quo* should be maintained.[4] This guaranteed the states such revenue as they already enjoyed from sources within the federal field. The proposal to maintain the *status quo*

1   *Speeches by the Marquess of Linlithgow* (Simla, 1944), ii, 130.
2   Mss. Eur. D.609/25B, Memorandum by Zetland, 27 July 1939. IOL.
3   *Indian States Enquiry Committee (Financial), 1932 (Cmd.* 4103). The Committee was appointed by HMG to report on the financial aspect of the proposed federation.
4   Mss. Eur. F.125/4/47, Linlithgow to Zetland, 19 Aug 1937. IOL.

involved a substantial alteration of the scheme on a point on which Parliament had already expressed its judgement.[1] It would have been neither wise nor proper to ask Parliament to reconsider that judgement merely because of the fears that the states would not assent to the scheme as it stood. To have done so would have been to reopen the whole controversy which the 1935 Act was intended to still. Moreover, in this connection the position of British India needed to be considered since its cooperation was also necessary for the success of the federation. There had already been much talk in the press to the effect that the federal scheme was unjust to British India and unduly favourable to the states, and any concessions to the states would inevitably intensify this feeling.[2] To this, however, Linlithgow replied that even if the question of the financial *status quo* were excluded, it would still be impossible to avoid some amendment of the Act before a final approach could be made to the states. Apart from details, there were still the outstanding questions of how and to what extent the states' extra-territorial rights were to be protected. If that protection was not found to be necessary, he argued, any contention based on the supposed sanctity of the Act must go by the board. With them went, said Linlithgow, any argument based on the exacerbation of the British Indian sentiment, for so long as the adjustments of the Act were not all in favour of the states British India would have little ground for complaint.[3]

Zetland, however, pointed out that if the princes were to retain their existing revenues, they would be obtaining from the pool more than they were putting into it; and at the same time their contribution to the federation would be considerably less than that contemplated by Parliament.[4] The concession of an individual item to a particular state might have comparatively little importance, but the cumulative effect of granting it all round could be prejudicial to the interests of the federation. Besides, it would be construed as a bias towards the states and thus provide the anti-federationists with a useful propaganda instrument.[5] Although Zetland appreciated the difficulty of trying to persuade the rulers to enter the federation under the Act as it stood, he was not prepared to make even temporary concessions. He was emphatic that the Act must remain inviolate. Indeed, he was certain that no amendment of the Act, nor of the Instrument of Accession, could

1 1935 Act, Section 140.

2 See editorial comment, *The Times,* 6 Nov. 1938.

3 Mss. Eur. F.125/4/47, Linlithgow to Zetland, 19 Aug. 1937; see also Mss. Eur. F.125/5/38, Linlithgow to Zetland, 23 June 1938. IOL.

4 Mss. Eur. F.125/26/92, Zetland to Linlithgow, 1 Nov. 1937. IOL.

5 Mss. Eur. F.125/5/3, Zetland to Linlithgow, 22 Jan. 1938; Mss. Eur. F.125/5/29, Zetland to Linlithgow, 12 June 1938. IOL.

maintain the states in an unduly preferential position in the federation for very long. Moreover, legal protection of that kind could not withstand the play of political forces, and maximum friction would be generated if those forces could establish equilibrium only by breaches of the constitution. Besides, such preferential treatment would be difficult to defend in the Federal Court. Zetland acquainted Neville Chamberlain with this dispute and found him averse to any course which involved legislation that might revitalize the 'diehards'.[1]

A prolonged correspondence stretching over a year ensued between the Government of India and the India Office, but the issue remained unresolved. Eventually, in the summer of 1938, Linlithgow came to Britain on leave and impressed upon Zetland the necessity for financial concessions. An unwilling Zetland obtained the approval of the cabinet for an amending bill that would make the concession possible.[2] Zetland finally gave way to Linlithgow's persuasion, but much time had been lost during which the Indian political scene had changed considerably.

Succinctly stated, the position was that although the princes initially accepted the idea of federation, they were all the while afraid of their powers being absorbed by the federal authority; and the clearer the federal proposals became, the more confused were the princes. Their attitude cooled still further when they realized that the federation would not bring any financial gains. The princes became increasingly conscious of the overriding powers of the federal authority. Lastly, they were suspicious of the motives of the British-Indian politicians, a suspicion which was heightened by the Congress-inspired agitation for responsible governments in the states.

For the accession of the states was not simply an issue between the government and the princes. The activities of the Congress and the Moslem League were also responsible for the failure of the princes to accede. The federal scheme was so designed that the combined influence of the princes and the Moslems in the federal legislature would outweigh that of the Congress. Unlike the provinces, the states' representatives in the federal legislature were not to be elected by the people but were to be nominated by the rulers. The prospect of the Congress obtaining a majority at the Centre was therefore doubtful. It was principally for this reason that the Congress was opposed to the federation. To counterbalance the states' representatives it would have to obtain support from

1   Mss. Eur. F.125/4/41, Zetland to Linlithgow, 6 Oct. 1937. IOL.

2   L/PO/436, Notes on discussion between Zetland and Linlithgow, (nd), IOR; John L. Dundas, *Essayez, the Memoirs of Lawrence, Second Marquess of Zetland* (London, 1956), pp. 241 ff.

other groups, some of whom were opposed to it. The Congress therefore opened a campaign against the autocratic rule of the princes and set out to democratize the states by a *tour de force*. Their object was to ensure that the representatives of the states to the federal legislature should be popularly elected and not nominated by the rulers.[1] In this way the Congress hoped to obtain a substantial number of seats reserved for the states. The 1936 election triumph was the fire that caused the Congress agitation to 'overlap frontier lines like sparks across the street', (to use the terms Montagu and Chelmsford had used about the implications for the princes of nationalism in British India).[2]

Before 1937 the Congress had refrained from interfering in the affairs of the states, ostensibly in deference to Gandhi's belief that the princes held power in trust for the people.[3] Gandhi was at this time taking a long term view of the problems of the states. Many of the princes were able rulers. At the Round Table Conference they had demonstrated their patriotism by identifying themselves with the cause of Indian independence. It would be a mistake, Gandhi had pointed out, to regard them as 'reactionaries' or as stumbling blocks in the struggle for independence. In the internal affairs of their states they were, no doubt, autocratic: the undemocratic character of the states was well known. What was also known to the Congress leader was that 'Indian India' had not only its own forces to suppress any agitation, but also the backing of the 'Paramount Power'. Gandhi therefore reasoned that it would be good strategy for the Congress and the princes to achieve a common front in the struggle for independence and leave the question of internal reforms to a later date. In any case many of the states were introducing liberal reforms. There was another consideration which determined Gandhi's attitude. He was reluctant to launch a struggle simultaneously against both the British and the princes because, prior to 1937, the Congress was not sufficiently organized to man a two pronged attack. Gandhi wanted to direct the full force of the Congress against the British. He believed that after the British had left India, there would be time enough to deal with the princes. As indeed there was.

But after 1937, the Congress began to take a greater interest in the affairs of the states. Its overwhelming success in the provincial elections had raised great hopes in the minds of many of the princes' subjects who also aspired to obtain the same measure of freedom as was enjoyed by the people in the provinces.[4] The Congress began to devote a great deal

---

1 *Madras Mail,* 2 Nov. 1938.

2 *Report on Indian Constitutional Reforms, 1918. Cmd.*9109, para. 157.

3 *Round Table,* No. 100, p. 763.

4 Government of India, *White Paper on the Indian States, 1950* (henceforth

of attention to such questions as fundamental rights, civil liberties, adult franchise and mass contact. With Nehru and Bose in the forefront of its leadership, the Congress began to consider the application of these principles to India as a whole. Thus interest in the affairs of the states became more animated. Agitations for democratic rights were witnessed in many states, particularly in Mysore where they reached a high pitch. In October 1937, the Congress, for the first time, openly censured the Mysore government for its policy of 'repression' and appealed to the people of India 'to give all support and encouragement to the people of Mysore in the struggle against the State for the right of self-determination'.[1] Gandhi resented this overt support for the states' people and criticized it for being contrary to the policy which the Congress had followed hitherto.[2]

Gandhi's rebuke was ignored. At the Haripura session in 1938, the Congress justified its earlier policy towards the states. The objective was reiterated, though the resolution was worded more cautiously and intended to soothe the agitation in the states. It was stated that the Congress stood for the same political and social objectives in the states as in British India and considered the states an integral part of India. The Congress, it was admitted, was not yet able to liberate the people of the states by itself operating within their borders, and therefore, 'the burden of carrying on the struggle for freedom must fall on the people of states'. The Congress as an organization could only offer moral support; but individual Congressmen would be free to render any assistance.[3] Nehru, who had been chafing at the hesitant policy of the Congress towards the states, now claimed that the Congress would work for the attainment of the goal defined at Haripura: 'There was no question of non-intervention; the Congress, as represented by the will of the Indian people, recognizes no bars which limit its freedom of activity in any matter pertaining to India and her people'.[4]

It was impossible, even for Gandhi, to draw a line which would separate the states from the general awakening that was taking place in British India. A strong left wing had emerged within the Congress advocating direct intervention in the states. The interests of the rulers had been safe in British India as long as law and order was under British control. But now, in the Congress-governed provinces at any rate, it rested with the Congress ministries in the first instance to

White Paper 1950) pp. 38-9.
1   IAR, 1937, ii, 361-2.
2   Harijan, 13 Nov. 1937.
3   IAR, 1938, ii, 299-300.
4   IAR, 1939, ii, 437-8.

prevent subversive action against the states; and it was only as a last resort that the states could be protected by the governor's special responsibility for 'the protection of the right of any Indian State and the rights and dignity of the Rulers thereof'.[1] The ministries of the provinces adjoining the states declined to use their statutory powers to prevent agitation being organized within their provinces and then launched beyond them.

The wave of popular awakening exerted a profound influence on the Congress leaders. This was particularly so with Gandhi whose attitude towards the states now appeared to undergo a definite change. He hailed the simultaneous awakening in the states as a product of the 'time spirit' and declared that there was no half way house between total extinction of the states and full responsible government.[2] The policy of non-intervention by the Congress was, in his opinion, 'a perfect piece of statesmanship when the people of the States were not awakened', but once the people had been politically aroused that policy would be 'cowardice'.[3] A policy of non-intervention, he warned, could not be guaranteed indefinitely:

> It is impossible for me to defend it in the face of injustice perpetrated in the States. If the Congress feels that it has the power to offer effective interference, it will be bound to do so when the call comes... [4]

The old Congress's respect for the princes' authority was gone for ever, and though the Congress as a body still refrained from direct intervention, its members, including Gandhi and Nehru, took an active part in the agitation in the states.

It was against this background that the Congress met at Tripuri in March 1939. In his presidential address, Bose advocated a policy of direct intervention in the states.[5] Accordingly the Congress made a reappraisal of its policy towards the states. It was stated: 'This policy [of non-intervention] was dictated by circumstances and recognition of the limitation inherent in the circumstances, but it was never conceived as an obligation'. The Congress, it was claimed, 'had always possessed the right ... to guide the people of the States and lend them its influence'. The 'great awakening that is taking place among the people of the States may lead to a relaxation or to complete removal of the

1   1935 Act, Section 52 (1) (f).
2   *Harijan*, 3 Dec. 1938.
3   *Times of India* (Bombay), 25 Jan. 1939.
4   M.K. Gandhi, *The Indian States Problem* (Allahabad, 1941), p. 104.
5   *IAR*, 1939, ii, 325-7.

restraints which the Congress imposed upon itself', thus resulting in ever increasing identification of the Congress with the States' people.[1] Thus the Tripuri resolution bridged the gulf between the Congress and the states.

The Congress's agitation for responsible government spread with great rapidity throughout the Indian states and did more than anything else to frighten away the princes from entering the federation. The Congress, which was most likely to be powerfully represented at the centre, now threw away even the cloak of 'non-interference' and began openly to champion the reform movement in the states, so that it could secure some of the seats assigned to the states in the federal legislature.

From the very beginning when the federal negotiations started the Congress had criticized the undemocratic character of the states.[2] Each state was governed by its prince with the 'advice' of a political officer appointed by the British Government who resided in the court of the prince to whom he was assigned. This 'advice' was in all important matters really a 'control', reducing the prince to the position of nominal ruler.[3] The British Government, as suzerain in India, did not allow the rulers to form alliances or enter into armed dispute, but so long as their action did not affect the interest or prestige of the British empire, the princes were allowed considerable freedom to administer the internal affairs of their states. The Congress disliked the autocratic character of the states, and was afraid that the representatives of the states, in the federal legislature, if selected by the rulers, would in effect constitute a new and more objectionable instance of the previous 'official bloc'; because of the extraordinary weighting given to the states the position of these princely representatives would be very strong. Numerically they would constitute a powerful bloc, forty per cent in the upper house and thirty-three per cent in the lower house. If they acted together they would be in a position to demand representation in any coalition government; and a party not possessing an absolute majority in both houses would find itself, in critical moments, at the mercy of states' representatives who, it was feared, could easily be swayed by the officials.[4] Furthermore, the Congress left-wing feared that the princely

---

1   *Ibid.,* pp. 336-7.

2   For an account of the political conditions in the states see A. Citizen (pseud), *Under the Rule of His Exalted Highness – Condition in Nizam's State* (Poona, 1938), p. 1; P.N. Bazaz, *History of the Struggle for Freedom in Kashmir* (Delhi, 1954), pp. 140-1; All-India States' Peoples Congress, *Orissa States' Enquiry Committee Report* (Bombay, 1939), pp. 1-60; D.N. Kachru, *The Jhabua Tragedy* (Bombay, nd.), pp. 16-26; and *White Paper, 1950, passim.*

3   Ramanda Chatterjee, 'The Feudal Third in India', *Asia* (August, 1939), p. 437.

4   L.F. Rushbrook Williams, 'Indian Constitutional Problems', *The Nineteenth Century and After* (Jan-June, 1939), p. 556.

representatives would throw their influence into the scale of caution and conservatism, and thereby impede radical legislation in the economic field.

In the face of the Congress's determination to democratize the states, the princes looked to the 'Paramount Power' to safeguard their interests. It was claimed that the British Government was bound by treaties to support its princely allies if their position were threatened by agitation for reforms. The obligations of the British Government had been defined by the Butler Committee in 1929 in the following terms:

> The promise of the King-Emperor to maintain unimpaired the privileges, rights and dignities of the Princes carries with it a duty to protect the prince against attempts to eliminate him, and to substitute another form of government. If these attempts were due ... not to misgovernment, but widespread popular demand for change, the Paramount Power would be bound to maintain the rights, privileges and dignity of the Princes; but it would also be bound to suggest such measures as would satisfy this demand without eleminating the Prince.[1]

The last point was significant. The Congress could point to a statement by Lord Winterton, a member of the Cabinet, to the effect that the 'Paramount Power would certainly not obstruct proposals for constitutional advance initiated by the Ruler of the State'.[2] It was clear that while the British Government was bound to protect the princes against any external interference or internal subversion, it was also duty bound to impress upon them the necessity of introducing reforms. Linlithgow realized that unless some radical changes were brought about in the states it would only be a question of time before they succumbed to the Congress's agitation.[3] The bigger states, with more resources and better administrative machinery, were capable of looking after themselves; it was the future of the middle-sized and smaller states which was of immediate concern.[4] Linlithgow felt that the policy of abstention from interference which the government had hitherto followed was no longer feasible and would have to give way to active pressure for administrative reforms, such as improving the standard of the officials, limiting the privy purse to ten per cent of the total revenue of the states, and publishing an annual administration report. On the constitutional level, Linlithgow wanted the rulers to

1 *Report of the Indian States Committee, 1928-29 (Cmd.* 3302, 1929), para. 50.

2 *Parliamentary Debates,* House of Commons, vol. 322, 21 Feb. 1938.

3 Marquess of Linlithgow, *Speeches and Statements* (New Delhi, 1945), pp. 183-6; Fitze, *Twilight of the Maharajas,* pp. 86-7; Glendevon, *The Viceroy at Bay,* p. 107.

4 *White Paper, 1950,* pp. 38-9.

sponsor representative institutions in the states. But these proposals were opposed by the Political Department which insisted that questions of constitutional advance should be left to the Chamber of Princes.[1]

Zetland was in general agreement with Linlithgow's proposal as regards administrative reforms. But on the vital issue of constitutional advance, he considered that the initiative should rest with the rulers themselves. He felt that constitutional development in the states, once begun, in the nature of things could not but be regulated and limited in the same way as administrative changes, and that no policy conceived by the British Government could by itself maintain the rulers or ensure against their eventual submission to the Congress's dictates.[2] Zetland thus tried to steer a middle course by encouraging administrative improvements without drastically altering the constitution. He sought a 'holding position'. The states should neither gallop nor remain stationary. Perhaps on paper this seemed a nice compromise, but in practice it was no answer to the reconciliation of the new India with the old.

In the late 1930s no solution to the states problem seemed to be possible. The contradictory policies of the past had rendered it intractable. Britain was 'on the horns of a painful dilemma'.[3] It could not openly oppose democratization of the states, yet the activity of the Congress was bound to scare away the princes from the federation. In 1940 the Jam Saheb of Nawanagar maintained that the hostility of the Congress towards the states proved to be the decisive factor in dissuading the princes from acceding to the federation. 'It was felt that the attitude of a large section of British India towards the Crown', Nawanagar told the Chamber of Princes 'and the recent experience of organized subversive movements from British India against the States do not in the present circumstances provide that basis which is essential for a close union between British India and the states.'[4]

Furthermore, the Congress's campaign against the states had two unfortunate effects. First, it further aggravated the tension between the Congress and the Moslem League, whose leaders perceived that the Congress, to whatever extent it may have been honestly animated by a desire to promote democratic institutions in the states, was really engaged upon a tactical manoeuvre with the object of securing power in the federal legislature.[5] Second, the Congress's assault upon the states

1 Linlithgow, *Speeches and Statements,* pp. 183-5.
2 Mss. Eur. D.609/26, Zetland to Linlithgow, 21 Mar. 1939. IOL.
3 Mss. Eur. F.125/6/48, Zetland to Carlton Heath, 19 Dec. 1939. IOL.
4 *Proceedings of Chamber of Princes,* (1940) pp. 42, 48.
5 See below, chapter 4.

from 1937 onwards violated the spirit of the federal constitution with its emphasis upon autonomous units. The princes resented the Congress interference in their states. They had envisaged federation as 'the coming together for certain purposes of Indian States and Provinces for joint action on matters of common interest', and if they had imagined that democratization of their states was to precede its accomplishment then 'the idea of federation would never have emerged into the realm of practical politics'.[1]

Undoubtedly the most difficult part of the scheme was the attempt to federate 'democratic' British India and 'autocratic' states in a single federation. But the Congress, in opposing the federation, had overplayed its hand. There were strong arguments against the Congress's proposal that British India should federate first, and that the states should be left to come in only when they had become more democratic.[2] Its greatest single advantage was constitutional unity. This unity derived from the fact that ultimate responsibility both in British India and in the states rested in the same person – the Viceroy. A federation of British India alone would begin to impair the unity, because British India would be governed on the advice of the ministers responsible to the Legislature, while Paramountcy in Indian India would be exercised with responsibility to the Secretary of State for India. If the organic unity of India was allowed to disappear, separatist influences would inevitably begin to operate.[3] The arguments which were circulating during the Round Table Conference would be revived: the bigger states should first group into a loose association or 'confederation' which would then negotiate on equal terms with British India.[4] But a voluntary union of separate 'sovereignties' has always been difficult.[5]

There were anomalies in the proposed federal scheme, but the price was worth paying to ensure that India started on her career of national self-government as a constitutional and organic whole. This seemed to be all the truer in so far as the movement for constitutional government inside the states was growing and the main objections to the federation might well have disappeared when it reached fruition. In due course basic civil liberties – for example, the right to *habeas corpus,* freedom of speech and political association – might well be established. And as

1   Mss. Eur. F.125/6/48a, Memorandum by C.P. Ramaswamy Aiyar Nov. 1938. IOL.

2   *Harijan*, 2 Sept. 1939.

3   *Manchester Guardian*, 19 June 1931.

4   Maharaja of Patiala, *Federation and Indian States* (Simla, 1931), *passim.*

5   See Lord Lothian's statement in the *Statesman,* 27 Jan. 1938; K.M. Munshi, *Pilgrimage to Freedom,* i, 389.

political consciousness grew, the princes like the monarchs of Europe might gradually become constitutional rulers. The powers of the Paramountcy would certainly not be used to deny their subjects the liberties and rights which had already been established in British India.

In retrospect it seems that a better policy for the Congress in the late 1930s might have been to placate the princes. In the long run the Congress stood a good chance of controlling the states' representatives through the progressive democratization of their states. The Moslem League at the time was still weak, it had not yet formulated the demand for Pakistan, and it would probably have accepted the terms approved by the government. But the Congress was too impatient to obtain control at the centre.

A point of great importance, often ignored by scholars, is the fact that the Congress was opposed to the federal scheme as envisaged in the 1935 Act, but not to the principle of federation as such. An essential clue to the Congress's opposition is missed if a distinction is not made between federation in general as a constitutional device, and the particular federation which the Act envisaged. It was agreed on all sides that some form of federation offered the only practical means of holding ʿthe country together. The diversity of cultures and the multiciplity of languages combined with the great size of the country militated against a unitary form of government.[1]

The most obvious defects of the federal scheme in Congress eyes lay in the various devices which sought to introduce a conservative element into the federal legislature. The Congress complained that a principle objective of the federation was to increase the weight of the conservative forces in order to prevent a nationalist party like the Congress from securing a majority in the federal legislature. Clement Attlee, the leader of the British Labour Party, had similarly objected to the federal scheme because he thought that it had been designed so as to exclude ʿthe Congress party from effective power in the new constitution. On many occasions provisions have been deliberately put forward with that end in view'.[2] An examination of the federal provisions will show that there was some justification in the Congress's complaints.

The federal legislature was to consist of two chambers: a Council of State and a Federal Assembly. The princes were to be given representation in both Houses out of all proportion to the size and population of

---

1 Nehru's speech at Faizpur, *IAR*, 1936, ii, 222-8; Congress resolution at Haripura, *IAR*, 1938, i, 298.
2 Parliamentary Debates, House of Commons, vol. 302, cols. 824-8, 4 June 1935.

their states — 104 out of 260 in the Council of State, and 125 out of 275 in the Federal Assembly.[1]

Another source of Congress grievance was the weighting devices governing the choice of the elected members. In the Council of State, of the remaining 156 seats only 75 were to be 'general' seats which would be open to direct election by an electorate estimated to number about 150,000 or 0·05 per cent of the population of British India. The remaining seats were to be allotted to the Moslems (49), Sikhs (4), Scheduled Castes (6), Women (6), Europeans (7), Anglo-Indians (1), Indian Christians (2), and other minorities.[2]

In the Federal Assembly of 250 seats allocated to British India only 86 were to be 'general'; seats open to indirect elections from the provincial assemblies. The rest were to be divided among various groups: Moslems (82), Scheduled Castes (19), Sikhs (6), Anglo-Indians (4), Europeans (8), Indian Christians (8), Commerce (11), Landholders (7), Labour (10), Women (9), and so on.[3]

It was apparent from such reservations that the chances of the Congress controlling the centre were nearly non-existent. For example, if the Congress won all the general seats (86), together with the seats reserved for labour groups (10) and women (9), it would still have only 105 seats. And even if the Congress could reach an agreement with the Moslems and acquire all the Moslem seats (82), the total number of seats would be 187 — one short of majority. The Council of State would still remain out of its reach.

Let us now examine the powers of the federal legislature. With regard to financial powers, the budget was to be divided into two parts: 'expenditures charged upon the revenues of the Federation' and 'other expenditures'. The first included all the heavier expenditure, such as debt interest, the official salaries and pensions, defence costs, etc, which were not to be put to the vote in the legislature.[4] These 'non-votable' items constituted three-quarters to four-fifths of total expenditure. The Viceroy could at his discretion determine whether any item of expenditure fell into the 'non-votable' category. With regard to remaining expenditure the legislature could only express an opinion, but it had no control.[5] No financial bill could be introduced without the prior

1   1935 Act, Section 18.

2   1935 Act, Schedule 1, Allocation of seats for representatives of British India in the Council of State.

3   1935 Act, Schedule 1, Table of seats in the Federal Assembly for representatives of British India.

4   1935 Act, Section 33.

5   1935 Act, Section 34.

recommendation of the Viceroy. If the Assembly refused or reduced any grant, the Viceroy could declare it to be necessary for the discharge of his 'special responsibility', and authorize the expenditure. Britain retained effective financial controls for safeguarding her economic interests in India. Congressmen cited Laski's dictum that the Act 'seems to me a supreme example of economic imperialism in action'.[1]

Defence was outside the purview of the legislature. The members of the covenanted services, civil and police, who were appointed by the Secretary of State, were protected by special provisions.[2] Within the remaining permitted sphere of legislation, the legislature still had no independent powers. If the legislature passed a bill which the government did not approve, the Viceroy could 'withhold' his assent altogether. Alternatively, he could 'reserve' it for further consideration, and if he kept it 'reserved' for twelve months, the matter dropped. Further, if the Viceroy, having given his assent, later changed his mind, he could disallow it and it would become 'null and void'.[3] On the other hand if the legislature failed to pass a measure which the Viceroy considered necessary, he could pass it as a 'Governor General's Act', and it would have the force of ordinary legislation. The Viceroy could also issue ordinances with force of law for six months at a time.[4]

No fewer than ninety-four sections of the Act conferred 'special discretionary powers' on the Viceroy. To these were added the 'reserved powers'. As 'Reserved Departments', the Viceroy held under his exclusive control Defence, External Affairs, Ecclesiastical Affairs and Excluded Areas.[5] Finally there were the 'special powers' which enabled the Viceroy to take any action necessary for the discharge of his 'special responsibility'.[6] Among other things the 'special responsibilities' included the 'prevention of any grave menace to the peace or tranquillity of India'; 'safeguarding the legitimate interests of minorities'; prevention of commercial or financial discrimination against British individuals or companies operating in India; prevention of discrimination against British imports into India; the protection of the rights of the states and the princes.

The limitations of the federal part of the 1935 Act have been discussed at some length in order to understand the Congress's objections

1   Herold J. Laski, 'The Indian Report', *Nation,* cxl (2 Jan. 1935), p. 15.
2   1935 Act, Section 240.
3   1935 Act, Section 32.
4   1935 Act, Sections 44, 43.
5   1935 Act, Section 11 (1).
6   1935 Act, Sections 12 (1) and (2).

to the federation.[1] But it should be pointed out that the Congress's opposition to the federal scheme arose in part from its failure to realize that the federal system, like the provincial system, rested not on the old system of dyarchy but on the principle of responsible government. This meant that the initiative over the whole field of federal government, except in defence and foreign affairs, would gradually pass, unless all experience elsewhere was falsified, to the ministry. The Viceroy, unless he could obtain the backing of public opinion (as he probably could if any party attacked the legitimate rights of the minorities) would increasingly have to accept the advice of his 'responsible' ministers, rather than provoke a crisis from which there was no easy exit. Even in the field of foreign affairs and defence there could be no arbitrary division, for the reason that no Viceroy would wish to certify a military budget but would inevitably like to carry the support of his ministry on defence and foreign policy.

The first shot in the campaign against the federation was fired by Nehru. In his presidential address at the Faizpur Congress in December 1936, Nehru declared that 'utterly bad as the Act is, there is nothing so bad in it as this Federation and so we must exert ourselves to the utmost to break this'.[2] The Congress adopted a resolution rejecting the Act because, in its opinion, the Act did not represent the will of the Indian nation, and because it was designed to facilitate 'further exploitation of the Indian masses'.[3]

A year later the All India Congress Committee passed another resolution reiterating their 'emphatic condemnation and complete opposition to the scheme', and their decision to combat it in every way open to them. But no detailed plans for combating it were drawn. The general opinion was that the only effective method of preventing federation was to compel the governors to suspend the constitution.[4]

At the Haripura session in February 1938, the Congress defined its policy towards the federal scheme and the moves to combat it. The resolution expressly rejected the federation and warned that every possible measure would be taken to prevent its introduction.[5] It will be

---

1   It may be interesting to note that the same 1935 Act, with a few amendments, remained in force both in India and Pakistan for quite some time after the end of the British rule in 1947. When these countries, India in 1950 and Pakistan in 1956, adopted their own constitutions framed by their respective constituent assemblies, they showed remarkable resemblance to the 1935 Act.

2   *Statesman,* 31 Dec. 1936.

3   *Ibid.*

4   *IAR,* 1937, ii, 327; *Statesman,* 4 Nov. 1937.

5   *IAR,* 1938, i, 297-8.

seen that the rejection of the federal scheme in this resolution was absolute and did not leave the door open for negotiations. This absolute rejection was based on the view that the federal scheme represented, not a possible step on the path of self-government, but a strengthening of the hold of the British Government.

What was to be the policy of the Congress in the event of Britain endeavouring to impose the federal constitution? To this crucial question no specific answer was given by the Haripura Congress meeting. Linlithgow believed that in the Congress's inner circle, however, the view was held that absolute rejection was a preliminary gesture, and would eventually give way to some form of acquiescence, as in the case of acceptance of office.[1] This view tallied with the known tendencies of the moderate elements who controlled the party machine. They were willing to enter the federation provided some modifications were made in the practical working of the Act.[2] There were indications to suggest that the opposition to the federation would quieten down.[3] Gandhi was opposed to giving prominence to federation other than by expressing condemnation of the scheme; and from the wording of the resolutions it appeared that no detailed plans to combat federation had been worked out. The moderates did not desire a deadlock as they were anxious to implement the election pledges. It thus seemed that the Congress would eventually try to bargain with the government for a modification of the federal scheme more acceptable to it. The Congress's resolutions, though emphatic in their rejection of the federation, were worded vaguely so that the Congress, while maintaining a show of consistency, would be able to adapt itself to any political exigency. Since the Congress had accepted office, retreat in the constitutional field would be detrimental to the Congress's objective. By staying in the government it would be in a better position to persuade the British Government to amend the federal scheme.

In private conversations the Congress leaders had mooted the possibility of an early establishment of the federation.[4] Gandhi had given Lord Lothian a note which though it embodied his 'personal view which I have not discussed with my co-workers', indicated that he would

---

1 Mss. Eur. F.125/5/26, Linlithgow to all Governors, 7 May 1938. IOL.

2 Mss. Eur. F.125/5/4, Memorandum by Lord Lothian, 24 Jan, 1938. IOL.

3 Mss. Eur. F.125/3/22, Linlithgow to Zetland, 17 Apr. 1936. See also Mss. Eur. F.125/3/26, Linlithgow to Zetland, 3 Sept. 1936; Mss. Eur. F.125/6/36, Brabourne to Zetland, 22 Oct. 1938. IOL.

4 Mss. Eur. F.125/5/8, 'Survey of secret information relating to the Congress attitude towards federation'. (nd.) IOL.

accept federation if certain modifications were made. He wanted guarantees that 'before taking in the Princes, elementary rights of the States' people are guaranteed and their representation takes place through elections.[1] Gandhi, shortly afterwards, told the Viceroy that 'he attached the utmost importance' to the formula which he had indicated to Lothian. 'I got the impression', wrote Linlithgow, 'that he would accept federation, if some large States introduced the principle of popular choice'.[2] During this period conversations also took place between officials and some Congressmen, G.D. Birla and Bhulabhai Desai, and rumours began to be heard that a compromise was in view.[3] These rumours were not entirely without foundation, both Desai and S. Satyamurti had admitted to Linlithgow that the Congress would accept federation.[4] In December 1937, Gopal Reddi, a minister in the Madras government was reported to have said that the Congress would accept the federation, although a 'show of combating federation would have to be maintained'.[5]

The left-wing in the Congress were suspicious that the moderates were secretly 'playing the federation game'. It was reported in the press that Desai, who was the Congress leader in the Central Assembly, had suggested that the Congress might work the federal scheme. This brought from Subhas Bose a denial that any Congress leader could think in terms of working the federation: he threatened 'civil war' within the Congress if the scheme was accepted by the Congress, and he would himself feel it his duty to 'lay down the burden of [President's] office in order to be free to carry on a raging and tearing campaign against the federal scheme'.[6] In order to strengthen the fight against the imposition of the federation, Bose, who had been the Congress President the previous year (1938), decided to contest the election for president again in 1939. In announcing his candidature, Bose claimed: 'I feel strongly that we should have, during this momentous year, a genuine anti-Federationist in the Presidential chair'.[7] For the first time the

---

1 Mss. Eur. F.125/5/4, Note by Gandhi, 'For Lord Lothian and responsible statesmen only', 20 Jan. 1938. IOL.

2 Mss. Eur. F.125/5/22, Note of an interview between the Viceroy and Gandhi, 15 Apr. 1938. IOL.

3 Mss. Eur. F.125/4/69, Note of an interview between the Viceroy and Birla, 3 Dec. 1937; F.125/4/53, interview with Desai, 7 Sept. 1937; see also F.125/4/75, Linlithgow to Zetland, 30 Dec. 1937. IOL.

4 Mss. Eur. F.125/3, Linlithgow to Zetland, 17 Aug. 1936; F.125/5/18, notes of an interview with Desai, 11 Apr. and Satyamurti, 12 Apr. 1938. IOL.

5 Mss. Eur. F.125/5/18, 'Secret Survey'. IOL.

6 S.C. Bose, Crossroads (London, 1962), pp. 47-50.

7 Statesman, 26 Jan. 1939.

presidential election was openly contested. Bose defeated his opponent, P. Sittaramayya, who was supported by Gandhi and the majority of the members of the Congress Working Committee.

The re-election of Bose marked the intensification of the opposition to the federation. Bose demanded that the 'drift towards constitutionalism' should cease, and that war against federation should be waged from all sides. He declared that there had been no change in the attitude towards the federation, and made it clear that the government should be under no illusion that, because office was accepted in the provinces, the federal scheme would also be accepted.[1] Bose, however, was unable to continue his anti-federation policy as his election had led to a crisis in the Congress. Gandhi considered it a personal defeat.[2] At his bidding, twelve out of fourteen members of the Congress Working Committee appointed by Bose tendered their resignation. In their resignation letter, the wording of which is significant, they said: 'We feel that the time has come when the country should have a clear policy not based upon compromise between different incompatible groups of the Congress'. The letter seems to confirm the correctness of Bose's earlier assertion that there was, over the question of federation, a prospect of compromise with the government, for otherwise the reference to 'incompatible groups' is hard to explain. Negotiations between Bose and Gandhi regarding the composition of the new Congress Working Committee ended in failure. In April 1939, Bose resigned the presidency; and Rajendra Prasad, a staunch Gandhian, was elected. His election indicated that the Congress opposition towards federation would be toned down. The federal negotiations were, however, abruptly ended by the outbreak of the war.

The main indictment brought by the Congress against the federation was that it was 'undemocratic': they objected to the 'special' and 'reserved' powers of the Viceroy, and the heavy representation given to the nominees of the princes. To an extent, as we have noted, these criticisms were due to a failure to understand how the Act would work. They were also due to the fact that the Act had been 'imposed' by Britain and was not framed by an Indian constituent assembly.

Another factor which helped to kill the federation was the hostility of the Moslem League. While many Moslems, including Jinnah, had

---

1 Mss. Eur. F.125/142-45, *Quarterly Survey of Political and Constitutional Position in British India* (henceforth *Qr. Survey*), No.4.

2 *IAR*, 1939, i, 320.

favoured federation in the early days, their attitude changed after the Congress ministries came to power in the provinces. Moreover, the Congress's campaign to democratize the states had frightened the Moslem leaders. How could the Congress's demand for self–governing democracy be reconciled with the League's insistence upon safeguards for the Moslem interests? It was this fundamental difference, and the failure to solve it, which led to the complication of Indian politics and subsequent deadlock which became an even larger part of the wider Indian problem ultimately 'solved' through the partition of India. While it has been noted earlier that without the consent of the princes the federation could not have been established, even if the princes had agreed and Congress had acquiesced the government would have found it difficult to implement the federal scheme without the cooperation of the Moslems.

The League was gratified by the provision of separate electorates and various safeguards to protect the interest of the minorities. One of the reasons why the Moslem League had agreed to work the 1935 Act was its hope that it would not only be able to control the Moslem majority provinces, but that the divisions among the Hindus would probably enable the Moslem bloc to play a balancing role in the federal legislature.[1] The election upset the League's calculations.

The failure of the Moslem League to control a single Moslem majority province, or to play a balancing role in the Hindu majority provinces, revealed to many Moslems that their prospects in the federation were bleak. In the proposed federation the Moslems had one-third of the total seats allotted to British India. If the provincial election was any indication, the Congress would probably obtain a majority of 'non-Moslem' seats, and if it succeeded in 'coercing' the princes to send elected representatives to the federal legislature it would probably capture most of the seats allotted to the states.[2] The possibility of the League playing a balancing role in the federation was doubtful.

Criticism of the federation had been a regular feature of the Moslem League resolutions. But now the point of attack shifted. Prior to 1937 federation had been denounced by the League for the same reason as by the Congress, it fell short of full self-government at the centre. After 1937, the federation was denounced because it would enable the Congress to capture power at the centre as it had done in the provinces, and thus exclude the Moslem League from any share in it. It was feared

[1] B.R. Nanda, 'Nehru, The Indian National Congress and the Partition of India, 1935-47', in Philips and Wainwright, (eds.) Partition of India, pp. 157-8.
[2] IAR, 1939, ii, 345.

that a predominantly Congress government at the centre would be rigidly controlled by the Congress Working Committee; that the safeguards for the protection of the minorities would not in practice be effective and that the federal government would be disposed to interfere in provincial matters, particularly in the Moslem majority provinces. If the federation was to be dominated by the Congress, the Moslem League declared that it would have nothing to do with it.[1] The League began to demand a constitutional review *de novo* and stepped up its opposition to federation which it regarded as 'a conspiracy to establish a Hindu Raj with the support of British bayonets'.

The Moslem League could and did play upon the feelings of Moslem princes (such as the Nizam of Hyderabad) so as to prevent the imposition of 'Congress' rule upon their co-religionists.[2] When Linlithgow visited Hyderabad in 1938, the Hyderabad Executive Council was still officially in favour of federation. But those who saw the Osmania University students demonstrate against the federation could not fail to notice that behind the students' protest was the Nizam's wish to keep out of the federation.[3] Clearly the Congress's agitation had frightened the Moslems. Early in 1940 the Aga Khan, who had earlier supported the federal scheme, was reported to have admitted to Linlithgow that the 'sugar had all come off the pill' the moment the Congress started demanding the election of states' representatives, 'for under such an arrangement the Muslims would not get from the States in the Central Legislature the support required to balance the Congress votes'.[4]

The Viceroy, for some time, could not discern the Moslem hostility to the federation and was confident that the League would come in provided the princes gave him the platform from which to launch the federal scheme.[5] Zetland, however, could perceive in 1937 that 'the strongest opposition' to the federation would come from the Moslems.[6] He could 'not resist a steadily growing conviction that the dominant factor in determining the future form of government would prove to be the All India Muslim League'.[7] This estimate of the Moslem League's strength in Indian politics is somewhat exaggerated but it shows the

1   Mss. Eur. F.125/7/8a, Linlithgow to Zetland, 28 Feb. 1939. IOL.

2   C.H. Philips, *The Partition of India, 1947* (Leeds, 1967), p. 17.

3   Mss. Eur. F.125/4/73, Report by Intelligence Officer, Nagpur, 13 Dec. 1937. IOL.

4   D.609/26, Linlithgow to Zetland, 27 Feb. 1940. IOL; see also the resolution of the Moslem League of December 1938, *IAR*, 1938, ii, 345.

5   Mss. Eur. F.125/7/22, Linlithgow to Zetland, 2 June 1939. IOL.

6   Mss. Eur. D.609/26, Zetland to Linlithgow, 6 Dec. 1937. IOL.

7   Dundas, *Essayez*, p. 247.

trend of Zetland's thinking. By April 1939, Zetland was 'almost certain' that the Moslems would refuse to work the federation.[1] Zetland, therefore, suggested the possibility of convening a tripartite conference of the Congress, the League and the princes in order to hammer out a solution. But the Viceroy was much more optimistic than his counterpart in the India Office. He preferred to 'let the situation develop', for he remained hopeful that the Moslems would accept the federation if it were 'imposed on them'. He did 'not expect any serious trouble' from that quarter. Linlithgow asserted that in May 1939 there was nothing new about the Moslem's fears; the approach of the federation had brought them to the surface. They had been apparent throughout the Round Table Conferences and the proceedings of the Joint Select Committee; and the British Government had conceded to the Moslems the maximum safeguards compatible with the legitimate claims of other communities. Yet a few months later, following the outbreak of war, Linlithgow made a complete *volte face,* and from then on to the end of his term in 1943, he refused to move for fear of Moslem opposition. Denied Congress support, he fell back on the Moslem League. His primary concern with every constitutional proposal was now whether it would be acceptable to the Moslems.[2]

The princes, the Congress and the Moslem League — the three main groups in the constitutional scheme — had all declared their dissatisfaction with the federation. But each group opposed the scheme for different reasons: the princes because of their unwillingness to surrender their 'sovereignty' to a central government in which 'unfriendly' voices were likely to have an important say; the Congress because popular control at the centre would be circumscribed by the various safeguards in the constitution; and the Moslem League, on the other hand, for primarily communal considerations — fear of Hindu domination at the centre. In some respects Moslem hostility was a much more serious obstacle than the opposition of the other groups, being based on communalism and to an extent on the legitimate fears of a minority, so that it represented a force which struck at the very roots of Indian unity.

The Congress argued that 'it would be pointless to minimize this unanimous opposition [to the federation] on the plea that each of these three parties is actuated by different and contradictory motives'[3] But an analysis of the demands and criticisms reveals that they were

---

1   Mss. Eur. D.609/26, Zetland to Linlithgow, May 22 1939. IOL.
2   Details in chapters 4 and 5 below.
3   *The Times,* 20 July 1939.

mutually destructive. Let us take 'defence' as an example. The princes insisted upon 'defence' being retained by the Crown; a Congress government, notwithstanding the reservation of defence, would be able to influence defence policy and successfully attack the privileged position of the Punjab in army recruiting, which meant so much to the Moslems of that province. In effect, while the Congress wished the safeguards eliminated, the minorities valued them and demanded their extension. Any attempt to satisfy a single party would alienate one or both of the others. This was inherent in the circumstances and would be found to apply with equal force to any conceivable scheme. The difficulties created by the demands of the three parties were the best argument for the 1935 Act, for it represented a common denominator.

The opposition to the federal scheme was not confined to India alone. The conservative 'diehards' must also share the responsibility for the failure of the federation. The Government of India Bill of 1934 had been passed by Parliament despite the opposition of the diehards. This did not mean, however, that the diehards had acquiesced in the federal scheme. For the federal provisions to come into force they required the approval of both Houses of Parliament. It was known that the diehards were still active and had not bound themselves to rubber-stamp this last step necessary before the federation could be achieved. It was further known that they kept a close watch on any sign of pressure being brought by the Viceroy or the Political Department on the princes to federate. To exert concerted pressure the diehards grouped themselves in the 'India Empire Society' and in the *Morning Post* they had a ready organ to denounce any move towards federation.[1]

Fear of a possible renewal of diehard opposition caused Zetland to adopt an extremely cautious approach. Linlithgow virtually worked with his hands tied. The India Office was indifferent to the federal scheme and showed no sign of wishing to expedite it. Zetland's position, is must be remembered, was made difficult by the incessant threat from the diehards. Churchill had warned: 'I should be ready to take on my shoulders the responsibility of persuading them [the princes] to stand out of it [Federation].'[2] He was as good as his word. His pressure upon the Maharajas of Patiala and Dholpur dissuaded them from acceding to the federation. Zetland was therefore apprehensive that any pressure by the government to persuade the princes would give the diehards a 'handle to make use of' against the federal scheme. Writing about his difficulties, Zetland said that he had been warned by Salisbury and other

1 See Mss. Eng. Hist C.610, 'Aims and objects of India Empire Society'. Bodleian Library, Oxford; *Sunday Times,* 26 March 1933.
2 Cited in Glendevon, *The Viceroy At Bay,* p. 20.

diehards that their acquiescence in the passage of various orders in council dealing with the establishment of provincial autonomy must not be taken as an indication of their attitude towards federation to which they were irrevocably opposed. At the same time Churchill had warned R.A. Butler, the Under Secretary of State for India, that he would keep a look out for any indication that pressure was being brought to bear on the princes.[1] Thus it is possible to understand Zetland's reluctance to back Linlithgow in applying pressure on the princes and pushing through federation.

In his memoirs Zetland claims that immediately after assuming office he was anxious to hasten the implementation of the federation, but his correspondence with the Viceroy reveals otherwise. His mind was distracted from Indian affairs by the abdication crisis and by his interest in British foreign policy. In his first letter to Linlithgow, Zetland promised that he would 'keep him *au courant* with the proceedings of the Cabinet and with their fortunes in Parliament and in the country, and also with the course of events in international arena. . . .'[2] Linlithgow was less interested in international affairs and more anxious to press ahead with the federation,[3] but he was given no guidance from the Secretary of State. In the correspondence between the two during the first few months, the question of federation received scant attention in Zetland's letters. Even later on his attitude towards the problem of federation was distant. He failed to press parliamentary counsel ahead with the preparation of the Instrument of Accession. The princes were 'shy birds . . . and might easily take fright'.[4] Linlithgow in vain pleaded that the situation was deteriorating and that time was not on their side. He wrote that he remained 'entirely unconvinced that the market will improve with delay and very apprehensive that the consequences of the delay will be most unhappy'[5] But Zetland maintained his stand that haste would 'frighten them [the princes] off'.[6]

Despite this evidence to the contrary, Linlithgow has been

1 Mss. Eur. F.125/4/25, Zetland to Linlithgow, 25 Sept. 1939; Dundas, *Essayez*, pp. 242-3.

2 Dundas, *Essayez*, p. 204.

3 For Linlithgow's desire to hasten the inauguration of the federation see Mss. Eur. F.125/3/12, Zetland to Linlithgow, 29 June 1936; F.125/3/10, dated 15 June 1936; F.125/3/13, dated 28 June 1936; F.125/3/14, dated 13 July 1936; F.125/4/47, dated 19 April 1937; F.125/4/32 dated 27 May 1937; F.125/4/63, dated 27 Oct. 1937; F.125/5/2 dated 13 Jan. 1938; F.125/5/28 dated 24 May 1938; F.125/18/189 dated 3 July 1939; F.125/18/162 dated 6 July 1939. See also Mss. Eur. D.609/13, dated 15 June 1936; and D.609/7 dated 28 June 1936.

4 Mss. Eur. F.125/3/28, Zetland to Linlithgow, 25 Sept. 1936. IOL.

5 Mss. Eur. F.125/5/2, Linlithgow to Zetland, 13 Jan. 1938. IOL.

6 Mss. Eur. F.125/4/15, Zetland to Linlithgow, 28 June 1936. IOL.

criticized for his failure to inaugurate the federation. It has become fashionable to blame Linlithgow for dragging his feet over the federation issue. 'Here was pre-eminently a case for striking while the iron was hot, but it was cold indeed before the Viceregal hammer began to descend in 1939.'[1] Sir Penderel Moon has also accepted this sweeping verdict in his appraisal of Linlithgow's policy. He thinks that the implementation of the federal scheme was 'quite beyond the scope of the more pedestrian talents of Lord Linlithgow and never seemed probable that the princes would yield to his method of persuasion'.[2]

Similar views have also been expressed by Sir Samuel Hoare and Lord Halifax. Hoare thought that the Government of India did not believe that the British Government were serious about the federation and, therefore, did not push the princes hard enough to make up their mind. He suggested that greater effort should have been made by Linlithgow.[3] Halifax agreed.[4] But Zetland has claimed that, far from the delay being caused by the Government of India, it was Sir Samuel who 'as the Secretary of State favoured a cautious approach'.[5] Coen tends to support Zetland's contention. He claims that Arthur Lothian, who was shown the first draft of Zetland's book, found in it evidence that Hoare had definitely advised delaying the federation during discussions in the Cabinet.[6] Zetland had subsequently to curtail his comment because, according to rules, Cabinet discussions could not be quoted. Coen further maintains that Lothian was firmly convinced that Hoare's criticism of the Government of India's effort was inaccurate. The explanation seems to be that Hoare may have advised 'go slow' tactics in the Cabinet meeting because he sincerely doubted the possibility of enticing the required number of princes to accede to the federation and shrank back from the day when the scheme would be pronounced a failure. But later he found that his advice was wrong. While writing his memoirs in retrospect, he tried to push the blame on Linlithgow's government. Zetland, in turn, tried to put the blame on his predecessor, and on Linlithgow's government, when in fact he himself bore a large measure of responsibility.

This discussion shows how uncharitable have been the criticisms of historians and contemporaries alike. Far from delaying the federation, it

1 Percival Spear in *The Oxford History of India* (Oxford, reprint 1961), p. 815.

2 Penderel Moon, *Divide and Quit* (London, 1961), p. 18.

3 Templewood, *Nine Troubled Years*, p. 102.

4 R.J. Moore, 'The Making of India's Paper Federation', in Philips and Wainwright (eds.), *Partition of India*, p. 55.

5 Dundas, *Essayez*, p. 241.

6 Coen, *Indian Political Service*, p. 105.

was Linlithgow who determined the tenor of the British negotiations with the princes and drove forward the attempt to inaugurate the federation.[1] He was not able to mould events as he wished because his freedom of action and initiative were circumscribed by the overcautious policies of the India Office, and by the complications of Indian politics.

The underlying concept of an all-India federation was to preserve the unity of the country. But in the clash of politics, the struggle for power, the wrangle for ascendancy, and the scramble for gains on the part of the political organisations, the politicians (including the Tory diehards) and the princes, the federal scheme became a tragic casualty. Linlithgow's drive towards federation was ended prematurely by the outbreak of the war.

1 Lothian, *Kingdoms of Yesterday,* p. 146. R. Moore.

4

THE GROWTH OF COMMUNALISM AND THE RISE OF THE MOSLEM LEAGUE, 1936-43.

There was nothing absolutely inevitable about the partition of India: prior to 1939 the demand for the partition of the country on a communal basis had never been seriously considered.[1] We have seen how Linlithgow strove to implement the federal section of the 1935 Act: the establishment of the all-India federation might have placed Indian unity on a secure foundation. Yet it is ironical that it was during the viceroyalty of Linlithgow that the demand for Pakistan had its start and early development.[2]

There is little doubt that before the outbreak of the second world war Linlithgow sincerely hoped to see the 1935 Act functioning, and functioning well. But once war was declared he single-mindedly pursued the short-term aim of tiding India — and the Empire — over war-time difficulties. In order to offset Congress hostility during the war Linlithgow encouraged the Moslem League to adopt an intransigent attitude towards the Congress. Such an attitude was natural enough in the circumstances. But Linlithgow's war-time policy at times went beyond a mere encouragement of opposition to the Congress: caught in the web of his anti-Congress manoeuvreings, Linlithgow at crucial junctures provided a certain amount of reasonably direct support to those within the Moslem League who were pressing for a separate Moslem state.

---

1 The Moslem delegation to the Joint Select Committee in 1934 said that 'Pakistan' was a 'students' chimera' which no responsible person or organization had put forward. See *Joint Select Committee on Indian Constitutional Reforms, Minutes of Evidence* (HMSO, 1934), ii, 1496; Sir Samuel Hoare also testified to the same effect: 'The idea of Pakistan had not yet passed beyond the romantic mind of a Moslem poet, and the very name, Pakistan, was practically unknown'. Viscount Templewood, *Nine Troubled Years* (London, 1954), p. 90. It has been erroneously claimed that the idea of 'Pakistan' was first put forward by Sir Muhammed Iqbal: he did not contemplate a separate sovereign Moslem state but merely the consolidation of the Moslem majority provinces in north-west India in one political unit of an all-India federation. His proposal distinctly contemplated a common centre for the whole of India. See M. Gwyer and A. Appadorai, *Speeches and Documents on the Indian Constitution* (London, 1957), ii, 435-40. Iqbal personally denied that he was the originator of the idea of Pakistan. Edward Thompson, *Enlist India for Freedom* (London, 1940), p. 58. Even Jinnah, as late as May 1939 had not committed himself to 'Pakistan'. See C. Khaliquzzaman, *Pathway to Pakistan* (Lahore, 1961), p. 211.

2 C.H. Philips and M.D. Wainwright (eds.), *The Partition of India; Policies and Perspectives 1935-47* (London, 1970), p. 18.

It has been noted earlier that both the Congress and the Moslem League had decided to contest the elections to the provincial legislatures in 1936, and it was during the campaign that the first open rift developed between the two parties. Jinnah had claimed that the Congress should acknowledge the League as the sole representative of the Indian Moslems.[1] In other words, the Congress should forsake its secular character and confine its activities to Hindus. Nehru was shocked by Jinnah's approach to politics and pointed out that such a demand implied that 'in politics and social and economic matters the Moslems must function separately as a group and deal with other groups as one nation deals with another'.[2] There were two reasons why the Congress was not prepared to accept the Moslem League as the sole Moslem organization: first, it wished to maintain its claim that as a secular party it represented both Moslems and Hindus; second, there were several other Moslem parties, such as the Ahrars, the Nationalist Moslems and the Jamiat-ul-Ulema, who were opposed to the League.[3] A concession of the sort Jinnah demanded would have amounted, wrote Rajendra Prasad, to 'denying its own past, falsifying its history, and betraying its future'.[4]

Nehru's basic premise was that the economic interests of the various classes of the Moslems were indistinguishable from those of similar Hindu classes.[5] This was to a great extent true. Nevertheless the Congress could have viewed Indian politics more realistically. While there is no doubt that it was truly national in its objectives and had large followings in all communities, it might in 1937 have accepted the League's desire to cooperate in the government. There were possibilities of coalition ministries in the United Provinces and Bombay, where the Moslem League had emerged as an important factor in the provincial assemblies. The League had secured 27 out of 64 Moslem seats in the former, and 20 out of 39 in the latter. Relations between the Congress and the Moslem League leaders in the United Provinces were generally

1   K.B. Sayeed, *Pakistan: The Formative Phase, 1857-1948.* (London, 1968), pp. 82-3.

2   *Statesman,* 14 Jan. 1937; Khaliquzzaman, *Pathway to Pakistan,* p. 88; M. Brecher, *Nehru: A Political Biography* (Oxford, 1959), pp. 231-2; S. Gopal, *Jawaharlal Nehru,* (London, 1975), pp. 85-7.

3   Nehru to Jinnah, 6 April 1938. *IAR,* 1938, i, 369-75.

4   Rajendra Prasad, *India Divided* (Bombay, 1946), p. 145.

5   Nehru to Syed Mahmud, 12 June 1926 and 12 Jan. 1927, cited in Brecher, *Nehru: A Political Biography,* pp. 98-9; J. Nehru, *An Autobiography* (London, reprint, July 1936), pp. 458-72; H. Mukherjee, *Nehru: The Gentle Colossus* (Calcutta, 1964), p. 593; K.B. Sayeed, *The Political System of Pakistan* (Boston, 1967), pp. 23-36; Basil Mathews, 'The New India: Some Trends and Personalities', *Asiatic Review* (1937), pp. 251-68.

cordial. All this created a hope that coalition governments might be formed in these two provinces. Negotiations took place, but no agreement was arrived at. The Congress thereupon formed ministries in the United Provinces and Bombay but no representatives of the Moslem League were included.

The immediate reasons for the failure to form coalitions are not difficult to find. The terms offered really involved a merger and not a coalition: the Moslem League was to cease to function in the assembly as a separate group, its members were to become part of the Congress party and to share fully its privileges and obligations; the Moslem League parliamentary board was to be dissolved in the United Provinces, and no candidates were to be put up by it at any by-elections. Not surprisingly, Khaliquzzaman, the League leader in the United Provinces, characterized these terms as the 'death warrant' of his organization and refused to accept them.[1] Azad's claim that the coalition negotiations broke down because of Nehru's insistence on giving only one seat instead of two demanded by the League[2] does not seem to be correct.

Nevertheless, the failure to form a coalition ministry in the United Provinces has been the subject of much controversy. Sir Penderel Moon maintains that had Congress not refused to form an alliance with the Moslem League, the course of Indian history might have been different. He regards this failure as the *'fons et origo malorum'* and argues that the Congress leaders were 'responsible though quite unwittingly' for the critical change in the Moslems' sentiment from readiness to contemplate cooperation in an all-India federation to insistence upon separation. The Congress 'passionately desired to preserve the unity of India. They consistently acted so as to make its partition certain'.[3] Mr Ian Stephens, a former editor of *The Statesman*, shares this view:

> The effect of this, simultaneously on many Muslim minds throughout India was of a lightening flash. What had before been guessed at, now leapt forth in a horridly clear outline. The Congress, a Hindu dominated body was bent on the Muslim's eventual absorption.[4]

This is to make a mountain of a molehill. The failure to form a coalition ministry in the United Provinces may have annoyed some

1 Khaliquzzaman, *Pathway to Pakistan*, p. 161.
2 Azad, *India Wins Freedom*, (Calcutta, 1959) pp. 161-2.
3 E. Penderel Moon, *Divide and Quit*, (London, 1945), p. 14.
4 Ian Stephens, *Pakistan* (London, 1963), p. 76.

Moslem Leaguers, but it was too trivial an event to set in motion currents which have determined the course of Indian history.[1] There were other, more deep rooted causes for the League's hostility to the Congress; the issue of coalition was used largely as a facade to cover up the real motives. These we must now examine.

The provincial elections of 1936 had marked a turning point in the political development of the United Provinces. Prior to this time politics in the United Provinces had been dominated by the landlords. The landlords were accustomed to the old political conventions of the United Provinces formed in a period when the franchise was restricted to a small and privileged group; and politics had been conducted on the assumption that the established hierarchy and landlord system were to remain undisturbed for a long time to come. But the 1935 Act not only extended the franchise to a very large population but also failed to provide that preferential treatment for the *zamindars* which they had hitherto been used to.[2]

The electoral contest had therefore involved a conflict about the very nature of the political system of the province. The defeat of the National Agriculturalist Party, the party of the landlords, signified the eclipse of the landlords and the end of their political power. The danger of losing political power was a serious threat to the *zamindars* as the popularly elected ministers under the new constitution would enjoy considerable powers. To add to their worries, a section of the Congress led by Nehru had established themselves as spokesmen of the tenants and had begun to adopt an increasingly hostile attitude towards the landlords. Nehru's writings during the period showed a strong socialistic bias and held out promises of a full scale attack on the landlords' 'exploitation of her [India's] people'. He declared that the goal of the nationalist movement was not only 'political independence', but 'economically and socially it must mean the ending of special class privileges and vested interests'.[3]

Coupled with the Congress's onslaught against the *zamindari,* the economic depression of 1929-34 also helped to undermine the authority and influence of the landlords. In those years, long-standing tenant grievances about rents, security of tenure, exactions of illegal payments and forced labour were sharpened by the difficulties caused

---

1 A. Prasad, *Rafi Ahmad Kidwai* (London, 1965), pp. 35-6.

2 P.D. Reeves, B.D. Graham and J.M. Goodman (eds.), *A Handbook to Elections in Uttar Pradesh, 1920-51* (Delhi, 1975), p. lxvii; see also chapter 2 above.

3 J. Nehru, *India's Freedom* (London, 1936), pp. 20-34; see also Bipan Chandra, 'Jawaharlal Nehru and the Capitalist Class, 1936', *Economic and Political Weekly* (1975), x, nos. 33-5, pp. 1307-25.

by the slump in prices for agricultural produce; as a result tenants were drawn into political movements which promised support for their economic claims. The most important of these movements was the Congress's civil disobedience movement of the early 1930s, which in the United Provinces took the shape of a 'no rent' campaign.[1] Thus the growing strength of the nationalist movement and constitutional reforms, together with a period of economic depression, ushered in a new and dangerous era of political activity which threatened the very existence of the landlords.

One of the first acts of the Congress ministry in the United Provinces was the enactment of the United Provinces Tenancy Act which provided for greater security of tenure. Land reforms had long been a part of the Congress policy, but the landlords had been confident that the Congress would not take so drastic a step. Moreover, they mistakenly believed that even if it did, the governor would intervene. When, however, the Congress revealed its 'evil' intention to abolish *zamindari*, and there was no sign of any intervention by the governor, the landlords sought the protection of political parties opposed to the Congress. Thus the Hindu landlords turned to the Hindu Mahasabha, and the Moslem landlords to the League.[2]

In the United Provinces most of the big *talukdars* and landowners were Moslems. The *zamindari* provided the means of livelihood not only for the upper classes of Moslems but also for a large number of government servants, for whom landed property provided a subsidiary source of income.[3] Thus a good many well-to-do Moslems, threatened by the abolition of *zamindari*, in their consternation turned to the League.[4] Assured of the financial backing of the landlords and the support of middle-class Moslems, the League rapidly expanded its organization in many districts of the United Provinces.

1   S. Gopal, *The Viceroyalty of Lord Irwin* (Oxford, 1957), chapters v and vi.

2   S.A. Husain, *The Destiny of the Indian Muslims* (London, 1965), pp. 105-6; J. Nehru, 'Parting of the Ways', *Asia* (Nov. 1940), p. 598. Even Hindu princes became sympathetic towards the ML. Jam Saheb of Nawanagar confided to B. Shiva Rao: 'Why should I not support Muslim League? Mr Jinnah is willing to tolerate our existence, but Mr. Nehru wants the extinction of the Princes'. Philips and Wainwright, (eds.), *Partition of India*, p. 420.

3   F.C.R. Robinson, *The Emergence of Muslim Politics in India* (Cambridge, 1946), *passim;* see also his 'Municipal Government and Muslim Separatism in the United Provinces 1883 to 1916', in J. Gallagher, G. Johnson and A. Seal (eds.), *Locality, Province and Nation, Essay on Indian Politics 1870 to 1940* (Cambridge, 1973), pp. 69-121; David Page, 'Prelude to Partition: All India Moslem Politics 1920-1932' (Oxford D.Phil. thesis, 1974), p. xxiv.

4   Husain, *The Destiny of Indian Muslims*, pp. 105-6; C.H. Philips, *India* (London, 1948), p. 125; Sayeed, *Pakistan: The Formative Phase*, p. 88; *Manchester Guardian*, 23 March 1940.

Yet the United Provinces episode, though no doubt an important factor contributing to the growth of Moslem separatism, could not in itself have been sufficient to bring about the partition of the country. It is suggested here that at the root of the communal problem lay economic rivalry which over a period of time manifested itself in various forms.

> Muslim separatism in UP (writes Brass) was, in origin, the ideology of an upper class and *upper middle* class elite attempting to preserve its privileged position in society through political means.[1]

Middle-class Moslems realized that their chances of success (meagre under the British and, as individuals, none too bright even in a free India) could be immensely increased if they stood together as a corporate Moslem body and fought for power.[2] To put matters in simple terms, this argument, when carried further, led to the demand for a separate state for the Moslems, where the Moslem elites would have an opportunity for investing their money; of dominating commerce, the 'professions', and government services; of raising tariffs to protect their industries, and so on.[3] The idea of a separate Moslem state, by offering 'a short cut to worldly success, attracted the interest and aroused the ambition of the Muslim middle classes, who, for historical reasons, had so far been left behind by the Hindus in the race for plums of commerce, industry and the government'.[4] It is necessary to remember that although the British conquest of India had placed the two communities on an equal level of subjection, as the process of conquest had proceeded from the sea coasts inwards, it affected the Moslem majority provinces of north west India last of all. This accident of history gave an early start to the Hindus in acquiring English education and thus contributed to the emergence of a Hindu middle class subsisting on government services, the 'professions' and trade.[5] The growth of a Moslem middle class was impeded by the

1 P.R. Brass, 'Muslim Politics in United Provinces. Social Contest and Political Strategy before Partition', *Economic and Political Weekly* (1970), v, nos. 3-5, p. 183; M. Mujeeb, *The Indian Muslims* (London, 1967), Imtiaz Ahmad, 'Secularism and Communalism', *Economic and Political Weekly,* (July, 1969), iv, nos. 28-30, pp. 1137-58; R. Russell, 'Strands of Muslim Identity in South Asia', *South Asian Review* (Oct. 1967), pp. 21-32.

2 H. Kabir, 'Even the Muslims Disagree', *Asia* (Aug. 1940), p. 437.

3 Moon, *Divide and Quit,* p. 22; G.D. Khosla, *Stern Reckoning,* (Delhi, n.d.), p. 21.

4 C.H. Philips, *The Partition of India 1947* (Leeds, 1967), p. 16.

5 Anil Seal, *The Emergence of Indian Nationalism, Competition and Collaboration in the later Nineteenth Century,* (Cambridge, reprint, 1971) chs. ii, iii; N.K. Sinha, *Economic History of Bengal from Plassey to Perment Settlement* (Calcutta, 1956), 2 vols. *passim;* R.G. Casey, *An Australian in India* (London, 1947), pp. 76-7.

Revolt of 1857, which many British tended to regard as a Moslem rebellion.[1] Moreover, Moslem theologians, by throwing their weight against English education, further handicapped the Moslems in competing for jobs.[2]

The communities in most parts of India were divided along distinct economic lines. In Bengal the landlords were nearly all Hindus and the tenants were mostly Moslems. In the United Provinces the picture was almost the reverse.[3] In the towns the shop owners, professional men and employers were largely Hindus; the craftsmen and workers were predominantly Moslems.[4] But since class division so nearly coincided with the communal division, it was not surprising that essentially economic conflicts were often described as communal. In the Punjab the Hindus were so much identified with the landowning and money-lending class that the Land Alienation Act, which aimed at assisting and protecting the peasants of both religions, became the basis of a bitter quarrel between the two communities. The introduction of representative institutions and the grant of the Communal Award further confused religion and economics.[5]

The fact that the partition of the country would not cure the poverty of the people was irrelevant. The argument was that the Moslems and Hindus were so different that they could not live together in one state. What this perhaps meant was that Moslem businessmen and Hindu businessmen could not co-exist in one state without undue competition.[6] Therefore the League, by its obstructionist tactics and its very intransigence, tried to drive a hard bargain with the Congress and the British in order to obtain concessions.[7] The principal, though not the sole, motive behind the demand for a separate state for the Moslems was the urge on the part of the educated Moslems to advance themselves economically.[8] The League leaders, of course, understood all this perfectly well, but when articulating the demands of the Moslems they did not express it in those terms. Instead they argued on a much higher plane: they spoke in terms of two races, the Hindus and the Moslems, and the wide gulf

1   Richard Symonds, *The Making of Pakistan* (Karachi, 1966), p. 28.

2   W.W. Hunter, *The Indian Musalmans* (Delhi, reprint, 1969), ch. iv.

3   J.P. Narayan, *Towards Struggle* (Bombay, 1946), pp. 111-12.

4   G.T. Garratt, 'Economic Realities', T.W. Wallbank *The Partition of India* (Boston, 1966), p. 11.

5   H.V. Hodson, *The Great Divide,* (London, 1969), pp. 15-16.

6   Sayeed, *Pakistan: the Formative Phase,* pp. 95-6.

7   W.C. Smith, *The Muslim League 1942-45* (Lahore, 1945), pp. 14-16.

8   E. Thompson, *Enlist India for Freedom* (London, 1940), pp. 59-60.

that separated their history, tradition and ways of life, with their consequent inability to live together.

In the summer of 1937 Jinnah was faced with the hard reality that his party scarcely figured on the political map of India.[1] But Jinnah was not the man to accept defeat. For him the moral of the 1936 elections was the necessity of building up the Moslem League as the spokesman of the Moslems. In this task he was helped not only by the course of events and the policies of both the Congress and the British Government, but also by his skilful strategy. 'In politics', he said, 'one has to play one's game as on the chess board'.[2] In his strategy the first step was to revitalize the Moslem League.

Since it would take time before it could become a strong rival to the Congress, the Moslem League should not be in a hurry to reach a settlement. Jinnah held that since the ultimate power was with the British, it was they who could confer or transfer power: he did not need to come to terms with the Congress. Meanwhile the best course open to the League was to consolidate its own organization and then negotiate with the Congress from a position of strength.

Jinnah called upon the Moslems to organize under the banner of the Moslem League. He declared in October 1937 that

> No settlement with [the] majority community is possible, as no Hindu leader speaking with authority shows any concern or genuine desire for it. Honourable settlements can only be achieved between equals, and unless the two parties learn to respect and fear each other, there is no solid ground for any settlement.[3]

The League session held at Lucknow in October 1937 was itself a striking proof of its growing strength. Provincial leaders who had fought elections on the tickets of their own organizations now joined it. This session was attended by Sir Muhammad Saadullah, Fazlul Huq and Sir Sikander Hyat Khan, the chief ministers of Assam, Bengal and the Punjab, who had previously refused to come to terms with Jinnah. Jinnah's prestige was further enhanced by the conclusion of the Sikander-Jinnah pact under which the Moslem members of the Unionist party in the Punjab joined the Moslem League and agreed to accept its policy in 'all-India' matters; in return Jinnah consented to refrain from interfering in the affairs of the Punjab.

At the same time the Moslem League changed its creed from 'full

[1] Mss. Eur. F.125/19/271, Linlithgow to Amery, 30 June 1940 IOL.

[2] *Star of India*, 31 Dec. 1938.

[3] Jamil-ud-din Ahmad, *Speeches and Writings of Mr Jinnah*, i (Lahore, 1943, 6th edn. 1960), p. 32.

responsible government' to 'full independence', and decided to take immediate steps 'to frame and put into effect an economic, social and educational programme'.[1] A socio-economic programme was evolved to bring the organization in touch with the masses. This included the encouragement of cottage industries, organization of volunteers for social service, ameliorating the condition of factory workers, reduction of agricultural indebtedness and the introduction of compulsory primary education.[2] The organization of the League was overhauled. Provincial and district branches were reshaped; the membership fee was reduced to two annas; the Council was to consist of 465 members elected by provincial branches and no one was to be so elected without being a member of the primary League. Jinnah's efforts to strengthen the Moslem League seem to have borne fruit: in April 1938 he was able to claim that Moslems in hundreds of thousands had joined.[3] Towards the end of the year the Madras Moslem League claimed a membership of 43,920; in 1940 it rose to 88,833.[4] It is quite certain that between 1937 and 1940 the Moslem League attracted a large number of Moslems. Its organization had started penetrating the countryside and numerous branches had been opened all over the country.[5]

The Congress ministries, lacking the representatives of the Moslem League, offered Jinnah the handiest pegs on which he could hang all the grievances of the Moslems, real or fancied. Allegations of the Congress tyranny over the Moslems in the Hindu majority provinces began to be heard. In March 1938, when the Congress had been in office for only eight months, the Moslem League appointed a committee to investigate the complaints of ill-treatment being meted out to the Moslems in the various Congress provinces. The committee, which was presided over by the Raja of Pirpur, submitted its report in November 1938.[6] This comparatively restrained document was followed a year later by a much more lucid account of the grievances of Moslems in Bihar,[7] and by a still more intemperate report by Fazlul Huq[8]

1 *Statesman*, 21 Oct. 1937.

2 *Pioneer*, 19 Oct. 1937.

3 *IAR*, 1938, i, 382.

4 *Dawn*, 9 Nov. 1941.

5 R. Coupland, *Indian Politics 1936-42* (London, 1943) p. 183; A. Aziz, *Discovery of Pakistan* (Lahore, 1957), pp. 297-8; Sayeed, *Pakistan, the Formative Phase*, p. 178.

6 *The Report of the Enquiry Committee appointed by the Council of All-India Muslim League to Enquire into Muslim Grievances in Congress Provinces* (Delhi, 1938).

7 *Report of the Enquiry Committee Appointed by the Working Committee of Bihar Provincial Muslim League to Enquire into some Grievances of Muslims in Bihar* (Patna, 1939).

8 A.K. Fazlul Huq, *Muslim Sufferings Under Congress Rule* (Calcutta, 1939).

Communal tension had been gradually rising since the Congress's assumption of office. The Congress could not altogether ignore the growing strength of the League and efforts had been made to reach an agreement by means of so-called 'unity talks' between Gandhi and Jinnah.[1] But nothing came of these personal contacts. The negotiations broke down owing to Jinnah's insistence that the Congress should recognize the League as the only organization representing the Indian Moslems. This was a novel demand. In retrospect it would seem as if this pre-condition was laid down by Jinnah to avoid coming to the negotiating table. This interpretation finds support in the memoirs of Khaliquzzaman who thought it was a 'piece of good luck' that the Congress fought shy of accepting Jinnah's demand because, if the negotiations between the two parties had really got off the ground, he wondered 'what positive demands we [the Moslem League] could have made'. Jinnah's 'sixteen points' had been substantially conceded by the 1935 Act and there was no demand by the Hindu community for the repeal of the 'Communal Award'.[2]

Apart from publishing stories, mostly unverified, about the 'atrocities' committed by the Congress governments, the main charges contained in all these reports were concerned with the Congress's 'campaign of mass contact' among the Moslems, the introduction of the Wardha scheme of education, the use of Hindi, the singing of *Bande Matram,* the hoisting of the Congress flag on public buildings, the playing of music before the mosques, and the ratio in service between the two communities.[3] These charges must now be examined.

The Congress' campaign of contacting the masses, Nehru claimed, had never been thought of in terms of Moslems alone. The Congress had worked among the Hindu masses and 'disabled the Hindu Mahasabha politically'; it had done successful work among the Indian Christians, Parsis, the Jews and the Sikhs.[4] It is difficult to understand how it became an offence on the part of the Congress, a secular organization, to try to reach the Moslem masses also, on the basis of an economic programme conceived in the interests of peasants and labourers.[5] The League's claim amounted to a denial of the right of any other party, Moslem or Hindu, to speak to the Moslems about political matters or any others of general interest.

1   D.G. Tendulkar, *Mahatma* (Bombay, 1951-4), iv, 303-5; *IAR,* 1938, ii, 302.
2   Khaliquzzaman, *Pathway to Pakistan,* p. 192.
3   Coupland, *Indian Politics 1936-42,* pp. 179-94.
4   *Statesman,* 2 July 1942.
5   Beni Prasad, *The Hindu-Muslim Question* (London, 1946), pp. 73-6.

The Wardha scheme of education was another source of resentment to the League.[1] It should be noted that the scheme was formulated by a committee which was presided over by an eminent Moslem scholar, Dr Zakir Husain. He was assisted, among others, by Khwaja Sayyedain, a Moslem religious leader. The scheme combined manual with mental training, thus shifting the emphasis from mere literacy to vocational efficiency. Educationists in Europe had already adopted this method.[2] The purpose of the Wardha scheme was to provide a well-rounded education. Apart from learning to read and write, 'scholars' also acquired knowledge of some trade - woodwork, bookbinding, weaving. They grew their own food. Thus by their labours the scholars earned their food while being educated; and all that the government needed to do was to provide buildings, text books and the salaries for the teachers.[3]

It was unfortunate that the confusion between Indian renaissance and Hindu revivalism which was rampant in the Indian mind of the time should have marred a scheme which otherwise had many features to recommend it. The Moslem League objected, and not without reason, to the introduction of a religious colouring into education, for this was bound to reflect the tone and temper of the majority community. It seemed a surreptitious attempt to impose the peculiarities in the culture of one community on members of another, and as such it provoked angry opposition. In a state composed of different religious denominations, education could best thrive by being secularized, and the necessary corollary to the separation of politics and religion was that public education should have been kept scrupulously free from the religious traditions of any community. The main indictment against the Congress was that by introducing religious elements in education it was turning its back on secularism, something it should have avoided in a plural society like India.

The question of a common language proved another source of dissension, for here also the League saw an attempt to impose Hindu culture on the Moslems. There was argument as to whether the Persian or the Devanagari script should be used. Hindi and Urdu are basically the same language, but differ in their scripts as well as in the proportion of Sanskritic to Saracenic words.[4] As a compromise the

---

1 M. Mujeeb, 'The Partition of India in Retrospect', Philips and Wainwright (eds.) *Partition of India,* p. 413.

2 Prasad, *India Divided,* p. 141.

3 Dorothy Hogg, *India: A Plea for Understanding* (London, 1943), p. 9.

4 P.R. Brass, *Language, Religion and Politics in Northern India* (London, 1974), chs iii and iv.

Congress decided to give equal status to both Devanagari and the Persian script. But what is interesting is that this language controversy was of little interest to the masses. Not even ten per cent of the people were literate. Steeped in poverty and faced with the pangs of hunger, the problem for them was not which script they would use but how to build a society in which they might have the leisure and the education which would permit them to read.

The singing of *Bande Mataram* was considered another source of conflict between the two communities. It may be mentioned that Jinnah himself was a member of the Congress when it used to be sung, and he had never found anything objectionable in it. Yet it now became one of the major causes of conflict. To soothe Moslem feelings, the Congress decided that only the first two stanzas of the song, which consisted of a praise of the motherland, would be sung. The possible objection to what may be called the religious aspect of the song was further removed.

The playing of music outside the mosques and the denial of the right to slaughter cows were two major items in the League's catalogue of grievances. Juridically, the Hindus had as much right to play music on the public road as Moslems had the right to kill cows on their own land. But the use of criminal law by the Congress Government in Bihar to prevent cow-killing was a mistake, for this was a restriction of the civil right of a community.[1]

The hoisting of the tri-colour Congress flag was also frowned upon by the League. It was not in any way a Hindu flag. Its colour had been determined to represent the various communities: saffron for Hindus, green for Moslems, and white for the other minorities.[2]

Another major cause of conflict was the question of the ratio in services and representation in the legislatures. This grievance assumed great importance although it affected the smallest number of people. It was inevitable that in a country like India, with heavy unemployment, there were likely to be cases of nepotism over appointments. In such a situation one of the necessary evils of party government may be the use of government patronage to oblige the party workers. It was only natural that the Congress ministries in making minor appointments should have given preference to their party workers who, as it happened, were in most cases Hindus. The conflict was heightened by the fact that in the United Provinces the Moslems were in a minority

1   H. Kabir, 'Even the Muslims Disagree', *Asia* (Aug. 1940), p. 436.
2   Prasad, *India Divided,* p. 140.

but occupied a favoured position in government services; whereas in Bengal they were in a majority, but the Hindus occupied most of the places in the services. Thus the Moslem League in the United Provinces could point out that under the Congress regime the Hindus were determined to oust the Moslems from their favoured position; while in Bengal the League could conveniently accuse the Hindus of having deprived the Moslems of their share in public services even though the Moslems were in the majority. Moreover some Congress ministers, in the first flush of power, occasionally went beyond the limits set by the high command. It was easy for the League to represent these as attacks on Moslem interests.

The reports on the alleged persecution of the Moslems by the Congress were brushed aside by the Congress press with contempt. The official rejoinder was, however, more carefully considered. The Bihar government published a reasoned reply to the *Pirpur Report*. After summarizing the government's attempt to further Moslem interests in Bihar by nominating Moslems to official posts, by expenditure on Moslem education and by grants to Moslem institutions, it answered the charges point by point. As regards cow sacrifice, it was claimed that the Congress ministers had made 'no change whatever in the traditional policy of the previous government'. They had permitted it where it was an established right, but had discouraged it where it had not hitherto been customary. The same applied to processions and music. Allegations that riots had been unfairly suppressed were denied; the police had treated peace breakers with impartiality. The charges were never put to the test of impartial investigation, but there is little doubt that these allegations were greatly exaggerated.[1]

In October 1939, Rajendra Prasad, the Congress president, wrote to Jinnah offering to have the complaints investigated by the Chief Justice of the Federal Court of India. Jinnah, however, refused to accept this suggestion because, as he claimed, the matter was under the Viceroy's consideration and that 'he is the proper authority' to deal with such questions.[2] Jinnah was apparently trying to avoid any inquiry because he knew that many of the charges would not stand up to judicial probing. His reluctance is understandable. The League was trying to convince neither the British nor the Congress: its propaganda was meant for 'home consumption', i.e., for the Moslems. In this it achieved remarkable success. The important point to bear in mind is not whether the Moslem grievances were true or exaggerated, but

1   Moon, *Divide and Quit*, p. 23.
2   Prasad, *India Divided*, p. 147.

whether many Moslems believed in them. 'Had not the Quran reminded them time and again that the infidel could never be expected to bear any good will towards Muslims?'[1] Anything which widened the rift between the Hindus and the Moslems and indicated that the difference between the two communities was unbridgeable proved Jinnah's thesis that a democratic structure was unsuited for India.

Jinnah's anti-Congress attitude admirably suited Linlithgow since it demonstrated to the people in Britain and the USA that there was a deep rivalry between the two communities. The government could thus claim that unless the two communities resolved their differences they could make no further constitutional advance. This was despite the fact that Linlithgow personally believed that there was little substance in the League's allegations; he had informed Jinnah that there was no evidence of 'any positive instance of real oppression'.[2] And to Amery he had confessed: 'As you know I never took these complaints seriously, and I should be surprised if they did not prove to be psychological in character'.[3] Linlithgow's public silence on this issue, however, is significant.

It could hardly be expected that the Viceroy would appoint a Royal Commission in the middle of the war to rake up such a controversy. Linlithgow had, however, made a departmental inquiry. The results of the inquiry showed beyond doubt that the Moslem League had exaggerated the stories of Congress 'atrocities'. Here is the official summary of the inquiry report:

> As a rule the Ministries showed themselves ready to accept the Governor's advice and even to err on the side of generosity in the hope of disarming Muslim hostility, but some ministers had difficulty in overcoming an instinctive communal bias: and in some provinces the Hindu Congressmen in the countryside used all opportunities for arrogant behaviour. [4]

Shortly afterwards the Viceroy asked the Governors of the United Provinces, Central Provinces and Bihar to report on the treatment of the Moslems in these three provinces. The replies show the shallowness of the League's charges. The following is an official summary of these replies pertaining to the 'specific' complaints of the Moslems:

[1] Cited in Sayeed, *Political System of Pakistan*, p. 38.

[2] Mss. Eur. F.125/8/20, note of an interview between the Viceroy and Jinnah, 5 Oct. 1939, IOL.

[3] L/P&J/8/690, Linlithgow to Amery, 8 Jan. 1942. IOR. See also Mss. Eur. F.125/7/19, Linlithgow to Zetland, 19 May 1939. IOL.

[4] L/P&J/8/645, 'Note on Use of Special Responsibilities and other safeguards by Governors in Congress Provinces, July 1937 to October 1939', n.d. IOR.

(A) *Moslem landlords arrested*

i.	The United Provinces	Moslems were no worse off than Hindus
ii.	The Central Provinces	Ditto
iii.	Bihar	Ditto

(B) *Promotion of officers who support the Hindu Mahasabha*

i.	CP	No case of this, but tendency of ministry to select certain officers
ii.	Bihar	Allegations unfounded

(C) Communial riots started by Hindus and investigation one sided:

i.	UP	Both sides to blame
ii.	CP	Ditto
iii.	Bihar	Allegations unfounded

(D) Forcing Hindu culture on Moslem:

i.	UP	No evidence of this
ii.	CP	Shukla, the chief minister, would like to do this but has no opportunity
iii.	Bihar	No evidence

(E) Wasting money on so-called village uplift and employing non-Moslems:

i.	UP	Allegations baseless as Moslems lived mostly in towns
ii.	CP	Government money used for party propaganda when possible
iii.	Bihar	Money was wasted, but Moslems also employed

(F) *Unfair enquiries against Moslem officers*

i.	UP	Some cause for complaint in the past but not in 1939
ii.	CP	Several instances
iii.	Bihar	Allegation routine

(G) *CP and Bihar ministries have no Moslem ministers*

i.	UP	There are two Moslem Ministers and Moslem Parliamentary Secretaries
ii.	CP	There is no Moslem Minister
iii.	Bihar	There is one Moslem Minister

(H) *Moslems do not get a fair share of public appointments*

    i.   UP   Allegations untrue

    ii.   CP   Ditto

    iii. Bihar   Ditto

The Governors of the United Provinces and Central Province attributed the sense of grievance which the Moslem League allegedly faced to the fact that it did not have a share in the government: it was in opposition in all the provinces. They considered that the only solution to the problem was that the Moslems should be given a share of power.[1] Similarly the governor of Assam confessed that he could not cite a single instance of a case of the oppression of minorities. Nor could he recall any case in which he had had to endeavour to protect the minority community against unfair treatment.[2] Similarly, Sir Francis Wylie, former Governor of Central Province and Berar, wrote many years later that 'the accusations of gross anti-Moslem bias on the part of the Congress ministries were of course moonshine'.[3]

Yet behind all this smoke was undoubtedly some fire. It is difficult to agree with Azad that the League's charges were absolutely unfounded.[4] There is no denying that the Congress made mistakes which contributed towards communal friction. The sense of power among the Congressmen in the villages, and even in the district levels, led them into arrogant and provocative behaviour. This tendency was worsened by the formation of what was called 'parallel government', whereby some Congress ministers sought to bypass governmental machinery and operate through the party organization and the leaders in the district.[5] The League fully exploited these mistakes to rally the Moslems under its own banner. While isolated cases of petty tyranny by local officials may have occurred in remote villages and towns in the Congress-controlled provinces, the theory of a concerted tyranny directed against the Moslem community would be difficult to sustain. It may be pointed out that during these years nearly half the members of the Civil and Police Services were still British.[6] They occupied

---

[1] L/P&J/8/686, 'Summary of the Reply of the Governors of CP, UP and Bihar', n.d. IOR.

[2] L/P&J/8/645, Sir R.N. Reid (Governor of Assam) to Linlithgow, 17 Dec. 1939; see also M.J.K. Sullivan to Laithwaite, 7 Jan. 1940. IOR.

[3] F. Wylie, 'Federal Negotiations in India, 1935-39, and After', Philips and Wainwright (eds.) *Partition of India*, p. 523.

[4] Azad, *India Wins Freedom*, p. 21.

[5] Khosla, *Stern Reckoning*, p.21.

[6] Coupland, *India: A Re-Statement*, p. 125.

almost all the key appointments in the secretariat, besides holding charge of the important districts. Almost all the Inspectors General of Police were still British. It is significant that there is hardly any evidence in the records of the India Office to support the theory of a 'Hindu raj' in the Congress-governed provinces. Law and order was, of course, a provincial subject, but the channels of communication between the Viceroy and his colleagues in the Executive Council on the one hand, and the British governors and the chief secretaries on the other, had not dried up. It is difficult to believe that any deliberate illtreatment of the Moslems would have gone unnoticed and unrecorded by the officials of the British government even in their confidential correspondence.

The argument may be concluded by quoting the verdict of Sir Harry Haig:

> In dealing with questions raising communal issues the Ministers, in my judgement, normally acted with impartiality and a desire to do what was fair. Indeed, towards the end of their time they were being seriously criticised by the Hindu Mahasabha on the ground that they were not being fair to the Hindus, though there was in fact no justification for such criticism.[1]

Nevertheless, the Viceroy continued to emphasize the communal differences and pleaded with the Home Government to give special importance to the point of view of the Moslem League. He said: 'We may have to go a good deal further than we have done in giving weight to their [Moslem] point of view'.[2]

The outbreak of the war and the subsequent resignation of the Congress ministries introduced a new element in Indian politics: the Congress lost its bargaining power.[3] As long as its ministries were in office, Linlithgow could not ignore the Congress in his reckoning. It was responsible for the government of eight of the eleven British Indian provinces, and so it had it within its power to impair the government's war effort. When, however, the Congress ministries resigned, Linlithgow's attitude naturally changed. There was no urgent necessity to placate the Congress for the sake of the war effort; parliamentary government had been suspended in the Congress provinces and the administration had been taken over by the Governors' direct rule. The British generally believed that in view of earlier commitments against

---

1 Sir Harry Haig, 'UP and the New Constitution', *Asiatic Review* (1940), p. 428.
2 Mss. Eur. D.609/18, Linlithgow to Zetland, 26 Oct. 1939. IOL.
3 Moon, *Divide and Quit*, p. 273; see also ch. 5 below.

fascism it was highly unlikely that the Congress would embark on a campaign of civil disobedience; international opinion, moreover, would condemn any action that might thwart the war effort. In any case the Viceroy was confident that the powers of the Raj were sufficient to deal with a Congress campaign of civil disobedience, as indeed he was to prove during the 'Quit India' campaign of 1942.

The Moslem League, late in 1939, by no means came out openly in support of the government's war effort, but at the same time it did not oppose it: the Moslem ministries of Bengal and the Punjab were allowed to render unconditional support.[1] But the Congress's insistence on a definition of British war aims before it would agree to cooperate caused Linlithgow to suspect that Congress was manoeuvreing to take advantage of Britain's difficulties so as to hasten India's independence. Thus in order to offset Congress hostility, and perhaps mindful of the dangers of Congress and Moslems combining in their hostility against the British as they had done during the Khilafat movement at the end of the first world war, the Viceroy sought support elsewhere. The obvious choice was Jinnah and his Moslem League. As might have been expected, Linlithgow felt it expedient to befriend the Moslem League and encourage it to become the rival of the Congress on the all India scene.[2] The government used the existence of 'internecine conflicts' between the Hindus and Moslems to consolidate its position. 'That such divisions and conflicts should be used as practical aids to imperial government was only to be expected', admits Linlithgow's constitutional adviser, 'for who with the daunting task of governing, with absurdly small force, an Indian district or province or all India would not use such useful means as lay to hand'.[3] This was a natural policy for an imperial power to pursue, particularly when it was engaged in a war of survival. It was also not surprising that the Viceroy should discountenance any move on the part of the Congress ministries to return to office except on his own terms.[4] It is significant that he should have insisted on a mutual settlement by the Congress and the League of their differences in the provincial fields as a *sine qua non* for the inclusion of political leaders in the Executive Council or for any other constitutional changes.

1 Menon, *Transfer of Power in India*, p. 59.

2 H. Tinker, *Experiment with Freedom, India and Pakistan, 1947* (London, 1967), p. 30; Munshi, *Pilgrimage to Freedom*, (Bombay, 1967) i, 61-2; Francis G. Hutchins, *Spontaneous Revolution: The Quit India Movement* (Delhi, 1971), pp. 186-8; F. Moraes, *Witness to an Era* (London, 1973), p. 105.

3 Hodson, *The Great Divide*, p. 6.

4 Menon, *Transfer of Power*, p. 69.

Jinnah was not slow to recognize the changed situation. He remarked: 'After the war began . . . I was treated on the same basis as Mr Gandhi. I was wonderstruck why all of a sudden I was promoted and given a place side by side with Mr Gandhi'.[1] From this he concluded that the Moslem League had become a power to be reckoned with.[2] Henceforth the League's points of view began to receive much more attention from the government.

In turning to Jinnah for support, Linlithgow knew that he could count on him. As early as August 1938, Jinnah had hinted to Lord Brabourne, the acting Viceroy, at the possibility of the Moslem League cooperating with the British and had ended up with the startling suggestion that (Brabourne's description) the British should 'keep the centre as it is now, that we should make friends with the Moslems by *protecting* them in the Congress provinces and that if we did that, the Moslems would *protect* us at the centre'.[3] Jinnah's disclosure did not surprise Zetland; it only confirmed his 'conviction that the dominating factor in India would prove to be the All India Muslim League'. He had long held the view that 'the solidarity of Islam is a hard fact against which it is futile to run one's head'.[4]

In March 1939 two Muslim League leaders, Chaudhuri Khaliquzzaman and Rahman Siddiqi, had called at the India Office and met Colonel J.H. Muirhead, Under-Secretary of State, who had recently returned from India, to inquire about his views on the position of the Indian Moslems. Muirhead said that he realized that British representative institutions were not best suited to the needs of the Indian Moslems, but there was little that the government could do as the Moslems had not yet formulated any alternative scheme. Khaliquzzaman had claimed that he thereupon suggested the separation of the Moslem majority provinces from the rest of India. Colonel Muirhead liked the idea and arranged for the two leaders to put their proposals to Lord Zetland. 'So my idea', wrote Khaliquzzaman, 'about the British attitude [sic] was coming true'.[5]

1 Cited in Menon, *Transfer of Power*, pp. 59-60. Menon does not indicate the date of this statement but it appears to have been made shortly after Jinnah met Linlithgow on 5 Oct. 1939.

2 Ahmad, *Speeches and Writings of Mr Jinnah*, i, 154

3 Mss. Eur. F.125/6/15, Brabourne to Zetland, 19 Aug. 1938. IOL. Sir Sikander Hyat had also assured Brabourne that 'given a fair deal' by the British, the Moslems 'would stand by [the British] through thick and thin'. *Ibid.*

4 John L. Dundas, *Essayez the Memoirs of Lawrence 2nd Marquess of Zetland* (London, 1956), p. 119.

5 Khaliquzzaman, *Pathway to Pakistan*, p. 205. Khaliquzzaman and Siddiqi had gone to London as members of a delegation sent by the Palestine

The meeting with Zetland, although unnoticed at the time, was of crucial importance to the future of India. It had a remarkable similarity to Lord Minto's reception of the Moslem delegation at Simla in 1906. In 1906 the Moslems had been assured separate electorates; little more than three decades later they were given the hope of a separate Moslem state.

The meeting took place on 21 March 1939. Khaliquzzaman told Zetland that the British were transferring power to Indian hands in such a way that when they left India the Moslems would find themselves 'the slaves of the majority'. At this stage Zetland again made the point which had been made earlier by Colonel Muirhead, namely, that the Moslems had not put forward an alternative plan. Khaliquzzaman's reply was prompt:

> You may partition the Muslim areas from the rest of India and proceed with your scheme of federation of the Indian provinces without including the Muslim areas which should be independent from the rest.[1]

His rather egoistic claim in his memoirs that he had put forward to Zetland a clear-cut scheme for partitioning India into Hindu and Moslem states may well be only partially true; nevertheless, in view of what followed, the claim has to be taken seriously. It is certain that at this stage some kind of common central authority had not been ruled out by such people as Khaliquzzaman and Siddiqi. Zetland's description of the meeting with these two leaders reveals that by way of 'a suggestion of constructive character' they had proposed the establishment of 'three or four federations of Provinces and States which would be coordinated by a small central body of some kind or another'. The object of the scheme was, the leaders had claimed, to give the Moslems as great a measure of control as the Hindus'.[2] The two Moslem leaders returned to India with the impression that the India Office might view sympathetically their idea of keeping the Moslem majority provinces out of an all-India federation. 'My own impression, after my talk with these two British officials, was that they would not oppose the demand [for partition] seriously . . . I could not help being thankful to Colonel Muirhead for having given me encouragement to discuss the question with Lord Zetland who in turn was quite sympathetic'. 'I brought back with me from London',

conference held in Egypt in October 1939 to put the Arab case regarding Palestine before the British Government.

1 *Ibid.* pp. 205-6.

2 Dundas, *Essayez*, pp. 248-9.

recalled Khaliquzzaman, 'hopeful dreams for the future of the Muslims of India'.[1]

Khaliquzzaman's impression is corroborated by the correspondence between Zetland and Linlithgow. Zetland was now confirmed in his view that the real opposition to the federation would come from the Moslems. In his letter reporting the conversation, he did not mention a single word in favour of the all-India federation to which the British Government was officially committed. His only concern was that the Moslem leaders were 'vague' about the details and had 'failed to consider the practical difficulties in the way of such a scheme'.[2] He was now convinced that the 'deep-seated dislike and fear of Hindu domination on the part of the 90 million Muslims is a thing which we cannot possibly brush aside.[3] Linlithgow correctly pointed out that Moslem apprehension would be inherent in any scheme of representative government at the centre because they contemplated the 'future course of Indian politics as an unending communal contest'.[4]

With the outbreak of war, however, the roles were reversed. It was now the turn of the Viceroy to stress the importance of giving due weight to the points of view of the League.[5] He did not regard this policy as wise or reasonable in the long run, but he realized that it suited the exigencies of the war.[6] He set about strengthening the League so that it would be on an equal footing with the Congress.[7] In reply to the Congress's demand for a definition of war aims, Linlithgow implicitly accepted the League's claim to speak for all the Moslems of India, while the Congress was dubbed a Hindu body.[8] The Viceroy conveniently ignored the fact that in the elections of 1936 the League had won only 105 out of 489 Moslem seats and did not control a single government in any of the Moslem majority provinces, while the Congress formed governments in eight provinces, including the NWFP with its 95 per cent Moslem population.[9]

1 Khaliquzzaman, *Pathway to Pakistan*, pp. 207-8.

2 Dundas, *Essayez*, pp. 248-9.

3 *Ibid.*

4 *Ibid.* p. 250.

5 Mss. Eur. F.125/8/10, Linlithgow to Zetland, 5 Sept. 1939. IOL.

6 Munshi, *Pilgrimage to Freedom*, i, 53.

7 Mss. Eur. F.125/8/10, Note of an interview between Linlithgow and Jinnah, 4 Sept. 1939. IOL.

8 Cmd. 6121 (1939), *India and The War: Statement Issued by the Governor-General of India on 17 October 1939.*

9 See chapter 2 above, pp. 25-7.

The Moslem League, of course, was quick to recognize 'with satisfaction that HMG recognized the fact that the all-India Muslim League truly represents the Muslims of India and can speak on their behalf'.[1] Later, in 1945, commenting upon the development following the outbreak of war, Jinnah remarked: 'There was going to be a deal between Mr Gandhi and Lord Linlithgow. Providence helped us. The war which nobody welcomes proved to be a blessing in disguise'.[2] Jinnah understood the benefits of collaborating with the British and took full advantage of the situation. In such circumstances he might have committed one of two mistakes. He might either have antagonized the British by trying to extract too many concessions or he might have adopted the opposite course of offering unconditional support in the war effort. He avoided both these pitfalls. He never rejected a British offer outright but no sooner had one of his demands been complied with than he came back with another. By playing his cards adroitly, he was able to secure for the League a status equal to that of the Congress. The Congress, on the other hand, displayed a lack of statesmanship and could not regain the initiative. 'The League', wrote Menon, 'grew rapidly in the sunshine of favour'.[3]

Jinnah was grateful to Linlithgow for his help in the consolidation of the League: in an interview Jinnah 'thanked me with much graciousness for what I had done to assist him in keeping his party together and expressed gratitude for this'.[4] Linlithgow's ostensible reasons for helping to consolidate the Moslem League were that he thought it was unsatisfactory that while the Congress should be well equipped to pursue its objectives, the League should be deprived of its due position by failure to secure an adequate mouthpiece. He therefore thought that the League's point of view should be more competently explained.[5] However, the real reasons which motivated the Viceroy were the exigencies of the war. The Congress was 'non-cooperating', and in order to counter its demands the Viceroy thought it necessary to have a powerful Moslem League as a counter-weight. The general consensus of opinion within the Government of India was against settlement with Congress and tended to incline

1   Eur. Mss. F.125/143 Quarterly Survey of Political and Constitutional Development in India, No. 9. IOL; see also Gwyer and Appadorai (eds.), *Speeches and Documents*, ii, 488-90.

2   Ahmad, *Speeches and Writings of Mr Jinnah*, ii, (Lahore, 1947, 6th edn. 1964), p. 245.

3   Menon, *Transfer of Power*, p. 437.

4   L/P&J/8/505. Note of an interview between Linlithgow and Jinnah on 5 Oct. 1939. IOR.

5   *Ibid.*

towards an accommodation of the Moslem League's demands. Lord Erskine, the Governor of Madras, who in 1936-7 had been advocating the necessity of enlisting the cooperation of the Congress, now took a hard line: 'Personally I think we should not bargain, for if the Congress go out [resign], it will be their funeral, not ours'.[1] There were others too, who preferred to strike the Congress a hard blow. The Commander-in-Chief, Sir Robert Cassels, insisted that the government should 'hit them [Congress] over the head while we are in a position to do so'.[2] Sir James Grigg, the Finance Member, expressed similar views.[3] At the same time there was a feeling among the officials that the government should endeavour to enlist the support of the League, even though it was recognized that the Moslems 'were apt to pitch their demands pretty high'.[4] Linlithgow wrote that this view 'tallied' with his own appraisal but he suspected that Jinnah was manoeuvreing for an acceptance of the principle whereby 'any minority is entitled to hold up progress completely'.[5] An assurance in this 'crude form' was out of the question. But in order to offset the 'dangerous' claims of the Congress Linlithgow was anxious to retain the League's goodwill. It should be remembered that he saw his primary task as Viceroy as keeping the Indian Empire intact during the war and maximizing India's war effort. He thus favoured publicizing the conflicting and irreconcilable demands of the minorities and insisted that agreement between the major parties must be a precondition for any constitutional progress.[6] He therefore urged Zetland to draw the attention of Parliament to various earlier statements in which the British Government had promised to safeguard the interests of the minorities. In this way the Viceroy hoped not only to demonstrate the supposed hollowness of the Congress claim to speak for the Moslems, but also to bring about a situation in which no constitutional changes could be contemplated until the two communities were agreed. And in response to Linlithgow's wishes, Zetland stated in the House of Lords

---

1 Telegram from Erskine to Linlithgow, cited in Mss. Eur. F.125/18/244, telegram from Linlithgow to Zetland, 16 Sept. 1939, IOL. For reports from other governors see Mss. Eur. F.125/18/222a, Linlithgow to Zetland, 5 Sept. 1939, Mss. Eur. F.125/18/248 dated 17 Sept. 1939 (for Wylie's report); Mss. Eur. F.125/18/249 dated 18 Sept. 1939 (for reports from the governors of Assam and Bihar)

2 Mss. Eur. F.125/7/8a. Linlithgow to Zetland, 28 Feb. 1939. IOL.

3 L/P&J/8/505, telegram from Linlithgow to Zetland, 31 Aug. 1939. IOR.

4 L/P&J/8/505. T.A. Stewart (Chief Secretary, Bihar) to Linlithgow, 23 Oct. 1939. IOR.

5 Mss. Eur. D.609/26, telegram from Linlithgow to Zetland, 22 Oct. 1939. IOL.

6 *Ibid.*

that the British Government felt the necessity for an agreement between the Hindus and the Moslems to be a precondition for any constitutional changes.[1]

This was a significant statement. It meant that as long as the two communities did not resolve their differences, the government could not be called upon to meet the Congress's demand for constitutional advance. From the government's point of view the immediate effects of the statement were satisfactory. It was hardly likely that Congress and the Moslem League would be able to find a mutually acceptable plan for quite some time to come. The government would thus be left free to carry on the war unhindered. But the long term results of the move were significant, too. It made it extremely difficult to resolve the impasse.

Early in November 1939, Linlithgow invited Gandhi, Rajendra Prasad and Jinnah to a joint discussion. He claimed that 'the lack of prior agreement between the major communities such as would contribute to harmonious working in the centre' was primarily responsible for delays in constitutional progress. He therefore asked them to meet among themselves and submit agreed proposals 'which could be considered for some expansion of the Governor General's Council at the Centre'.[2] It seemed that Linlithgow was not prepared to allow the Congress to return to power save on his own terms. The Congress rejected the Viceroy's proposals on the grounds that the crisis in India had been caused by the Viceroy's declaration of India as a belligerent without the consent of the people. The Congress had not resigned because of any conflict with the League, for which reason there was no fresh necessity to work out 'agreed proposals'.[3] The negotiations, the Congress claimed, had failed because of the fundamental differences between the Congress and the British Government.

However, Linlithgow did not, in his public statement on the failure of his talks, refer even once to the conflict between the British and the Congress, but only to that between the Congress and the League, thus giving ground for suspecting that his main objective in arranging these talks was to use them for advertizing these differences and to claim that they persisted despite British efforts.

[1] House of Lords, *Parliamentary Debates*, vol. 114, cols, 1695-98, 7 Nov. 1939; see also Sir Samuel Hoare's statement in the House of Commons, vol. 352, cols. 1634-44, 26 Oct. 1939.

[2] *IAR,* 1939, ii, 411.

[3] L/P&J/8/506, telegram from Linlithgow to Zetland, 4 Nov. 1939. IOR.

The Congress leaders did meet Jinnah but no agreement could be reached. Jinnah's position was delicate. He could not openly refuse to be a party to the Congress demands for a declaration of war aims. If he did so he would be branded as unpatriotic and 'pro-British'. At the same time he was aware that by supporting the Congress without first obtaining some concessions for the League he would not only earn the disfavour of the government but also strengthen the Congress at the expense of the League. He therefore side-tracked the main discussion by putting forward five conditions as his price for cooperating with the Congress: coalition ministries should be formed in the provinces; no measure should be passed by the legislatures if two thirds of the Moslem members objected to it; the Congress flag should not be flown on public buildings; the singing of *Bande Mataram* should be abandoned; and the Congress should stop its campaign of 'mass contact of the Moslems'.[1] It was hardly likely that the Congress would concede these demands. Thus, by an extremely astute move, Jinnah threw the onus of reaching a settlement back on the Congress.

There is some evidence to suggest that Jinnah at this stage might have been working in collaboration with the Viceroy. In an interview with Linlithgow, Jinnah admitted that Gandhi had enquired of him whether it was possible for the Congress and the Moslem League jointly to demand the declaration for which the Congress had been pressing the British Government. Jinnah was thus placed in an embarrassing position and had difficulty in refusing to support Congress demands. The Congress leaders warned that unless Jinnah was prepared to join them in putting up a demand, he would be exposed before the public as the one real obstacle to India's independence.[2] In this situation Linlithgow decided to call off the idea of an all-parties conference which he had planned to convene in order to expose the 'hollowness' of the Congress's claim to speak for the whole of India. The Viceroy realized that while such a conference would, no doubt, destroy the Congress's claim to represent all India, it would also confirm the Congress allegation that Jinnah was a 'stooge' of the British Government. While reporting to Zetland the summary of his interview with Jinnah, Linlithgow candidly admitted:

> He [Jinnah] had given me very valuable help by standing against the Congress claims and I was duly grateful. It was clear that if he,

1 Quarterly Survey, no. 10. IOL.

2 L/P&J/8/506, Note of an interview between the Viceroy and Jinnah on 4 Nov. 1939. IOR.

Mr Jinnah, had supported the Congress demand and confronted me with a joint demand, the strain upon me and His Majesty's Government would have been very great indeed. I thought therefore, *I could claim to have a vested interest in his position.*[1]

This is a crucial document. It explains in plain terms the reason behind the British efforts to encourage the League: the British Government was engaged in a war and it would have been virtually impossible not to concede the Congress demands (which effectively amounted to independence) if those demands had been backed by major parties and communities. Thus it was necessary to prevent the League from joining hands with the Congress, at least for the duration of the war.

The Viceroy, however, gave a different version for public consumption. He said that he had 'begged' the leaders in 'most earnest manner to spare no endeavour to reach agreement', and emphasized that it was essentially a question affecting Indians alone and on which agreement between the Indians themselves was essential.[2] However, the India League, an organization headed by Krishna Menon and representing the Congress in London, guessed what Linlithgow was up to. It issued a rejoinder denying that the talks between the Congress and the Moslem League had broken down on 'communal issues' and claimed that Jinnah had raised no such objections. It claimed that the breakdown did not 'mean communal disagreement but rather the intensification of differences with British policy and a break with the British government which refuses to make a satisfactory declaration'.[3]

The India League's statement created consternation in the India Office. Wishing to have it refuted, Zetland asked Linlithgow if it would be possible to persuade Jinnah to issue to *Reuters* a statement contradicting the India League's assertion.[4] Such a reply would be given the widest publicity, both in Britain and the USA. Jinnah evinced much interest and promised to give a befitting reply on a 'suitable occasion'.[5]

There is no clear evidence to show that Jinnah ever gave the

---

1 *Ibid.* Emphasis added.

2 *IAR,* 1939, ii, 411.

3 Mss. Eur. F.125/18/304, cited in telegram from Zetland to Linlithgow, 16 Nov. 1939. IOL; see also *The Times,* 8 Nov. 1939.

4 Mss. Eur. F.125/18/303, telegram from Zetland to Linlithgow, 18 Nov. 1939; see also Mss. Eur. F.125/18/492, telegram from Linlithgow to Zetland, 28 Nov. 1939. IOL.

5 Mss. Eur. F.125/18/511, telegram from Linlithgow to Zetland, 28 Nov. 1939. IOL.

'befitting reply' he had promised. In the third week of December 1939, however, while correspondence was going on between Nehru and Jinnah with a view to exploring means for a *detente* between the Congress and the League, Jinnah suddenly called upon the Moslems to celebrate 'deliverance day'.[1] This was supposed to be deliverance from the 'tyranny, oppression and injustice during the last two and a half years' of Congress rule. Jinnah also urged the Government of India to enquire into the 'anti-Moslem' policy of the Congress ministries. Attempts to persuade him to call off 'deliverance day' failed, and his statement was construed as an open attack on the Congress.[2] The negotiations between Nehru and Jinnah came to an end. In the absence of any definite evidence it would be hasty to suggest that Jinnah's call was inspired by the Government, but Linlithgow inclined to regard it as a 'convincing reply' to the India League's statement. He claimed in his correspondence with the Secretary of State that Jinnah's statement calling for 'deliverance day' would prove that the communal problem was a live issue.[3] Meanwhile, in order that the position of the Moslems might be better explained to the British Cabinet and Parliament, Linlithgow proposed to send Sir Sikander Hyat Khan to Britain.[4] But Zetland considered the idea of approaching the Cabinet and members of Parliament to be 'misconceived'. He felt that propaganda could not be confined to a negative insistence that the Moslems could not be a party to self-government in India on the principle of unqualified majority. In order to be successful, it would have to indicate the terms and conditions on which the Moslems would be prepared to accept self-government.[5]

Linlithgow therefore began to urge the Moslem League to put forward 'concrete proposals' to counteract the Congress's demand for independence and a constituent assembly to frame a constitution for India. Linlithgow spoke to Jinnah on several occasions, telling him that it would be impossible to educate public opinion in Britain and 'more particularly' the 600 odd representatives in the House of Commons by a submission of a formal memorandum to the

---

1 *Hindustan Times* (Delhi), 3 Dec. 1939.

2 S.S. Pirzada, (ed.) *Leaders' Correspondence with Mr Jinnah* (Bombay, 1944), p. 147.

3 Mss. Eur. F.125/18/521, telegram from Linlithgow to Zetland, 8 Dec. 1939; see also Mss. Eur. F.125/8/30, Linlithgow to Zetland, 7 Dec. 1939, IOL.

4 Mss. Eur. F.125/19/6a, telegram from Linlithgow to Zetland, 12 Jan. 1940. IOL.

5 Mss. Eur. F.125/19/6, telegram from Zetland to Linlithgow, 16 Jan. 1940, IOL.

British Government and emphasizing that if Jinnah did not wish to let the Moslem case to go by default it was essential that the League should formulate plans immediately.[1]

Reporting to Zetland the substance of these talks, Linlithgow wrote:

> I again put forward the familiar argument for formulating and publishing a constructive policy and in the light of our discussion he said that he was disposed to think that it would be wise for his friends and himself to make public at any rate the outlines of their position in good time.[2]

Still not very strong, the League was probably not in a position to commit itself definitely on the constitutional issue, but it could not afford to postpone its commitment for long. Both the Congress and the Moslem League had rejected the British Government's scheme, embodied in the 1935 Act, to establish an all-India federation. The Congress had countered it with its alternative plan of a constitution framed by a constituent assembly. The League, while opposing both the British and the Congress, had no plans of its own. Previously it had nominally subscribed to the idea of a loose federation for India. The results of the 1937 elections had, however, clearly shown that despite separate electorates and reservation of seats, the League could not hope to play a decisive role in the proposed federation. Adherence to the concept of an all-India federation would be a mistake. The way Jinnah's mind was working about this time is revealed in an article published in January 1940. He pointed out that the League was irrevocably opposed to any federal objectives because it would bring about a Hindu majority rule. He suggested that the British Government should revise India's future constitution *de novo*: 'To conclude, a constitution must be evolved that recognises that there are in India two nations who both must share the governance of their common motherland'.[3] It is significant that Jinnah still spoke of 'common motherland' and there was as yet no hint of partition.

In the third week of March, however the League at its Lahore session adopted a resolution demanding the partition of India with separate states for Moslems and Hindus as a solution to the communal problem.[4] This was the League's reply to the demand for complete

---

1 Mss. Eur. F.125/131/12, note of an interview between the Viceroy and Jinnah, 6 Feb. 1940. IOL.

2 Mss. Eur. F.125/19/6, telegram from Linlithgow to Zetland, 16 Jan. 1940. IOL.

3 *Time and Tide* (London), 19 Jan. 1940.

4 L.A. Sherwani, *Pakistan Resolution to Pakistan, 1940-47* (Karachi, 1969), p. 21; see also Jinnah's presidential address to the ML session at Lahore in

independence made three days before by the Congress at Ramgarh.[1] The Lahore resolution radically altered the dimensions of the communal problem. All solutions hitherto thought of - separate electorates, composite cabinets, reservation of seats - suddenly became out of date. 'For the moment', wrote a British newspaper, 'Mr Jinnah has re-established the reign of chaos in India'.[2] The 'Pakistan resolution' as it came to be called, added to the complexities of the constitutional controversy which the Congress leaders had hitherto regarded as a simple issue between themselves and the British Government. The original demands for a declaration of Indian independence were lost sight of in a welter of acrimonious accusations between the two communities.

From Jinnah's point of view, the 'Pakistan resolution' was a part of his carefully planned strategy. He knew that the idea of a Moslem state, within or without India, would prove to be a catch-all.[3] He shrewdly refused to spell out the details of 'Pakistan' which his followers were thus left free to picture according to their own imagination.[4] The orthodox dreamed of a State representing the purity of pristine Islam. Those Moslems with a more secular outlook succumbed to the prospects of financial benefits from their 'own State'. Moreover the vision of a sovereign Moslem State was reminiscent of the past glories of Moslem rule. While most Moslems took up the idea enthusiastically, at least a few accepted it rather regretfully as offering perhaps the only possible solution to the intractable Hindu-Moslem problem.

It would be hasty to suggest that this demand for partition came as a direct response to Linlithgow's persistent request for a 'constructive proposal'. The final verdict must await further research but such a possibility cannot be ruled out altogether in view of Linlithgow's

March 1940. N. Mansergh, *Documents and Speeches of British Commonwealth Affairs, 1931-52* (Oxford, 1953), i, 609-12.

1 *IAR*, 1940, i, 228-9, see also R.J. Moore, 'British Policy and the Indian Problem 1936-40', Philips and Wainwright (eds.), *Partition of India*, p. 93.

2 *Manchester Guardian*, 2 Apr. 1940.

3 S.R. Mehrotra, 'The Congress and the Partition of India', Philips and Wainwright (eds.), *Partition of India*, p. 204.

4 It seems that Jinnah himself was not too sure of the implications of the 'Pakistan' resolution, and it may have been put forward merely to counter Congress demands. See Durga Das, *India from Curzon to Nehru and After* (London, 1969), p. 95; Menon, *Transfer of Power*, pp. 104-5; Moon, *Divide and Quit*, p. 21; Tara Chand, *History of the Freedom Movement in India* (Delhi, 1961-72), iv, 327-8; W.R. Crocker, *Nehru: A Contemporary's Estimate* (London, 1966), n.1, pp. 91-2.

reports to Zetland six week earlier.[1] The idea of partition was first mooted by the League Working Committee in February 1940, about the time that Linlithgow had for the first time insisted that the League should formulate a 'constructive' plan to counter the Congress's demand for a constituent assembly. When discussion was in progress, Sir Sikander Hyat and Fazlul Huq went to see Linlithgow, and, on their return from the interview, informed the Committee that the Viceroy had told them 'that he was doing his best for the League and advised them to send a League Delegation to London to place its case before the Prime Minister and the Secretary of State'. Although the demand for partition was not made public till 23 March, according to Khaliquzzaman the decision had been communicated to the Viceroy several weeks before by Jinnah.[2] Linlithgow kept quiet and did not even mention it to Zetland. But when the 'Pakistan resolution' was finally adopted, the Viceroy seems to have feigned surprise; he described it as a 'preposterous claim' put forward for 'bargaining purposes' and 'partly to dispose of the reproach that Moslems had no constructive scheme of their own'.[3] Nevertheless the resolution brought much relief to Linlithgow, as it provided some answers to the British dilemma. It had, as he said, 'offset the extreme Congress claim to independence . . . Congress contention that Congress is the mouthpiece of India . . . [and that] a constituent assembly on the basis of adult suffrage is the only machinery for deciding future progress'. In commending the 'Pakistan' demand to the British Government, Linlithgow said that he was personally not in favour of assuaging Jinnah to the extent of recognizing the claim for partition. But the refusal of the Congress to cooperate in the war effort, and its increasing militancy, had created a situation, which, he said, called for sympathetic consideration of the League's demands. He therefore urged that some 'specific reference' be made in Parliament to the League's demands, and that it should be stated in plain terms that 'we [the British Government] cannot possibly ignore the views of 80 to 90 million Mussalmans in India'.[4] Linlithgow, despite his self-professed personal dislike for the 'Pakistan' scheme, was endeavouring to secure a broad acceptance of the League's demand from the British Government.

---

1   See above pp, 115-6 Linlithgow had also asked Sikander Hyat to press Jinnah to produce a 'constructive scheme'. Mss. Eur. F.125/131/10, note of a conversation between the Viceroy and Sikander Hyat, 25 Jan. 1940. IOL.

2   Khaliquzzaman, *Pathway to Pakistan*, pp. 233-4.

3   Mss. Eur. F.125/19/21, telegram from Zetland to Linlithgow, 4 April 1940. IOL.

4   *Ibid.*

Zetland did not share Linlithgow's point of view. He considered the League's resolution to be 'a counsel of despair' and wholly at variance with the policy of a united India which British rule had achieved and 'which we aim to perpetuate after British rule ceases'. He therefore insisted on 'pouring much cold water on the Moslem idea of partition . . . though not necessarily at this stage rejecting it'.[1] His successor, Amery, was still more critical of the 'Pakistan' scheme. He asserted that the break-up of India 'on Ulster or Eire lines' would be disastrous, and that partition, by destroying the natural boundaries of the country, would lay India open to external dangers.[2] He emphasized that the 'absurdity of the idea should be exposed' so that Jinnah should be under no illusion as to the attitude of the British Government.[3]

But Linlithgow opposed the ruling out of the League's demand. 'Silly as the Moslem scheme for partition is, it would be a pity to throw too much cold water on it at the moment'. He was in no hurry to discuss the period after British rule had ceased. Such a day was 'very remote', and till then the least said the better.[4] Linlithgow refused to take the claim for 'Pakistan' seriously. It was, he judged, a matter which would have to be dealt with after the war: 'For God's sake leave the post-war period to post-war men'.[5] He may have been right. But the important point is that once the Congress, and the Moslem League had taken up their extreme positions they could not recede without loss of face. Furthermore, the longer the positions were held, the greater would be the number of firm adherents.

It is necessary to explain the complacency, if not active connivance, with which Linlithgow and many of the British officials viewed the demand for Pakistan. It is possible, though by no means certain, that if from the outset the British Government had made it clear that they would have nothing to do with any scheme that threatened the unity of India, the demand for partition would have died down. But it may be argued that it was very difficult for Linlithgow to advise the British Government to make such a pronouncement.[6] The demand for

1 Mss. Eur. F.125/19/94, telegram from Zetland to Linlithgow, 4 April 1940. IOL.

2 Mss. Eur. F.125/9/33, Amery to Linlithgow, 16 Sept. 1940. IOL.

3 Mss. Eur. F.125/10/3, Amery to Linlithgow, 25 Jan. 1941. IOL.

4 Mss. Eur. D.609/19, Linlithgow to Zetland, 5 April 1940. IOL.

5 Linlithgow's comment of the margin. See Mss. Eur. F.125/10/38, Amery to Linlithgow, 11 Dec. 1941. IOL.

6 L/P&J/8/508, Amery to Linlithgow, 17/21 Feb. 1941, and L/P&J/8/690, Linlithgow to Amery, 1 Mar. 1941. IOR.

Pakistan had come in March 1940, when Britain was engaged in the war, and when the Congress was not only clamouring for independence but also threatening civil disobedience, which would have hampered India's war efforts. In these circumstances it would have been inexpedient for Linlithgow to antagonize the principal Moslem party by rejecting its demand out of hand. Moreover, Linlithgow could not ignore the effect of refusal on the Moslem majority province of the Punjab which supplied a very considerable portion of the recruits for the army. As the representative of His Majesty's Government in India, Linlithgow knew the importance of India to the Allied cause, and his policy was therefore dominated by realization of this fact. This policy demanded the holding of India in the Empire for the duration of the war. What Linlithgow could be blamed for is his failure to bridge the chasm that had opened between Hindus and Moslems.

It would, however, be far from correct to suggest that Linlithgow was not aware of the implications of the League's demand.[1] But he had his own reasons for not making an official pronouncement on the issue because 'it would not only be a mistake but it would be very near a breach of faith were we to do anything of the sort: and . . . we must refrain as rigidly from ruling Pakistan out in deference to Hindu pressure as we must refrain from accepting Pakistan as a solution in deference to the pressures [from the Moslem League]'.[2] In official circles the 'Pakistan' scheme was welcomed as a means of checkmating the Congress demands.[3] Many British officials did not trouble themselves about the merits of the partition scheme. It provided the British with a convenient case to argue that no constitutional advance could be made unless the Congress and the Moslem League 'came to an agreement among themselves'. There was little chance of other parties accepting the proposal; political deadlock was likely to last indefinitely, and the only alternative was the continuance of British rule.[4] It is clear, however, that this support by the British officials was not due to any affinity with the Moslem leaders. Their support was to a large extent dictated by the exigencies of war. To Amery, Linlithgow confided: 'I am in no hurry to face up to this matter [of Pakistan] and

1   For example, Sir Penderel Moon has claimed that 'The British at first noticed these developments with mild complacency . . . Later, when they woke up to the fearful consequences that might ensue, they made desperate but unavailing efforts to avert them', Moon, *Divide and Quit*, p. 14.

2   L/P&J/8/690, Linlithgow to Amery, 1 Mar. 1941. IOR.

3   Mss. 'Political Report' by Professor Edward Thompson (Dec. 1939), p. 10, Rhodes House, Oxford. See also Mss. Eur. F.125/135/122. Laithwaite to Clauson, 3 Nov. 1940. IOL.

4   M. Edwardes, *The Last Years of the British in India* (London, 1963), p. 73.

I would propose to leave them alone and not to get into it too closely for some considerable time to come . . . I am not a bit fussed about the post-war period'.[1]

At the same time it must be added, somewhat regretfully, that Linlithgow's policy did much to give the 'Pakistan' proposal that air of feasibility which was needed before it could gather support even among the Moslem masses.[2] In his long awaited public statement of August 1940, Linlithgow assured the Moslem League that the Government would not contemplate any constitutional changes to which the Moslems were opposed. This assurance had given the League the power to veto any constitutional advance which it did not approve. This meant that Jinnah could bide his time, build up his organization, and eventually force the Congress to yield to his demand that the Moslem League was the sole organization of the Moslems.

The theoretical validity of the League's demand was recognized by the British Government through the Cripps proposal of 1942 which provided that any province which did not wish to accede to the Indian Union could opt to remain out of it.[3] It will be argued later that the process of non-accession provided in the plan was such that it would have been very nearly impossible for the Moslem provinces to secede from the Indian Union. But the important point to note is that it conceded the League's demand in principle.

It is interesting to note that the Moslem League resolution demanding partition was put forward on behalf of 'Muslim India'; thus the British Government accepted the League's claim to be the spokesman for the Indian Moslems. The question may be asked to what extent the demand for partition was actually supported by the Moslems.

If the results of the 1936 elections are taken as the criteria for determining the support of the Moslem masses for the policies of the League, it appears that the League at that time had a small following among the Moslems. In the absence of exact figures, Professor Wilfred Cantwell Smith advances a possible estimate: the League in 1940 was supported by virtually all the Moslem upper class, most of the Moslem upper-middle class and a very considerable portion of the rest of the Moslem middle class.[4] This would suggest that the League's

1 L/P&J/8/690, Linlithgow to Amery, 8 Jan. 1941. IOR.

2 Mss. Eur. F.125/19/26. telegram from Linlithgow to Amery, 12 Aug. 1940. IOL.

3 For details see chapter 6 below.

4 W.C. Smith, *Modern Islam in India* (London, 1946), pp. 255-6.

support at this time was essentially confined to the upper echelon of the Moslem community. There were several sections of the Moslem community which remained outside the fold of the League and were opposed to the partition of the country.

Khan Abdul Ghaffar Khan's *Khudai Khidmatgar* was a Pathan nationalist movement, which endeavoured to preserve the unity of the country. They were the dominant Moslem party in the North West Frontier Province. The *Jamiyat-ul-Ulema-i-Hind* never accepted the doctrine of the two nations as propounded by the League. From its very inception it stood for a 'United Indian nationalism',[1] the very core of the Jamiyat-League differences[2] The Ahrar Party in the Punjab had refused to join the League and declared its determination to 'crush it because it is a party of reactionaries'.[3] The Ahrar Party accepted the political objectives of the Congress and wanted to extend its economic implication still further. In Bihar, the Momin Ansar Conference (party of Moslem weavers) remained opposed to the League. The Momins constituted a large section of the Bihar Moslems, but educationally, economically and politically a backward section of the community. They demanded from the League almost the same safeguards which the League demanded from the Congress on behalf of the Moslems[4] Similarly the demand for 'Pakistan' was opposed by the *Ittehad-e-Millat*, another important organization in the Punjab[5] In addition, the nationalists of Baluchistan, organized by Allama Mashriqui, were also opposed to the division of the country.[6] Furthermore, there were in the Congress itself a large number of nationalist Moslems who were opposed to the League. Many organizations with Moslem members, such as the Shia Conference, the States Peoples Conference, Trade Unions, and Kisan Sabhas had adopted the same political platform as the Congress had done.[7]

Nor did the League command much support in the Moslem majority provinces. In the Punjab, the Unionist Party was outside its control. Sir Sikander Hyat Khan, premier of the Punjab from 1937 to 1942, as long as he lived continued to voice his opposition to

[1] H.A. Madani, *Muttahida Qaumiyat aur Islam* (Delhi, 1938), (in Urdu).

[2] Z.H. Faruqui, *The Deoband School and the Demand for Pakistan* (Bombay, 1963), p. 103.

[3] *Amerasia* (Aug. 1940), p. 279.

[4] H. Kabir, *Muslim Politics 1906-1942* (Calcutta, 1943), pp. 36-8.

[5] M. Noman, *Muslim India* (Allahabad, 1942), p. 331.

[6] Prasad, *India Divided*, p. 145.

[7] J. Nehru, *A Bunch of Old Letters* (Bombay, 1958), p. 407.

'Pakistan'. 'If Pakistan meant "Muslim raj in Punjab" he would have nothing to do with it'.[1] In Bengal, Fazlul Huq and his Krishak Proja Party had not in their hearts accepted 'Pakistan', although they were committed to it publicly.[2] No Moslem Leaguer had been elected to the Sind Legislature in the 1936 elections. Allah Buksh, who was Prime Minister of Sind in 1940, was hostile to the demand for 'Pakistan'.[3] In the North West Frontier Province, where the Moslems were overwhelmingly dominant, the League had little influence and the government was in the hands of the *Khudai Khidmatgars,* who, as we have noted, were opposed to the League. Such leadership was lacking, however, among the Moslem leaders in the Moslem minority provinces where the separatist movement first gathered momentum. Once the cry for 'Pakistan' had been raised it became difficult to silence it. The term 'Pakistan' became synonymous in the popular mind with 'Moslem raj', a state where the Moslems would be supreme.

After the arrest of the Congress leaders in August 1942, political activities in India came to a standstill. The Congress was outlawed for three years, its ablest cadres imprisoned, its funds seized and its organization virtually broken. In this peculiar vacuum the Moslem League flourished. It denounced the 'Quit India' movement as an attempt to establish the 'Hindu Raj' and to 'deal a death blow to the Muslim goal of Pakistan'.[4] The League's tirade was useful to the Government of India which had switched its publicity machine against the Congress to represent it as pro-Axis.[5]

The political field now being open to Jinnah, he made the best political use of it in strengthening the hold of his party over the Moslem masses. Jinnah modelled his campaigning style on Congress lines. Between the years 1937 and 1943 the Moslem League grew from strength to strength. As the League never published its membership figures, it is difficult to ascertain its precise strength. However, it is possible to have some idea of its growing popularity. Towards the end of 1941 the Madras Moslem League claimed a membership of 112,078. Typical was the report from the South Kanara district Moslem League: 'Last year there were only 4,200 members. This year

1 Mss. Eur. F.125/28/262, telegram from Linlithgow to Amery, 12 Mar. 1941. IOL.
2 Moon, *Divide and Quit*, p. 22.
3 *IAR,* 1940, ii, 325.
4 Sherwani, *Pakistan Resolution to Pakistan,* pp. 72-3.
5 See chapter 6 below.

there are 7,759 members'.[1] In the Central Provinces the membership increased from 23,000 in 1938 to 56,541 in 1943.[2] In Bengal the growth of the Moslem League was phenomenal: in 1944 the League was claiming 550,000 members.[3] In Sind the membership rose to over 300,000 in 1944.[4] All over India there was an upsurge of the League's strength. Sixty-one by-elections were held for Moslem seats in the legislatures during 1937-43, and of those 47 were won by the Moslem League, 10 by independent Moslems, and only 4 by the Congress.

From being a highly elitist body of aristocratic gentlemen for whom politics was a form of leisure, the League changed into a mass gathering of fervent men who threw aside their balance and moderation for what they regarded as a righteous cause. The irony of the situation lay in the role of Jinnah who had retired from the Congress during non-cooperation days when that body had adopted a programme of direct and unconstitutional action. His fate pursued him and made him the instrument through which the Moslem League was transformed into a body advocating direct, if necessary unconstitutional action.

A conference of the presidents and secretaries of all the provincial Moslem Leagues was held in November 1941, with the aim of establishing a link between the centre and the provinces for coordinating their activities. In order to intensify the League's programme, provincial committees were enjoined to convene regular district conferences and to train a large number of workers who were to tour the province to propagate the ideals of the Moslem League among the Moslem masses. The provincial committee was also required to embark upon a recruitment campaign to enrol at least ten per cent of the Moslem population as primary members of the League.[5] There was a visible increase in the League's activities; *Dawn* carried a column 'Week-ful of the League's activities' highlighting the various meetings and programmes of the Moslem League. To educate and convert Moslem opinion, special 'Pakistan conferences' were organized by the district and provincial committees. Prominent Moslem leaders from other provinces were invited to address the gatherings.[6] In order to keep in touch with the districts, the central and provincial leaders worked out a programme of extensive touring: the highlight being a visit by

1 *Dawn*, 9 Nov. 1941.
2 *Ibid.*, 24 Oct. 1943.
3 *Ibid.*, 18 Jan. 1944.
4 *Ibid.*, 14 May 1944.
5 *Ibid.*, 2 Nov. 1941.
6 *Ibid.*, 2 Nov. 1941.

Jinnah himself.[1] Speakers were trained to do propaganda work for the Moslem League. Some of the full-time workers were paid from party funds and lived in party premises.[2]

A separate information, propaganda and publicity department was created. A committee of writers was appointed to write pamphlets on the social, economic, and political problems of the Moslems. These were published under the titles of *Pakistan Literature Series* and *Home Study Series* so that the 'Public may receive without delay and trouble all literature, pamphlets and books of the all-India Muslim League'.[3] At about the same time the Moslem Youth Study Circle started a monthly journal, *Spirit of Youth,* to serve as a 'beacon of light to Muslim young men all over the country, thus rallying them round the banner of Islam in India'.[4] Leaflets and brochures were issued by the Moslem League publicity department and were distributed free of cost to public libraries.[5] Poetry and songs on Pakistan were recited publicly. A particularly popular song was: *'Moo mein kalma, hath mein talwar, larke lenge ham Pakistan'.* ('With Quranic verse on the lips and a sword in hand, we shall fight for Pakistan'). Congress had used similar publicity tactics: Dr G. Pandey writes that the 'people of surrounding areas gathered at an appointed place on an appointed day every week, a speaker read out a song concerning a political event of that week, and then distributed leaflets containing the song'.[6]

The most significant step in the development of the League's propaganda work was the foundation of *Dawn* in October 1941. 'The *Dawn*', wrote the editor, 'supplies the long felt want of a suitable medium for the Muslims and others whose voice could not be heard above the din and clamourous pro-Congress propaganda going around'.[7] The Moslem League rapidly built up a strong press - either by starting new newspapers or by taking over older established ones and persuading them to adopt the Moslem League line. Thus Dehli had *Anjam, Jung* and *Manshoor;* Lahore produced *Inqilab, Nawa-i-waqt, Paisa Akhbar* and *Zamindar; Hamdan* and

1 *Ibid.,* 26 Oct. 1941.
2 *Ibid.,* 24 Nov. 1942.
3 *Ibid.,* 24 Nov. 1941.
4 *Ibid.,* 9 Nov. 1941.
5 *Ibid.,* 18 Feb. 1942.
6 G. Pandey, 'Mobilization in a Mass Movement: Congress "Propaganda" in the United Provinces (India), 1930-34', *Modern Asian Studies,* ix, 2, (1975), pp. 219.
7 *Dawn,* 26 Oct. 1941.

Asre-Jadib came from Lucknow and Calcutta respectively. There were a host of other lesser known regional newspapers. The gruesome stories contained in the Pirpur report were serialized in *Dawn* and *Manshoor* under the title, 'It Shall Never Happen Again'.

The Moslem League leaders knew that it would be much easier to mobilise popular enthusiasm upon simple religious issues than upon complicated socio-economic questions. Moreover, questions such as representation in the legislatures and services were of interest mainly to the educated Moslems; the vast masses had little interest in them. To arouse in them a passionate opposition to the Congress it was necessary to excite religious fears. A newly awakened consciousness easily responds to semi-religious calls, and the Congress itself had used that type of appeal to rouse mass consciousness among the Hindus. The Moslem League now used it with equal success. It secured the services of the Pir Saheb of Manki Sharif, Pir Jamait Ali Shah and Makhdum Raza Shah of Multan. The *modus operandi* of the *pirs* and *mullahs* was to appeal to the latent religious prejudices. They raised the cry of 'Islam in danger' and exhorted the Moslems to support the demand for Pakistan. Sir Malcom Darling writes about the Punjab thus:

> The cry was raised "Islam is in danger", within certain areas very crude variations, threatening those who opposed the League with hell and damnation and even with exclusion from burial in a Muslim cemetery.

Few Moslems, Sir Malcom recalls, could resist the call of Islam. 'It was religion, too, as expounded by *mullah* and *Pir* which drew so many women to the polls, nearly all, of course, to vote as their husbands'.[1] When these religious preachers told the simple Moslem peasants in resounding political speeches about their manifold disabilities, from which the magic of 'Pakistan' would free them, they would have been less than human if they had not believed. The Indian cultivators were no more proof against propaganda than is the small farmer in any other country - particularly when a new heaven and a new earth were being promised if they would only vote a certain way. The growth of the League's popularity may to a large extent be attributed to the efforts of the *pirs* and *mullahs.*

The League also relied heavily for its campaign upon the voluntary efforts of students, particularly from Aligarh Moslem University and Dacca University.[2] The foundation of the all-India Moslem Students'

---

1 Malcolm L. Darling, *At Freedom's Door* (Oxford, 1949), p. 86.
2 M. Husain, 'Dacca University and the Pakistan Movement', Philips and Wainwright (eds.), *Partition of India,* pp. 369-73.

Federation did much to make the League a mass party. The purpose of the Students' Federation was to 'rouse political consciousness' amongst the Moslem students and to prepare them to take their proper share in the struggle for the freedom of the country; and within three years Jinnah complimented the students for having 'succeeded in awakening the political consciousness of Muslim India from one end to the other end of this subcontinent'.[1] A uniformed Moslem national guard was formed. The main purpose of enlisting and training the national guards was to 'create in them a spirit of service and sacrifice and to make them a disciplined body of enthusiastic self-less workers for the social, economic and political uplift of the masses'.[2]

During the 'first five year plan' (1937-41) of the Moslem League, the League activities spread all over the country. The Moslem League 'established a flag, a platform, and demonstrating the complete unity of the entire body of the Moslems', defined its goal of a separate homeland for the Moslems.[3] Towards the end of 1941, the Moslem League launched its 'second five year plan'. This consisted of planning and building up 'the departments of national life of Muslim India'. In this the increased emphasis was on the educational, social and economic uplift of the Moslems.[4] Shortly afterwards the League decided to appoint a National Planning Committee, which was to prepare the Moslems 'to participate in the national developments in the direction of commercial and agricultural expansion, and industrialisation, and be ready for a gigantic and coordinated drive in the field of economic reconstruction, and then in the postwar reconstruction'.[5] The committee consisted of technicians, economists, men of commerce and practical businessmen.

Jinnah also endeavoured to establish a Moslem Chamber of Commerce with a view to encouraging commercial and industrial enterprise.[6] The help of wealthy Moslems like the Raja of Mahmudabad, M.A.H. Ispahani, and Habib was enlisted. The Moslem Chamber of Commerce was finally to come into being in April 1945. Jinnah was also to initiate other economic ventures including banks, an insurance company, shipping lines and an airline. These ventures gave great impetus to the commercial aspirations of the Moslems.

1 Ahmad, *Speeches and Writings of Mr Jinnah*, i, 238-9.
2 *Dawn*, 15 Nov. 1941.
3 *Ibid.*, 3 May, 1942.
4 *Ibid.*, 2 Nov. 1941.
5 *Ibid.*, 29 Dec. 1943.
6 *Ibid.*, 10 Mar. 1943.

After 1943, there was hardly any organized group of Moslems opposed to the Moslem League. The Congress Moslems had lost much of their political importance. Of the various Moslem leaders of the Congress, some had switched to the Moslem League; others like Azad were still important inside the Congress, but their popularity among the Moslems had declined. The Ahrar party in the Punjab had virtually disintegrated; the Krishak Proja party in Bengal had lost much of its following. After the assassination of Allah Buksh, Sind came under the influence of the Moslem League. Similarly, the sudden death of Sir Sikander removed Jinnah's most formidable rival in the Punjab. With the single exception of the Khuda-i-Khidmatgars in the North West Frontier Province there was virtually no opposition to the Moslem League from Moslem groups.

Separatism had won the day. The seeds of 'Pakistan', watered in the flood of frustration, fear and fury soon raised their heads above the soil.

5

WAR AND CONSTITUTIONAL IMPASSE:
FIRST ATTEMPTS AT SOLUTION

In September 1939, when the war broke out, Linlithgow was still vigorously pushing forward the federal scheme and was confident that federation might be inaugurated by July 1941.[1] The provincial governments had been functioning satisfactorily for a little over two years. It appeared that after years of turmoil India under Linlithgow was treading the constitutional path and a complete transfer of power might be hoped for in the not too distant future. As the war became imminent, Linlithgow showed a desire to work in close collaboration with the Indian leaders. The day before the outbreak of hostilities, he wrote to Zetland:

> You know how strongly I feel that it is not only desirable but essential to find some way out of the present impasse . . . I agree as to the importance . . . of association of princes and representatives of British India with defence [but] I am a little inclined to doubt whether it is wise to confine ourselves to the Central Legislature. For a good part of the year it will not be sitting, and apart from that it is very unrepresentative, I am attracted by the thought of an *ad hoc* committee; and it occurs to me that one possibility might be to extend the field of selection beyond the Assembly and to ask leading political parties . . . to nominate representatives who could be kept confidentially in touch with developments irrespective of whether or not Assembly was in session.[2]

The war, however, found Linlithgow 'at bay'.[3] He had to reconcile his imperial duties as the Viceroy of the King with conflicting, and sometimes exorbitant, demands from the various Indian parties. Although a man of great courage and resolution, Linlithgow failed during the war to grapple with the Indian problem. The result was unfortunate. A political deadlock ensued which remained unresolved during his prolonged viceroyalty and after.

Although it has been suggested that the Indian problem was 'an inextricable muddle and not a soluble riddle' (Professor Moore's description), it is nevertheless arguable that a little imagination and courage in the first few weeks of the war might have reversed the process

---

1 Mss. Eur. F.125/8/13, Linlithgow to Zetland, 14 Sept. 1941; see also Linlithgow's marginal comment in Mss. Eur. F.125/8/12, Zetland to Linlithgow, 5 Sept. 1939 IOL; John Glendevon, *The Viceroy at Bay*, (London,1971), p.134.

2 L/P&J/8/505, telegram from Linlithgow to Zetland, 31 Aug. 1939. IOR.

3 The phrase has been taken from Lord Glendevon's book, *The Viceroy at Bay*.

of distrust which subsequently made an agreement almost impossible. Neither Delhi nor London was prepared to take the initiative. 'In the absence of effective diplomacy during the first year of war', writes Professor Moore, 'the gap between British policy and Congress demand became a gulf, the communal rift became a chasm, and party resolutions hardened into ultimata.'[1]

Ever since the early 1920s, the Congress had begun to take an increasing interest in foreign affairs. It developed a foreign policy based on the elimination of political and economic subjection everywhere and the cooperation of free nations. This was consistent with the demand for Indian independence. In 1920 a resolution was passed by the Congress in which India's desire for cooperation with other nations was emphasized.[2] In 1927 the Congress had passed another resolution criticizing British foreign policy and affirming India's refusal to be involved in war without her consent.[3]

After 1927, the Congress does not seem to have paid much attention to the international question. The next resolution on the subject came nine years later, in 1936, when the Congress condemned the German and Italian wars of aggression and warned the British Government that the fascist powers were grouping themselves together with the intention of dominating the world and crushing political freedom.[4] The protest was repeated at the Haripura session of the All India Congress Committee in February 1938. The Congress offered support for 'collective security' and condemned the British 'appeasement' of fascist aggression.[5] The tragedy which befell China, Abyssinia (Ethiopia), Austria, Czechoslovakia, Spain, Albania, a sequence of helpless suffering, struck the popular consciousness of India. In March 1939, as Hitler seized Czechoslovakia, the Congress voiced its annual warning in terms of desperation:

> The Congress records its entire disapproval of British foreign policy culminating in the Munich Pact, the Anglo-Italian Agreement and the recognition of rebel Spain. This policy has been one of deliberate betrayal of democracy, repeated breach of pledges, the ending of the system of collective security and cooperation with governments which are avowed enemies of democracy and freedom.[6]

---

1 R.J. Moore, 'British Policy and the Indian Problem 1936-40', in C.H. Philips and M.D. Wainwright (eds.), *The Partition of India* (London, 1970), pp. 84-5.
2 J. Nehru, *The Discovery of India* (Henceforth *Discovery*) (Bombay, reprint, 1969), p. 416.
3 *IAR,* 1927, ii, 53.
4 *IAR,* 1936, ii, 202.
5 *IAR,* 1938, i, 296-7.
6 *IAR,* 1939, i, 341-2.

The Congress further urged that India must direct its own foreign policy, 'thereby keeping aloof from both Imperialism and Fascism, and pursuing her path of peace and freedom'.[1] Thus the Congress resolution laid down a dual policy in regard to the war: an opposition to fascism and an emphasis on India's freedom.

The despatch of Indian troops to Aden, Egypt and Singapore in August 1939, as part of the general defence preparations, further antagonized the Congress against the British Government. The Congress charged that the government had flouted the Central Legislative Assembly and defied public opinion by sending Indian troops abroad, and it called upon the members of the Central Assembly to refrain from attending the next session of the Assembly. The Congress provincial governments were asked to refrain from assisting in the war effort.[2]

The government had been alerted by the repeated resolutions that a declaration of war on behalf of India without its consent might complicate the political situation. Forewarned, the government began to forearm. Zetland and Linlithgow discussed their policy in the event of war. Linlithgow had proposed that federal negotiations should be put in cold storage as the question was generally disliked by both the British Indian politicians and the princes, and urged that for the duration of the war the government should refuse any constitutional change. He had been encouraged in this view by Erskine and Lumley, the governors of Madras and Bombay, who had assured him that the Congress ministers wished to continue in office and would be extremely hesitant to resign even if asked to do so by the Congress Working Committee.[3]

Meanwhile Linlithgow also prepared contingency plans to deal with the situation likely to arise if the Congress ministers resigned from office. At his insistence, the British Parliament rushed through the Government of India (Amendment) Act in April 1939, whereby a new section (126A) was inserted in the 1935 Act, authorizing the central government, during the operation of the proclamation of an emergency resulting from war or threat of war, to give directions to the provincial governments about the way in which executive authority was to be exercised, enabling the central legislature to make laws in the provincial field and conferring executive authority on the central government. The provincial

1 *Ibid.*

2 *IAR*, 1939, ii, 214-15; see also J. Nehru, 'India's Demand and England's Answer', *Atlantic Monthly* (Aug. 1940), p. 450.

3 Tara Chand, *History of the Freedom Movement* (Delhi, 1961-72), iv, 280. K.M. Munshi has recorded: 'Rajagopalachari and I had hoped that Gandhiji would be prepared to make cooperation unconditional'. *Pilgrimage to Freedom* (Bombay, 1967), i, 55.

governments were directed to strike against any organization which tried to impede the war effort. At the same time Linlithgow was, at this stage, eager to explore alternative avenues so as to avert a direct clash — argument, appeal and concessions which involved no substantial transfer of executive authority during the war.[1]

The war in Poland broke out on 1 September 1939 and on the 3rd Chamberlain announced in Parliament that Britain was at war with Germany. Constitutionally speaking, Britain's declaration of war on Germany automatically turned India into a belligerent. Linlithgow briefly informed India over the radio of the circumstances in which 'we find ourselves at war with Germany today', and expressed his confidence that India would make her contribution on the side of human freedom against the rule of force.[2]

Linlithgow had presented India with a *fait accompli*. His declaration provoked an old issue in a new and critical form. By declaring India at war without consulting the Indian leaders, Linlithgow had committed a tactical indiscretion from which further misunderstandings arose. 'That was a fatal mistake', said the critics, 'without which all would have been well and everybody working in agreement',[3] The Congress complained that when the war came Eire (a Dominion) was allowed to remain neutral; in Australia and New Zealand the declaration was confirmed by Parliament; South Africa hesitated for three days; and Canada for one week remained quasi-neutral. Only British India, they argued, was made a belligerent without its consent.[4] The Congress perhaps forgot that India was not yet a Dominion and therefore not entitled to the same treatment. Nevertheless, the feeling of being treated as inferior to the dominions was very genuine. 'Indians', wrote the author and journalist, John Spender, 'feel their self respect to have been wounded when they were taken into the war without their consent.'[5] Disregard of Indian feeling, said Sir Reginald Coupland, 'inevitably flamed the wound which inequality of national status inflicts on Indian minds'.[6] It must be said that Linlithgow, with his years of experience in India, ought to have anticipated the consequences of pursuing the course which he laid down.

1   Tara Chand, *History of the Freedom Movement,* iv, 280.

2   *Gazette of India,* 3 Sept. 1939.

3   Cited in Sir George Schuster, 'The Indian Political Situation', *Asiatic Review* (1941), xxxvii, 439.

4   See statement by Pandit Pant, the chief minister of the UP. *Statesman,* 28 Oct. 1939.

5   *The Times,* 16 Jan. 1941.

6   R. Coupland, *Indian Politics 1936-42* (London, 1943), p. 212.

He was aware that the Congress had repeatedly warned Britain against plunging the country into a war without the consent of the people.[1] This exercise of authority revealed a disturbing incapacity to understand not only the psychology of a nationally conscious but still dependent people but also the whole trend of Commonwealth development in recent years.[2] But it must be noted that, as stated earlier, the constitutional responsibility for declaring war lay with the Viceroy.[3] As the representative of the King-Emperor, he thought it right that India should come into the war. Consultation with political leaders apparently would have made little difference to his decision.[4] If the political leaders had said 'no' or made impossible demands, Linlithgow would still have had to declare war. If the nationalists took it as an affront to their self-respect, the system rather than Linlithgow was to be blamed. It was an unfortunate reality that, when the war came, the central government was still being run by the officials. The causes of the failure to establish responsible government at the centre have been examined elsewhere.[5] Irrespective of who was to be blamed for the failure to implement the federation, the indisputable fact remains that the Viceroy and his officials were responsible for the central government. The Department of External Affairs, which had the power to decide whether India should go to war, was under the exclusive jurisdiction of the Viceroy. The position would have been somewhat different had the federal part of the 1935 Act been in operation when war broke out. Even after the establishment of the federation, External Affairs would have continued to be under the control of the Viceroy, but it could hardly be expected that he would have shaped foreign policy without consulting other members of the Council. In modern warfare it is almost impossible to separate the departments of External Affairs and Defence.

Constitutionally Linlithgow's action in declaring India at war was unimpeachable. But it might be suggested that something might have been done to give India an opportunity of going to war by a political act of her own, performed by her existing representatives. The Congress was an unofficial organization, but there were the central and provincial

1 See above pp. 129-31.

2 N. Mansergh, Survey of *British Commonwealth Affairs: Problems of External Policy 1931-39* (London, 1952), pp. 410-11.

3 Coupland, *Indian Politics 1936-42*, pp. 211-12; Sir Frederick Whyte, *India: A Bird's Eye View* (New York, 1943), p. 31.

4 Munshi believed that 'in the circumstances that existed, no consultation would have yielded satisfactory results'. *Pilgrimage to Freedom*, i, 54.

5 See chapter 3 above.

assemblies. It would have been tactical and wise to have provided these bodies with an opportunity to declare by resolution the determination of the people of India to cast in their lot with the Allies.

Linlithgow's failure to consult the Indian leaders was a tactical indiscretion. But it would be incorrect to say, as Nehru did, that India's participation in the war was taken for granted.[1] This is not true of all people. Sir Muhammad Zafrullah Khan, the Law Member of the Executive Council and leader of the Central Assembly, had declared in September 1939: 'I am certain that every one of us here fully realizes the gravity of the crisis and is determined to do his duty to King and country'.[2] The statement was accepted without any protest. A similar comment was made in the Council of State. On 11 September Linlithgow addressed a joint session of both Houses. He declared his trust that 'India will speak and act as one and that her contribution will be worthy of her ancient name'.[3] Discussion of this address would have been out of order, but there were other ways in which members of either house could have indicated their dissent if they had wished. Not one of them did so.

When the war broke out there was no doubt that the Indian leaders were anti-Nazi. The Congress had given ample evidence of its stand. For years, as we have seen, they had denounced fascism. There was no place in India for the Nazi creed of state worship, brute force and racial arrogance.[4]

The initial response of the Congress to the war was realistic and wise. In an interview with the Viceroy, Gandhi stated that his own sympathies were with the British: 'I am not just now thinking of India's deliverance, it will come, but what it will be worth if England and France fall or if they come out victorious over Germany ruined and humbled'.[5] Nehru gave expression to similar statements. He said that India was not out to bargain, nor did she approach the problem with a view to taking advantage of Britain's difficulties.[6]

1 *Modern Review* (Jan. 1942), p. 26.

2 *Legislative Assembly Debates,* iv, no. 4, 4 Sept. 1939, pp. 279-80.

3 *Ibid.,* no. 7, pp. 431-4.

4 Tara Chand, *History of the Freedom Movement,* iv, 277; T.A. Raman, 'Can the Indian Deadlock be Broken', *Asia* (Aug. 1941), p. 429; Sir Albion Bonerji, 'The Indian Attitude Towards War Aims of the Allies', *Asiatic Review* (1940), xxxvi, 312.

5 Mss. Eur. F.125/18/222b, telegram from Linlithgow to Zetland, 5 Sept. 1939. IOL. Subsequently Gandhi had modified his statement to mean that 'support' in accordance with the principle of non-violence 'could only mean moral support'. *Harijan,* 4 Nov. 1939.

6 *Statesman,* 10 Sept. 1939; see also *News Chronicle,* 10 Oct. 1939;

Gandhi had expressed his sympathies for Britain and France 'from a purely humanitarian point of view.' His first impulse was therefore to adopt the course which he had pursued during the first world war. Writing to the then Viceroy, Lord Chelmsford, he had said: 'If I could make my countrymen retrace their steps, I would make them withdraw all the Congress resolutions and not whisper "Home Rule" or "Responsible Government" during the pendency of the war'? The history of India might have been different if such a policy had again been adopted in 1939. From 1937 the Congress had been in power in eight of eleven British Indian provinces, and except for a few minor difficulties, the ministries were functioning with vigour. It is arguable that, as the premier organization of the country, its duty was to remain in office during the war years to protect popular interests and to establish its claim to independence by supporting the Allies. Gandhi, however, allowed his earlier decision to be swayed by, amongst other things, his obsession with non-violence.

The Congress Working Committee met at Wardha and deliberated for nearly a week over its course of action. If India was willing to cooperate in the war, the Congress argument ran, she expected some generous response to her long wish for political freedom at home. The psychological moment had arrived to make it clear that a new order in Asia, as in Europe, was to result from the victory of the Allies. In defining its policy, the Congress Working Committee had to reconcile the points of view of the various groups within the Congress and adopt a policy consistent with its previous declarations. There were four groups within the Congress: first, the Gandhians with their insistence on non-violence; second, the financial supporters of the Congress like Birla, Tata, Dalmia, Mafatal and Walchand Hirachand, who generally felt that the Congress should not obstruct the war effort because, amongst other things, the war would bring higher profits to Indian industrialists and agriculturalists; third, the group headed by Nehru who wished to throw in their lot with the Allied powers fighting for democracy and freedom; and finally the more extreme section – the Forward Bloc – headed by Subhas Bose who felt that 'Britain's difficulty was India's opportunity'.[3]

Manchester Guardian, 28 Nov. 1939.

1 Mss. Eur. F.125/18/221a, telegram from Linlithgow to Zetland, 4 Sept. 1939. IOL.

2 Gandhi to Viceroy, 29 Apr. 1918, cited in B.R. Nanda, *The Nehrus: Motilal and Jawaharlal* (London, 1962), p. 155.

3 See the resolution of the Forward Bloc, 18 Sept. 1939. *Quarterly Survey,* no. 9, p. 25.

On 14 September the Congress declared that if the war was to defend the *status quo,* colonies, vested interests and privileges, then India would have nothing to do with it. If, however, the issue was democracy and freedom, India would throw her weight on the side of democratic powers, provided democracy also functioned in India. But it was absurd, the resolution said, for a subject India to become the champion of liberties abroad which were denied to her at home. The Congress therefore invited the British Government to declare its war aims in regard to the new democratic order that was envisaged, and in particular, how these aims were going to apply to India during the war. A declaration of Indian independence was asked for, and the recognition of the right of the Indian people to frame their own constitution through a constituent assembly.[1]

The resolution revealed a conflict between a sympathy with the professed objective for which Britain was engaged in the struggle and a suspicion of British intentions towards Indian aspirations. It was caught in an equivocal position. The inconsistency was apparently recognized by Nehru, the exponent of the Congress foreign policy. The demand for war aims, he explained, was not put forward in 'the spirit of the market place'.[2] It was the inevitable outcome of India's long struggle for freedom and an essential preliminary to the success of India's war effort.[3] This explanation was correct in so far as Nehru was concerned. But there were certain others in the Congress who were not actuated by the same ideals. The group led by Subhas Bose had been impressed by the Irish and Russian examples. Ireland had revolted against Britain during the first world war and remained neutral during the second. The Bolsheviks had taken advantage of the Russian government's wartime difficulties in 1917. Why should not India seize the opportunity to win its independence? Bose therefore advocated the serving of an ultimatum on the British Government to declare India independent by a certain date, failing which the Congress should launch a campaign.[4]

The Congress had posed two basic questions: what were the ideals

---

1 *IAR,* 1939, ii, 226-8.

2 *Manchester Guardian,* 5 Oct. 1939; Mss. Eur. F.115/4-7, Note of an interview between Sir Harry Haig and Nehru, 21 Sept. 1939. IOL.

3 J. Nehru, 'India's Demand and England's Answer', *Atlantic Monthly* (Aug. 1940), pp. 423-40; see also Edward Thompson's letter to *Manchester Guardian,* 28 Nov. 1939; Nehru, *Discovery,* pp. 423-40. Nehru had made it clear that the only way to deal with Nazi aggression was to liquidate the empire and replace it with freedom. As Nehru put it, 'we could never separate these two [Fascism and Imperialism], for us, they were twin brothers'. See L/P&J/8/668, copy of a letter from Nehru to Miss Eleanor Rathbone, the British MP, 22 June 1941. IOR.

4 *Selected Speeches of Subhas Chandra Bose* (Government of India, New Delhi, 1962), p. 75.

for which the Allies were fighting? and second, would India be given a foretaste of that freedom for which she was being called upon to fight? To many British statesmen such a demand smacked of impractical radicalism, if not of cynical opportunism. Far-reaching constitutional changes could not be attempted in the midst of a war. From the British point of view there were obvious difficulties in meeting the Congress demand, but it is perhaps possible that a little imagination and courage in the first few weeks of the war might have reversed the process of mistrust which subsequently made an agreement impossible. It is true that there was no responsible government at the centre, but Linlithgow might have summoned the premiers of the provinces and enlisted their support. In view of the initial sympathetic response of Gandhi and Nehru, it seems probable that the Congress might not have raised too many difficult objections. Having been consulted for their views, the premiers could have been asked to draw up an agreed resolution declaring India's support for war, which could then be passed by the provincial assemblies.

It was not only the Congress that felt that a declaration of the British war aims was a desideratum. Robert Boothby, a Conservative Member of Parliament, had asked for such a declaration in regard to the future of Czechoslovakia, and Chamberlain had given an assurance that the independence of Czechoslovakia would be one of Britain's objectives.[1] In fact it could be said that sections of the Congress were looking to the British Government to provide proof that Britain had taken up arms not merely in defence of its interests but in the hope of creating a new world order out of victory. The doubts that had prompted such pressure could not be really justified, though Britain by its past actions had helped to rouse the pressure. The British Empire had already gone far in the progress from empire by way of trusteeship to a free association in the British Commonwealth of Nations. The Dominions had proved that the road was the correct one. A hundred years earlier Lord Durham in his report on Canada advocated responsible government as a cure for rebellion.[2]

The Congress demands received a sympathetic press in Britain. The

[1] *Hindu* (Madras), 15 Sept. 1939. Anxiety was voiced in several American liberal publications about the absence of a clearly enunciated war aim by the Allies. 'It is not enough for the British and French to reply merely that there can be no peace with the present rulers of Germany', wrote the *New Republic*. 'It is high time for them to state what kind of world they envisage and how they propose to get from here to there'. Cited in J.J. Martin, *American Liberalism and World Politics* (New York, 1964), ii, 1972. *Common Sense* featured an editorial 'Peace Terms Now', and *The Nation* carried on a debate on the theme. *Ibid.* pp. 1085-91.

[2] E.M. Wrong, *Charles Buller and Responsible Government* (Oxford, 1926), *passim.* (I owe this reference to Sir Edgar Williams).

Manchester Guardian praised 'Pandit Nehru for pressing us to face the larger issue', and urged the government to assure India that the 'free and equal association of nations is the object of the British policy'. The newspaper concluded: 'The words of Queen Victoria to another generation of Indians should be remembered today — "In their prosperity will be our strength, in their contentment our security, and their gratitude our best reward".'[1] Another newspaper suggested that the only solution to the Indian problem was to give a 'promise that full Dominion Status will be granted in a specified number of years'. It was argued that if the Indians knew the date when Dominion Status would be accorded, they would not only be satisfied but would also use the interval to qualify themselves for their new duties and responsibilities.[2] The fixing of a date presented a difficulty which the newspaper ignored. It may be recalled that the 1919 Act had provided for a revision of the Act after ten years. The result had been that most of the important parties had immediately begun to indulge in criticism of the Act and in making claims for changes in the next constitution. The same process could have occurred in 1939 and the years immediately following if a date for Dominion Status had been fixed. It must also be remembered that the announcement of a date for the granting of Dominion Status might have aggravated the communal situation. The communal leaders would then have been inclined to put up their demands and a more acute communal wrangle might have ensued.

The nationalist press in India supported the Congress case. It generally overlooked the political and constitutional difficulties, but claimed that Indo-British relations would improve if India's independence were recognized. The Indian Liberal press regretted that the Congress had raised the issue at such a time, urged the country's unconditional collaboration with the British war effort, and believed that Dominion Status would be attained at the end of the war by mere force of events. The British-owned press, with few exceptions, was sympathetic towards the demand for war aims but urged the need for Hindu-Moslem unity as a preliminary to further constitutional changes.[3]

Immediately after the publication of the Congress resolution, the Moslem League passed a resolution expressing satisfaction at the suspension of the federal scheme, but urging the British Government 'to review and revise the entire problem of India's future constitution *de novo*'. The resolution declared its opposition to any system of govern-

---

1 *Manchester Guardian,* 5 Oct. 1939.

2 *Nottingham Guardian,* 30 Sept. 1939.

3 L/I/1/745, Summary of newspaper reports. IOR.

ment which would result in majority rule on the ground that 'such a constitution is totally unsuited to the genius of the peoples of the country, which is composed of various nationalities and does not constitute a national state'. After cataloguing the Moslem grievances against the Congress rule in the provinces, the resolution came to the war crisis. It condemned Nazi aggression and concluded by saying that if Moslem cooperation were to be obtained the government must secure justice and fair play to the Moslems.[1] This was apparently the best that Jinnah could do if he was to avoid a breach between those who were in favour of offering unqualified help to Britain, and those who wanted to strike a bargain. The Premiers of Bengal and the Punjab were also satisfied that the terms of the resolution would not hamper them in cooperating with the war effort.

The conflicting demands of the Congress and the Moslem League at once threw into dramatic prominence all the complicating factors which had marked the Indian political experience in the preceding twenty years. It had raised in wartime, and in acute form, those very problems which the politicians of both the countries had been unable to resolve in time of peace. No doubt the Congress leaders had a genuine faith in the 'national' character of their demands, and asserted that no sectional motives inspired them. Congress, which claimed to base its faith on democracy as practised in Britain, held that divergent opinion would vanish if the British declared Indian independence and left the people to determine their own constitution. It promised, no doubt with sincerity, to safeguard the special interests of the minorities. But it might be argued that in national questions, where the interests of the minorities conflicted with those of the majority and where no compromise was possible, the will of the majority would prevail. Congress was certainly the focus of Indian nationalism, but since most Congressmen were Hindus, it was difficult to convince the Moslems that a constituent assembly convened on a democratic basis would safeguard minority rights. The Congress leaders had sincerely tried for years to alter this state of affairs, but even these efforts were regarded by the Moslem League as designed to further the political ends of the Congress.

This does not mean, however, that the other parties opposed constitutional advance, but only that they were apprehensive about advancing along purely Congress lines. The Congress's demand for independence, based on a constitution framed by a constituent assembly

---

1   Resolution of the AIML, 17-18 Sept. 1939, M. Gwyer and A. Appadorai (eds.) *Speeches and Documents on the Indian Constitution 1921-47* (London, 1957), ii, 488-90.

and not the imperial parliament, conflicted with the British intentions, but it conflicted even more with the policies of the League. The League feared that the application of majority rule would mean the political subjection of the Moslems.[1] In India no constitution had much prospect of permanence which was not acceptable to the Moslems, and to attempt to impose one upon them against their will was to run the risk of insurrection.

Here were two quite different points of view. The Congress claimed to speak for the whole of India. The Moslem League denied that right, urged the British Government to protect the Moslems against the Hindus, and repudiated the ideal of democratic government as unsuited to India. The triangle of forces that was to endure until the partition in 1947 was already in evidence. It was against this background of conflicting claims that Linlithgow's policy must be viewed. Linlithgow's primary task was to prosecute the war effort by enlisting the support of the Indians. Concessions to one group might have alienated the other.

Linlithgow believed that the Congress, despite its initial refusal to cooperate in the war effort save on its own terms, would eventually agree to cooperate provided it was given an 'excuse' for doing so. Constitutional changes during the war seemed out of the question. He would therefore be prepared to associate political leaders in some sort of a defence liaison committee.[2] But he was resolutely opposed to a definition of British war aims:

> Nothing could be more foolish, I suspect, on our part as a nation than to start at this point to commit outselves to a series of objectives, which may at the moment indeed appear reasonable and easily attainable, but which might as the war goes on call for a very substantial revision.[3]

Zetland was anxious not to take a rigid stand which would lead to an open rupture with the Congress.[4] He and Linlithgow exchanged a number of telegrams to work out a strategy to deal with the Congress demands. Linlithgow, however, was confident that he could hold India to the empire during the war despite the intransigence of the Congress. He remained opposed to defining war aims and advised that the 'wise course' would be to take 'refuge in generalities'. The British Government, he said, had not defined their war aims with any precision, and since India was not the only country affected by the war, its future could

1 See Jinnah's statement, *Manchester Guardian,* 21 Oct. 1939.
2 Mss. Eur. D.609/18, Linlithgow to Zetland, 25 Sept. 1939. IOL.
3 *Ibid.*
4 See War Cabinet Conclusion 29(39)12, Cab. 65/1, dated 27 Sept. 1939. PRO.

not be considered in isolation. Moreover, as the international situation was very uncertain, it was unnecessary to incur a premature commitment of any sort. At this early stage it could only be stated that Britain's motives in entering the war were essentially 'the upholding of the principles of fair and honest dealing between nation and nation, man and man'.[1] He further proposed that he would commence his declaration with an exposition of the opposing claims of the Congress and the Moslem League, and emphasize their incompatibility.[2]

In order to satisfy himself about the 'trend of feeling' in the country, Linlithgow summoned fifty-two leaders, representing various parties and communities, to meet him in Delhi.[3] As was to be expected, these leaders presented Linlithgow with a formidable dossier of differences.[4]

While these conversations were going on, the Congress, on 10 October, adopted a resolution embodying the substance of the resolution of 14 September, with this addition: 'India must be declared an independent nation and present application [sic] must be given to their status to the largest possible extent'.[5] In view of the developments in the course of the next four years, it should be observed that at this time the Congress was apparently not asking for *complete* independence immediately, but only for as much of it as might be possible.

Having completed his talks with the leaders, Linlithgow published an official statement on 17 October. War aims were stated in vague terms. After commenting on the differences of opinion which emerged in the discussions with the various leaders, the statement contained two points: first, that at the end of the war the British Government would be willing to enter into consultations with different groups 'with a view to securing their aid and cooperation in framing such modifications [in the constitution] as may be desirable'; second, that a consultative group consisting of selected Indians would be called in to help with the war effort.[6]

1   Mss. Eur. F.125/18/288, telegram from Linlithgow to Zetland, 24 Sept. 1939. IOL.

2   Mss. Eur. F.125/18/305, telegram from Linlithgow to Zetland, 27 Sept. 1939. IOL.

3   Mss. Eur. F.125/18/327, telegram from Linlithgow to Zetland, 3 Oct. 1939. IOL.

4   P. Sitaramayya, *The History of the Indian National Congress,* (Bombay, 1947), ii, 137.

5   All India Congress Committee, *Congress and War Crisis* (Allahabad, 1942), pp. 27-30.

6   Linlithgow, *Speeches and Statements, 1936-43,* pp. 204-11. For a discussion in the War Cabinet see WCM 47(39)12, Cab. 65/1 dated 14 Oct. 1939. PRO. See

This was the long awaited reply of the Viceroy. Not only were the war aims not clearly explained, but, also, India's political goal remained as uncertain as before. The 1935 Act might be revised, but nothing would be done before the end of the war. For any modification of the Act, however, a general agreement amongst the various groups and communities would be necessary. The only concession to the Congress was the agreement to establish a consultative group, and even this was not to be nominated by the political parties. It would consist of a panel of names to be nominated by the political parties upon whom the Viceroy would, from time to time, be able to draw for discussion of a particular subject.[1] The Viceroy's statement had a mixed reception in Britain.[2] In India, however, the reaction was more critical. The Congress condemned it as 'unsatisfactory'. The statement, Gandhi claimed, showed that there would be no democracy for India if Britain could prevent it. He concluded, obviously hinting at non-cooperation, that the Congress 'will have to go into the wilderness again before it becomes strong enough to reach its objectives'.[3] Nehru and Azad also rejected the offer. Jinnah preferred to sit on the fence and did not commit himself either way. The Moslem League neither accepted nor rejected the Viceroy's offer. It acclaimed the British Government's repudiation of the Congress's claim to represent India and noted with satisfaction the recognition of the League as the only representative organization of the Moslems. But before offering its cooperation, the League desired various clarifications.[4]

Apart from the fact that Linlithgow's statement offered precious little to persuade the main political parties to cooperate in the war effort, there were other constraints which influenced the policies of the Congress and the League. They were both largely bound by their previous declarations, and felt that if they agreed to participate in the government, they might find it difficult in future to revert to the extreme positions which they had adopted for the purpose of bargaining. Moreover the Congress was also faced with the possibility of a split in

also Mss. Eur. D.609/26, telegram from Zetland to Linlithgow, 27 Sept. 1939, IOL; L/P&J/8/505, Extract from conclusions of War Cabinet 34(39)12 dated 2 Oct. 1939. IOR.

1   See Zetland's speech of 18 Oct. 1939. *Parliamentary Debates,* House of Lords, vol. 114, cols. 1445-53; see also Mss. Eur. D.609/26, Memorandum by Zetland, 12 Oct. 1939. IOL.

2   *The Times,* 18 Oct., *Manchester Guardian,* 18 Oct., *New Statesman and Nation,* 21 and 28 Oct. 1939.

3   Cited in Mss. Eur. F.125/28/66, telegram from Linlithgow to Zetland, 19 Oct. 1939, IOL; see also *The Times,* 30 Sept. 1939.

4   *Quarterly Survey,* no. 9.

its ranks if agreement with the British were reached. It was quite likely that its left wing would refuse to accept the invitation contained in the Viceroy's statement, while the remainder, by identifying with the government, would lose their *raison d'etre,* which hitherto had been that of unyielding opposition to the government.

As the Viceroy's reply was an implicit refusal of the Congress demands, the threat of resignation had either to be withdrawn or to materialize. Face would have been lost if it were withdrawn, and — perhaps more important — Subhas Bose, the recalcitrant Congress leader, might have used the opportunity to overthrow Gandhi's leadership.[1]

It was, however, not an easy task to persuade the Congress ministries to resign. The decision to resign was essentially made by the Congress Working Committee, but the CWC and the various Congress ministries did not see eye to eye on this issue. It was difficult for the ministries to abandon power at the dictate of the Congress Working Committee which had no share in the ministries. Furthermore there was a tendency among the ministers to give no more than lip service to the principle advanced by Nehru in 1937 that the primary duty of the Congress was to achieve India's independence and the consequent necessity to avoid being entangled too much in bureaucratic matters. The ministries had become increasingly interested in performing the task of administration creditably and showed signs of developing independence of outlook and resistence to central control. They also showed sympathy for provincial interests which modified the Congress's role as a mass nationalist movement.[2] Further the Congress ministries had alienated some of their supporters by their failure to fulfil their election pledges.

Taking all these considerations into account, the Congress leaders might have felt that the Congress had little to gain at the national level by continuing in office. All these were important considerations leading to the decision to resign from office, but in themselves might not have sufficed. Any misgivings which the Congress leaders might have had were removed by Linlithgow's statement. On 22 October the Congress Working Committee announced that the Congress could not support the British war effort and called upon the Congress ministries to resign.[3]

1   L/I/1/777, Confidential Appreciation of the Political Situation in India, 17 Sept. 1939, IOR; Mss. Eng. Hist. C.627, 'The Proposed Federation' by Sir Louis Stuart, pp. 80-81; Munshi, *Pilgrimage to Freedom,* I, 59 and 393.

2   See Mss. Eur. F.125/6/36, Brabourne to Zetland, 22 Oct. 1938, IOL; Munshi, *Pilgrimage to Freedom,* i, 44 and 48.

3   *IAR,* 1939, ii, 326.

The decision to resign was unfortunate. It showed a lack of appreciation of the realities of power, or at least of the extent to which those
realities were bound to change in an India which had moved from peace
into war, and did more than anything to shake the foundations of
Congress power. In retiring from ministerial office the Congress leaders
had perhaps acted hastily, hoping that in the void which they had
created they would be called back to office with enhanced prestige.[1]
This was a miscalculation. By surrendering power the Congress left the
field open to the Moslem League. Moreover, the Congress opposition to
the war effort, and the League's *de facto* support for it, convinced many
British that 'the Hindus' generally were their enemies and 'the Moslems'
their allies — a consideration that must have added force to the official
support for the Moslem League. It was a heaven-sent opportunity, and
Jinnah did not fail to take full advantage of it.

By 10 November the Congress ministries in eight provinces had
resigned and the administration was taken over by the governors under
Section 93 of the 1935 Act.[2] The twenty-seven-months-old experiment
in Government-Congress collaboration had ended. The break completed
the deadlock which was to persist to the end of Linlithgow's Viceroyalty.

It was unfortunate that Linlithgow missed the opportunity to
enlist the support of the Congress. It is conceivable that if he had
openly stated that a war of freedom could only end in the freedom of
India, as in fact it did, Nehru might have been able to swing the Congress
in favour of cooperation. In 1936, Nehru had warned Britain of the
menace of war in Europe, and since then he had been extremely
critical of the British policy of 'appeasement' and had accused Britain
of 'a deliberate betrayal of democracy'. But whatever may have been
his opinion about British policy prior to the outbreak of war, he felt
that condemnation of Britain was out of date in 1939. He desired that
India should join hands with the Allies in fighting against the aggressors
because he believed that 'England and France have still the instinct of
democracy'.[3] He chided his colleagues: 'How then can you now say
that you will oppose them [Britain] when they have gone to war for a
righteous cause?'[4] But Linlithgow ignored Nehru's desire to cooperate
in the war. He felt that he could carry on India's war effort without
the cooperation of the Congress. His statement was so ill-calculated to

[1] A. Hamid, *Muslim Separatism in India* (Lahore, 1971), p. 229; Munshi,
Pilgrimage to Freedom, i, 55.

[2] *Quarterly Survey,* no. 10.

[3] Coupland, *Indian Politics 1936-42*, pp. 208-9.

[4] Cited in L/P&J/8/505, Mahadeo Desai to Laithwaite, 12 Oct. 1939. IOR.

appeal to the Congress, writes Sir Penderel Moon, that 'cynics said it was purposely designed to ease Congress out of office'.[1] As indeed it might have been.

Contrary to the expectations of the Congress Working Committee that the Congress would be recalled to resume office with greater prestige, its resignation had apparently come as a 'relief' to some of the governors and senior civil servants.[2] Congress 'cooperation', it was felt, would take the form of regular and exasperating obstruction to which 'non-cooperation' or even active hostility would be preferable.[3] The Government of India *Quarterly Survey* recorded:

> . . . a respite is everywhere welcomed from the dust and turmoil of party government: the pace had been too fast for comfort and many people have suffered some jostling. Whether or not "good government is no substitute for self-government" it is pleasant to rest a while before resuming the noisy progress of democracy. The change over to administration under Section 93 in seven provinces took place quietly, and ushered in a period of calm such as most Governors had not known in the days of normal administration.[4]

A section of officials were not keen to have the Congress in office for the duration of the war. In the short term at least there was something to be said for this view, and Linlithgow apparently ensured that events would conform to it.[5] And the Congress was to find that Linlithgow was not prepared to allow it to return to power except on his own terms.

Linlithgow emphasized that unless there was a mutual understanding between the communities, the British Government would be unable to make any constitutional advance. While it is no doubt true that it would have been unwise to make constitutional changes without a degree of unanimity among the communities, Linlithgow's decision to withhold political advance *sine die* apparently encouraged the Moslem League to adopt an intransigent attitude, and it steadfastly refused to come to an agreement with the Congress. Indeed Linlithgow's policy revealed a lack of foresight. It is however possible that because of his earlier success in persuading the Congress to accept ministerial offices in the provinces in 1937, Linlithgow may have been over-confident of his

---

1 E. Penderel Moon, *Divide and Quit,* (London, 1961), p. 25.

2 Francis G. Hutchins, *Spontaneous Revolution: The Quit India Movement* (Delhi, 1971), pp. 180-82.

3 Moon, *Divide and Quit,* p. 25.

4 *Quarterly Survey,* no. 10.

5 Moon, *Divide and Quit,* p. 25.

persuasive ability to secure cooperation now. Moreover, he genuinely believed that the Congress leaders were trying to bargain and that if only the government could hold on long enough the leaders would be bound to lower their demands. This time, however, he failed to read the Congress attitude.

Congress accused Linlithgow of side-tracking the main issue and reiterated its demand for a declaration of war aims.[1] While not denying the existence of the communal problem, Congress argued that its gravity could be over-stated, and that it was created by the British Government. These were misconceptions, though held by Congress leaders with sincerity. While it was no doubt true that many Moslems had joined the Congress and there was a fair degree of mutual tolerance between the two communities, there were unfortunately many in both communities whose outlook was limited by their faith. The Moslems were a minority in almost the same sense as the Protestants of Ireland or the Sudeten Germans in Czechoslovakia. There particularism might be deplorable but to ignore it would be a mistake.

Nevertheless Linlithgow might have done something to compose the communal difficulties and pave the way for cooperation between the communities. Instead he made agreement of communal groups a prerequisite for any further consideration of the political problem and shrank back from any initiative that might have ended the impasse.

It was quite apparent that a policy of *non possumus* would not suffice. The government would have to make further efforts if it were to prevent the Congress from resorting to civil disobedience which would be likely to impede the war effort. Whilst Linlithgow procrastinated, Sir Stafford Cripps took the initiative. Cripps had long been interested in the Indian problem and was reputed to be a close friend of some of the Indian nationalist leaders. He informed Zetland that he proposed to go to India on a private visit during which he would explore with the Indian leaders the possibility of setting up a constituent assembly. On the basis of the provincial election returns of 1936, and with conjectural figures for the states, Cripps had prepared a plan for the composition of a constituent assembly. Out of a total of 2,000 representatives, over 700 would be Congress, about 450 Moslem League, 400 other parties and 500 for the representatives of the states. Taking this as a starting point, he hoped that it might be possible to get broad acceptance for the composition of a constituent assembly from the

---

[1] L/I/1/745, 'Note on Indian Reactions', 6 Nov. 1939, IOR. See also J. Nehru, *The Unity of India* (London, 1941), p. 347.

leaders of important parties. If he failed to obtain an agreement on this, the plan would collapse. But if there emerged a substantial consensus, he would propose that the British Government should summon a constituent assembly which would proceed to frame a constitution for India by a two-thirds or three-fifths majority. If the assembly failed to agree, Cripps pointed out, the government would have at least established its good faith in relation to India.[1] Cripps proposed to meet 'the difficulties' over the minorities, the states and defence by means of a treaty between Britain and India.[2]

Zetland was impressed by Cripps's plan. He was himself convinced that the war would usher in far-reaching changes, that it would be impossible to maintain the *status quo* and that the pace of India's progress towards self-government would inevitably have to be speeded up.[3]

> I do not believe [Zetland wrote to the Prime Minister] we shall find it possible at the end of the war to pick up the threads where we have dropped them and carry on as if nothing had happened. War on the grand scale seems to be accompanied by churning of the ocean of thought. As in the case of Plank's quantum theory in the domain of physics, so in the case of peoples, progress seems to proceed not smoothly but by jumps; and I do not believe that the picture of India moving towards the goal which we have set before her by smooth, measured and leisurely stages – which is what we have hitherto had in mind – is likely to be realised.[4]

Zetland's predictions about the future course of Indian politics were of course to be proved remarkably accurate. Even in early December 1939 Chamberlain agreed 'that in the circumstances brought about by the war a new approach might well have to be reconsidered'.[5] But before taking any action it was decided to seek 'the views of the man on the spot'. This was natural as the Cabinet had no clear appreciation of the communal situation in India. Here it is necessary to note the prominent role played by Linlithgow in the structuring of evidence placed before the Cabinet. He made sure that, both in Britain and in India, facts and arguments were so marshalled that the Cabinet's decision would conform to his own prescriptions. The Viceroy's reply to the Cabinet's request for his views was not enthusiastic.[6] In a most

1 For an outline of Cripps's scheme see Mss. Eur. F.125/18/308, telegram from Zetland to Linlithgow, 23 Nov. 1939. IOL.
2 L/PO/251, Zetland to Linlithgow, 6/7 Dec. 1939. IOR.
3 Mss. Eur. F.125/9/7, Zetland to Linlithgow, 4 Feb. 1940. IOL.
4 L/PO/251, Zetland to Chamberlain, 1 Dec. 1939. IOR.
5 Cited in L/PO/251, Zetland to Linlithgow, 6/7 Dec. 1939. IOR.
6 John L. *Essayez: The Memoirs of Lawrence, Second Marquess of Zetland* (London, 1956), pp. 275-7; see also Mss. Eur. D.609/18, Linlithgow to Zetland, 21 Dec. 1939. IOL.

adroit letter Linlithgow set out arguments against any premature attempt at a new approach. The Congress leaders were overbidding their hands, but the trump card, Linlithgow believed, was his. As long as the Congress failed to secure the cooperation of the Moslem League, its demands need not be met. The existing discords between the two parties could strengthen Britain's control in India 'for many years'.[1] But, significantly, he scarcely displayed any appreciation of the fact (so carefully summed up in Zetland's letter to Chamberlain) that the war was swiftly changing the destinies of the land whose future Britain was striving to shape. He persistently maintained the position he had taken up since the outbreak of war.

> I am strongly in favour of taking no action and of lying back . . . my considered judgement is that we should now make no further move towards Congress beyond repeating our readiness to help . . . and that we should be ready, if Congress make a break inevitable, to deal with the civil disobedience resolution and, without delay, to use full powers of censorship and pressure so far as the Congress is concerned and spare no effort in my power to bring home to Parliament and public that responsibility for the fact that India has not advanced to a point, and now seems unlikely to advance to a point, to which we have and are anxious to bring her [sic] is not ours; and that the predominant responsibility rests with Congress and the intransigence of its profound uneasiness which that attitude has caused to minorities as well as to Princes.[2]

Linlithgow continued to proffer this advice, at the same time warning against 'swapping horses or doing anything which might lose us Muslim support'.[3] By using the pretext of the minorities and the princes, he tried to build up a strong case against reopening negotiations with the Congress during the war.[4]

Nevertheless, Zetland's efforts succeeded in eliciting from Linlithgow an alternative plan.[5] On 10 January 1940, speaking at the Bombay Orient Club, Linlithgow stated that the British Government's object was to grant India the 'full Dominion Status . . . of the Statute of Westminster variety', and assured his audience that the government would do its best to 'reduce to the minimum the interval between the existing state of things and the achievement of Dominion Status'. For the duration of the war he offered to expand the Executive Council so as to include the representatives of the political parties, together with the

1   Mss. Eur. D.609/18, telegram from Linlithgow to Zetland, 18 Dec. 1939. IOL.
2   Mss. Eur. D.609/26, telegram from Linlithgow to Zetland, 8 Mar. 1940. IOL.
3   Mss. Eur. F.125/18/409, telegram from Linlithgow to Zetland, 25 Oct. 1939. IOL.
4   Mss. Eur. D.609/18, Linlithgow to Zetland, 4 Nov. 1939. IOL.
5   Mss. Eur. D.609/26, Linlithgow to Zetland, 21 Dec. 1939. IOL.

appointment of a defence consultative committee.[1] The speech, which was somewhat in contrast to his earlier views, was favourably received in India. Gandhi saw in it 'the germ of a possible settlement', and asked for an interview with the Viceroy to explore the possibilities of ending the deadlock.[2] This time the hopes of a settlement seem to have been higher than at any previous stages of discussions. It was hoped that with reasonable accommodation on both sides a compromise formula might be evolved.

The reaction was somewhat different in Britain. Linlithgow's mention of 'Dominion Status of Westminster variety' evoked protests from the diehards who tried to bring pressure on Zetland to dissuade Linlithgow from coming to terms with the Congress, The difficulty, as Morley had complained thirty years before, lay in synchronizing clocks in different hemispheres. 'It was not easy to devise a formula that could pass for self-government in India, and for the British Raj at Westminster.'[3] Sir Henry Page-Croft, a diehard who was to become a parliamentary Under-Secretary in the Churchill Government, declared himself 'astonished' that in order to placate the Congress 'the Viceroy should have gone out of his way to stress that Dominion Status was of the same kind as that provided by the Statute of Westminster'. A few days later he again warned Zetland:

> The Viceroy seems to have made a most definite statement which goes far beyond the intention of Parliament, which statement some of us regard as most dangerous and seriously to embarrass Parliament in dealing with any alteration of the constitution should it become necessary, at the end of the war.[4]

Diehard criticism of his speech put Linlithgow on his guard: in future he avoided the use of the phrase 'Dominion Status of the Westminster variety'. Nevertheless, he obtained from Jinnah the conditions for his agreement with the Congress: not simply abandonment of the singing of *Bande Mataram* and similar other demands, but also the formation of coalition ministries in the provinces and a provision that no measure should be passed by the provincial legislatures if two-thirds of the Moslem members opposed it. Nor was Jinnah willing to accept a democratic government based on a popular vote, or the

1 Linlithgow, *Statements and Speeches*, pp. 227-30.

2 Mss. Eur. F.125/28/118, telegram from Linlithgow to Zetland, 21 Jan. 1940. IOL.

3 Cited in Nanda, *The Nehrus*, p. 317.

4 L/P&J/8/504, Page-Croft to Zetland, 8 and 16 Feb, 1940. IOR. Churchill raised strong objections to Linlithgow meeting Gandhi. For discussion in the Cabinet see War Cabinet Conclusions 30(40)4. Cab. 65/5 dated 12 Feb. 1940. PRO.

collective responsibility of the ministers to the legislature. Jinnah's demands were exorbitant. It will be remembered that the legislatures of several provinces did not have a single Moslem League representative, but Jinnah did not explain how he could nominate his men to the coalition cabinet when none were available. However, surprisingly enough, Linlithgow felt that if Gandhi was 'prepared to be reasonable then there is . . . some chance of settlement'.[1] Gandhi, however, was uncompromising. After two fruitless hours of talk between the two of them, the negotiations broke down. Gandhi would not accept Jinnah's demand for coalition governments in the provinces and reiterated the Congress demand for a constituent assembly. Subsequently Gandhi stated that 'the vital difference between the Congress demand and the Viceroy's offer consists of the fact that the Viceroy's offer contemplates the final determination of India's destination by the British Government, whereas the Congress contemplates the reverse [*sic*]'.[2]

After this abortive meeting, Zetland again began to press on the Cabinet the necessity of bringing the Indian party leaders together. He pointed out that Linlithgow's argument for a policy of inaction was based on the mistaken assumption that the only alternative to inaction was complete surrender to the Congress demands. Moreover, Zetland added, if the Congress were to adopt at the forthcoming Ramgarh session (March 1940) the resolution demanding 'complete independence', the policy of 'lying back' would not serve for long. 'There seems to me', Zetland further argued, 'every advantage in securing the initiative for ourselves, even if the Congress do not resort to civil disobedience; and if they do, it would I think be essential that we should have some constructive plan of action'.[3] He therefore suggested that the government should endeavour to accommodate the Congress point of view. This would require the acceptance of a constitution framed by the Indians themselves, provided the states and political parties agreed to the composition of the constitution-making body. He believed that no agreement would be forthcoming unless the discussions among the Indians to solve the communal problems were undertaken with the clear knowledge that they alone would be responsible for finding such a solution. Both the Cabinet and the Viceroy failed to appreciate the merits of Zetland's plea; apparently they tended to minimize the dangerous consequences a civil disobedience campaign might have on

1   Mss. Eur. D.609/18, Linlithgow to Zetland, 3 Feb. 1940. IOL.
2   117/A/7, 'Review of all-India Constitutional Development since Outbreak of War', (n.d.), p. 7. IOR.
3   Mss. Eur. D.609/26, Memorandum by Zetland, 9 Apr. 1940. IOL.

the British war effort. The Cabinet deferred a final decision and called for an appreciation of the situation from Linlithgow.[1]

It seemed a short-sighted policy to allow the political situation in India to deteriorate until, at the end of the war, Britain's relations with India were like those with Ireland at the end of the first world war. It might have been a better policy for the British Government to have taken the initiative, while this was still possible, by firmly announcing that the responsibility for framing India's constitution would be in the hands of the Indians themselves.

Just as Zetland had predicted, the situation was further complicated when on 20 March the Congress adopted the resolution demanding complete independence;[2] and three days later the League's adoption of the resolution demanding the partition of India introduced an entirely new feature into Indian politics.[3] Zetland, while admitting that further reflection would be necessary before making any new move in India, recorded his opinion that inaction on the part of the government would not solve the problem: 'When the time is ripe a solution on the lines I have advocated will require serious consideration.'[4] But before he could take up the matter again, Neville Chamberlain resigned, and Zetland was replaced at the India Office by L.S. Amery. Amery's appointment was somewhat surprising: during the debate on the India Bill in 1934-5 he had distinguished himself by opposing Churchill and the diehards. Amery has himself recorded his surprise:

> What neither of us can have expected was that Churchill should within five years invite me to be Secretary of State for India in his great war Government, to renew, in the privacy of the Cabinet, the same fundamental divergence of outlook which had separated us on the floor of the House for many years.[5]

Despite the suspicion among nationalists that Amery was anti-Congress, his record, initially at least, shows that he had profound sympathy for Indian aspirations.

Throughout this critical period following the outbreak of the war, Linlithgow not only himself refused to take the initiative but also frustrated Zetland's attempts at a solution. But it should be remembered that Linlithgow was carrying enormous responsibility at the head of the British Indian Empire. No doubt he ought to have enlisted the coopera-

1 L/PO/77, Extract from the War Cabinet Conclusions, 15 Mar. 1940. IOR.
2 *IAR,* 1940, i, 228-9.
3 *Ibid.* p. 312.
4 Mss. Eur. D.609/26, Memorandum by Zetland, 9 Apr. 1940. IOL.
5 L.S. Amery, *My Political Life* (London, reprint, Nov. 1955), iii, 109.

tion of the Indian leaders, but that he believed had to be subordinated to his primary goal – the maximization of India's war efforts. He realized very shrewdly that Congress's cooperation would have to be secured on his own terms; otherwise he would be giving in at the thin end of the wedge. This would lead to friction between the Viceroy and the Congress ministers, thereby impeding India's war effort. The Congress claimed that only a popular government could arouse enthusiasm for the war among the masses. This would have been a weighty consideration if India, like France, had been the centre of the war. But in 1940 India was still far away from the scene of battles, and the question of resistance or guerrilla warfare was as yet remote. Linlithgow's task was to increase the supply of the sinews of war, and this he was accomplishing satisfactorily. The size of the Indian army was vastly increased. To Linlithgow, the problem was not one of enlisting soldiers, but one of providing them with guns and ammunition; and above all of preventing Hindu-Moslem conflicts among the soldiers.[1]

Amery at first continued his predecessor's policy. And indeed he was soon able to claim, in a letter to Zetland, that Linlithgow had 'come round very markedly to our point of view'.[2] In his first statement in Parliament as Secretary of State for India, Amery defined the goal of the government as the attainment by India of free and equal partnership in the British Commonwealth. He declared that it would be for the Indians themselves to devise a constitution best adapted to their needs and reiterated the promise that the 1935 Act would be open to re-examination at the end of the war, which, he added, necessarily implied discussion and negotiations and not dictation. Although no final agreement on the major issues was immediately possible, Amery was confident that provisional arrangements could be made which would permit the resumption of office in the provinces, and the appointment of political leaders to the Viceroy's Executive Council.[3]

Shortly afterwards Amery asked Linlithgow if the 'situation as affected here is not developing to a point at which some initiative on your part might not after all become possible'.[4] Linlithgow, while admitting the necessity of overcoming the 'real and solid' difficulty, warned Amery against the risk of taking a 'false step'. He emphasized that the Congress claim to speak for India as a whole was 'particularly

1 Mss. Eur. F.125/28/141, Linlithgow to Zetland, 8 Mar. 1940. IOL.

2 Mss. Eur. D.609/26, Amery to Zetland, 1 July 1940. IOL.

3 *Parliamentary Debates,* House of Commons, vol. 361, cols. 283-5, 23 May 1940; see also Mss. Eur. F.125/19/137, telegram from Amery to Linlithgow, 18 May 1940. IOL.

4 L/P&J/8/506, telegram from Amery to Linlithgow, 2 June 1940. IOR.

unreal' in the face of the opposition from the Moslems and the princes. Explaining his reluctance to take any initiative, Linlithgow pointed out that repeated failure would diminish the value of action by the Viceroy and impair his position as a mediator. He once again advised that 'we should continue as before, and should make no move until circumstances are more propitious for one, and there is some likelihood that it would produce results of value'. Against the possibility of the Congress launching a civil disobedience movement, he was confident that such a step, apart from its 'nuisance value', would not 'stop my war effort here, nor does their aloofness in the slightest degree limit that war effort which is basically conditioned by arms and equipment, and by limits of training facilities'.[1] Linlithgow's reply was in accord with the attitude which he had advocated earlier: the policy of 'lying back'. A remarkable feature of his reply was that it took no account whatever of an emphatic swing of Indian opinion in favour of cooperation with the war effort.[2] Linlithgow shied away from taking an initiative or otherwise endeavouring to bring about some provisional settlement with the Indian leaders such as Amery had appealed for in the House of Commons.[3] In Amery's proposal there was no direct reference to restoring self-government in the 'Congress provinces' nor to the expansion of the Viceroy's Council, but it was not intended to oust such an idea. Indeed, the natural assumption seemed to be that if discussion could be initiated on the lines indicated in the telegram of 2 June,[4] and if a spirit of accommodation showed itself, there might well be a provisional settlement. Had his telegram elicited a favourable response from Linlithgow, Amery had contemplated going to the Cabinet. It seemed hardly likely that the Cabinet would agree to a policy with which the Viceroy had expressed himself as being in entire disagreement.

Linlithgow's *non possumus* arguments were based on the assumption that his offer of 17 October 1939 was a 'generous one'. Yet it merely consisted of a reassertion that Dominion Status was the goal of British policy, an offer to examine the whole Act of 1935 after the war, the establishment of a Defence Advisory Committee for the duration of the war, and the inclusion of political leaders in the Viceroy's Council.

Meanwhile, in Europe, the war took a serious turn. In April, Denmark and Norway were invaded, then Holland and Belgium. As the Germans swept into France, the British forces were pushed into the sea, escaping

---

1 L/P&J/8/507, Linlithgow to Amery, 11 June 1940. IOR.
2 See below pp. 154-5.
3 See above p. 152
4 See p. 152 n.4.

from Dunkirk in June 1940. There was a marked upsurge in India of public sympathy for the victims of Nazi aggression and a desire to cooperate in the war effort, a sympathy resulting in many cases from the rather limited motive of safeguarding India's security. To many it seemed that if Britain were invaded there was nothing to prevent Germany from dominating the Mediterranean and marching on to India.[1] Several Congressmen, led by Rajagopalachari, favoured a relaxation of the uncompromising Congress attitude towards the war. Rajendra Prasad and Asaf Ali quite freely gave vent to their feelings on the subject. Nehru expressed his abhorrence at taking advantage of Britain's difficulties: civil disobedience would be like siding with the Axis.[2]

The Congress Working Committee met on 21 June to discuss its response to the war situation in Europe. It was at this crucial moment that Gandhi decided to bring matters to a head by raising the highly controversial issue of the application of the principle of non-violence to external aggression. He claimed that the time had come to declare that India would defend its liberty, not with the help of arms, but with 'force of non-violence'.[3] This was not the first occasion on which the question of non-violence had been raised in this form. Gandhi had mooted it first in September 1938 and again, a year later, on the outbreak of war. But he now insisted that in view of the deteriorating international situation a decision on a fundamental issue of this character could no longer be postponed. He declared that India could only be defended 'non-violently' and called upon every Briton to 'accept the method of non-violence'.[4] However, after a prolonged deliberation the Congress Working Committee rejected the principle in the sphere of national defence, while retaining it in the struggle for freedom.[5] For the first time in many years, Gandhi had failed to swing the Congress to his own point of view.

The Congress offered cooperation subject to two conditions: the declaration of Indian independence to take effect after the war; and a national government to be set up immediately as a token of that promise. The armed forces should remain under the British Commander-

1   B.R. Nanda, *Mahatma Gandhi* (London, 1958), pp. 435-6.

2   Mss. Eur. F.125/134/43, Laithwaite to Clauson, 23 June 1942 (enclosure), 'Congress and the War' by G. Ahmed. (The author was an officer in the police department); *Times of India,* 9 May 1940.

3   *Harijan,* 8 June 1940.

4   *Harijan,* 6 July 1940. See also *Harijan,* 29 June 1940.

5   L/P&J/8/507, Reuters message from Wardha, 21 June 1940. IOR. See also Sitaramayya, *The History of the Indian National Congress,* ii, 200-1; Nehru, *A Bunch of Old Letters,* pp. 414-24; Nehru, *Discovery,* p. 527.

in-Chief, and the Viceroy's position would remain unchanged, though he would be expected not to use his veto except in cases of emergency. The Congress believed that it had considerably brought down its terms for cooperation with the government and had even thrown away the leadership of Gandhi.[1]

The Congress claimed that the resolution, by providing for a provisional government to be so constituted as to command the confidence of the central legislature, sought to meet the claims of the Moslem League. Azad wrote to Jinnah that 'National Government' meant 'a composite cabinet not limited to any single party'.[2] The resolution appeared to be an attempt to rectify the indiscretion which Congress had committed in 1937 when it had failed to include a Moslem League nominee in the United Provinces and Bombay provincial governments. In some ways it was also the most constructive suggestion emanating from the Congress, which since the outbreak of the war had shown a lack of statesmanship and which for want of a definite policy had drifted towards non-cooperation and civil disobedience.

The resolution aroused lively interest in official quarters. *Prima facie,* it appeared to be simple, and a substantial toning down of the Congress demands. But a closer study revealed that it was open to more than one interpretation and did not really change the Congress position. The central demand, that of complete independence, remained, even though what was urged was its acknowledgement, not its immediate realization. The real ambiguity arose over the meaning of the term 'National Government'. All that was said about the 'National Government' was that it would command the confidence of all the parties in the legislature. Did that mean only that it would be a national coalition like the 'National Government' in Britain? A 'National Government' in this sense would mean a change in the constitutional status: it would subject the Government of India to the same kind of parliamentary control as the governments of Australia or Canada. Besides, the phrase 'the defence of the country' did not necessarily mean cooperation in the Allied war effort. When Azad suggested this interpretation,[3] Nehru remonstrated:

> The words in the original draft [of the resolution] were changed from "war effort" to "defence of the country" at my instance. I stated that it was conceivable that we might later have to take part in the rest of the war effort and therefore I could not rule it out

1   Nanda, *Mahatma Gandhi,* p. 437.
2   Sittaramayya, *The History of the Indian National Congress,* ii, 202.
3   *Hindustan Times,* 13 July 1940.

completely. But I was not prepared to commit myself to any such position at this stage.[1]

It was also not without significance that another resolution was passed at the same time by the Congress which spoke of its inability to apply the principle of non-violence to 'free India's national defence'. Independence, which was visualized as a possibility in one, was assumed as a reality in the other.

After months of procrastination, Linlithgow realized the need for associating non-officials in the prosecution of the war. What immediately prompted him into action is not clear. The disastrous effects of the German *blitzkrieg* in Europe and the plight of Britain may have warned him of a similar danger in India. As a patriotic Briton Linlithgow felt the necessity to do something. Moreover, he could not altogether ignore the recent Congress overture. So it was that for the first time since the outbreak of the war, Linlithgow approached the War Cabinet with a plan for ending the deadlock.[2] He sought the Cabinet's approval for a declaration to the following effect:

i. Britain's aim in India was dominion status

ii. The 1935 Act would be open to revision at the end of the war

iii. Full consideration would be given to the views of all interests

iv. Subject to Britain's continuing interests being protected, the British Government 'would be perfectly content to abide by conclusions of any representative body of Indians on which various political parties could agree'; and finally

v. The government 'would spare no effort to bring about 'Dominion Status within a year after the conclusion of the war'.

Linlithgow recognized that these ideas were 'somewhat revolutionary', but he felt it desirable to announce them with all possible speed.[3]

Linlithgow's proposals, though modest and short of Congress demands, were realistic. Britain had previously announced that her aim was to establish Dominion Status in India. However, as long as she indicated neither the date nor the method, she remained open to the charge that she was insincere and merely playing for time: until she did so her exhortations to the Indians to agree amongst themselves would meet with no response and merely add to the suspicion that Britain was deliberately procrastinating. Linlithgow's proposal clearly envisaged Dominion Status within a year of the end of the war.

Amery, while commending the proposals to the War Cabinet,

1 Cited in Mss. Eur. F.125/124/43, 'Congress and the War' by G. Ahmed.
2 Mss. Eur. F.125/19/27, Linlithgow to Amery, 1 July 1940. IOL.
3 Mss. Eur. D.609/18, telegram from Linlithgow to Zetland, 1 July 1940. IOL.

suggested that the renewal of effort by Linlithgow ought to be accompanied by a precise statement of the British Government's intention on the future constitutional development, the method of approach, and the time-table. He insisted that the declaration must be precise and warned against far-reaching but vague generalities as in the previous declarations.

> Our declarations hitherto [he continued] could not have been more sweeping in their general purport. Dominion Status of the Statute of Westminster variety . . . implies complete independence, including the now admitted right of a free decision to participation or neutrality in war, and indeed the power, if not constitutional right, to secede.

Amery was also in favour of conceding the right of the Indians to frame their own constitution. This, he argued, was not only the core of the Congress demand but also a natural corollary to the British pledges.[1] In a letter to Linlithgow, Amery further manifested his anxiety to end the impasse:

> Somehow or the other, by hook or crook, one wants to get Indian opinion deflected from the mere barren and aggravating restatement of opposite points of view to the seeking for solutions which may harmonize them.[2]

Amery's draft statement followed the lines of Linlithgow's proposal: at the earliest practicable moment after the war, India should become an equal partner in the Commonwealth; immediately after the war the Indian constitution should be examined anew by whatever constituent body Indians might agree upon; Britain's continuing interests and obligations would be safeguarded through a treaty; and Indians would be invited to join the Executive Council and the War Advisory Council[3]

The Cabinet, however, was not willing to go as far as Amery would have liked. It approved the expansion of the Executive Council and the establishment of the War Advisory Committee, but Amery was required to redraft his statement.[4]

The new draft embodied considerable changes, of which the main one transposed the sequence of the paragraphs in order to put in the forefront the responsibilities and obligations of the British Government and to emphasize that the constitutional scheme devised by the Indians must be subject to the fulfilment of these obligations. The new draft also

1 Mss. Eur. D.609/26, Memorandum by Amery, 6 July 1940. IOL.
2 Mss. Eur. F.125/9/28, Amery to Linlithgow, 4 July 1940. IOL.
3 Mss. Eur. D.609/26, Memorandum by Amery, 6 July 1940 (Appendix B). IOL.
4 L/P&J/8/507, War Cabinet Conclusions W.M. (40) 201st, 12 July 1940. IOR.

omitted the sentence committing the British Government to accept the constitutional scheme that would emerge from an Indian constitution-making body, and left the government free to object to any features of the constitution that were 'patently absurd and unjust'. The British Government was to be the sole judge of absurdity or injustice. In deference to Linlithgow's objections, Amery dropped the word 'constituent body'. While Dominion Status was promised, Linlithgow's phrase 'equal partner in the Commonwealth' was expunged.[1]

Amery had much difficulty in getting the revised draft through the Cabinet, mainly owing to Churchill's stonewalling. In the end Amery's 'clear-cut draft declaration has become a much more long winded and imprecise document, for the style of which I [Amery] should like, in private at any rate, to disclaim any responsibility.'[2] Amery's draft appeared as Linlithgow's August offer of 1940.

The August offer gave no definite assurances. It stated that Dominion Status for India was the objective of the British Government, but neither the date nor the method of introducing it was indicated. It stated that 'with the least possible delay' following the war the British Government would set up a representative body to devise India's constitution. The Viceroy, in the meantime, was to invite a certain number of representative Indians to join his Executive Council and the War Advisory Committee. A guarantee was given to the Moslems that the British Government would not contemplate transferring power to any system of government in India the authority of which was denied 'by large and powerful elements in India's national life'.[3]

The offer was rejected by all the major parties. It was ironical that when Linlithgow, who had himself frustrated Zetland's attempts to solve the impasse, at last took the initiative, his effort should have been defeated by the War Cabinet.

Congress rejected the offer as it fell short of its demands.[4] In his Orient Club speech,[5] the Congress argued, Linlithgow had spoken of Dominion Status of the Statute of Westminster type, and now he was doing no more than using the expression 'free and equal partnership'. The Congress resolution asserted that if free partnership meant the right of secession, there was no reason why a declaration could not be made

1 L/P&J/8/507, Memorandum by Amery, 13 July 1940. IOR.
2 Mss. Eur. D.609/26, Amery to Zetland, 3 Aug. 1940. IOR.
3 *Cmd. 6291* of 1940.
4 *IAR*, 1940, ii, 196-7.
5 See above pp. 148-9.

to the effect that India would be independent. Azad, the Congress President, refused to discuss the offer with Linlithgow since it was, he said, totally at variance with Congress policy.[1] Gandhi regretted that the offer had widened the gulf between India and Britain.[2] While publicly Gandhi regretted the announcement, in private he is reported to have welcomed it as 'a god-send' from the point of view of non-violence.[3] The whole concept of Dominion Status, claimed Nehru, was 'as dead as a door nail'.[4] Seven years later, in August 1947, the Congress not only accepted Dominion Status but also acquiesced in the partition of India.

The Congress leaders had apparently not fully understood the meaning of Dominion Status. Since the declaration of 1926, and the Statute of Westminster of 1931, it was difficult to explain how Dominion Status differed from 'complete independence'.[5] The dominions had acquired self-government, both legislative and executive. They had become independent states on an equal footing with Britain, 'in no way subordinate in any respect of their domestic or external affairs'. They were 'united by a common allegiance to the Crown and freely associated as members of the British Commonwealth of Nations'; but those ties did not infringe their liberty.[6] In dominion matters the monarch could act only in accordance with the advice of his dominion ministers. The independence of the dominions had already been proved when, after the outbreak of the war, Eire preferred to remain neutral, and there was no pressure from Britain to force it to change its stand. The Congress leaders, true to their doctrine of British perfidy, brushed aside all these developments as mere pretences intended to disguise the truth that Britain did not mean to loosen her imperial grip on India.

The Congress decision to reject the August offer was unfortunate. It antagonized the new Secretary of State, Amery, who had so far taken a

1   Mss. Eur. F.125/19/363, telegram from Linlithgow to Amery, 11 Aug. 1940. IOL; Azad, *India Wins Freedom*, p. 36.

2   *News Chronicle*, 14 Aug. 1940.

3   Mahadev Desai, *Maulana Abul Kalam Azad* (London, 1941), p. 179.

4   *Hindustan Times*, 12 Aug. 1940.

5   A useful definition of Dominion Status has been provided by Peter Fraser, a former prime minister of New Zealand: 'The people of the British dominions do not regard dominion status as an imperfect kind of independence. On the contrary it is independence with something added and not independence with something taken away. It carried with it membership of a free and powerful association from which every element of constraint has vanished, but one in which a way has been found for the practice of mutual confidence and cooperation in the full respect of the independence, sovereignty, and individuality of each member'.

6   K.C. Wheare, *The Statute of Westminster and Dominion Status* (Oxford, 1938), pp. 122-38.

sympathetic view of the Congress demands. He now came round to Linlithgow's belief that no business could possibly be done with the Congress.[1] This was yet another blunder by the Congress which not only gave leverage to the Moslem League but also meant that it forfeited any chance of its returning to office in the provinces. While the Congress saw nothing good in the offer, the Moslem League claimed that it had implicitly conceded its demand 'for a clear assurance to the effect that no future constitution, interim or final, should be adopted by the British Government without their approval and consent'. But while not forbidding cooperation in the war effort, the Moslem League did not offer it openly either.[2]

After rejecting the August offer, the Congress had to decide its course of action. Gandhi remained opposed to participating in the war under any conditions. Within the Congress there were some differences on the line to be taken, but all were agreed that India must withhold support to the British in the existing situation. The conflict between Gandhi's creed of non-violence and the group that advocated the use of force in defence against foreign aggression therefore remained a theoretical one. The attitude of the British, wrote Azad, 'united us in action even though our basic approach remained different.'[3] Nevertheless, as a political organization the Congress could not simply remain silent while tremendous events were happening in India and abroad. To sit by idle would mean the disintegration of the Congress as many of its members were tired of debate and discussions and were clamouring for action. While Gandhi was negotiating with the British, a civil disobedience campaign had already been launched by the Forward Bloc of Subhas Bose. This campaign appeared to have considerable support from many Congress workers, particularly in Bengal.[4] If Gandhi wished to keep his leadership of the Congress, he would have to harness the enthusiasm of the younger members.[5] They had been repeatedly asked not to cooperate in the war. To reverse this advice, without obtaining some satisfaction from the British, would lead to loss of face. The only course left open was to launch a civil disobedience movement. Consequently on 15 September, the All India Congress Committee reconsidered the earlier resolution offering Congress cooperation in the war. Gandhi, who had been formally absolved of responsibility for

---

1   Mss. Eur. F.125/9/37, Amery to Linlithgow, 14 Oct. 1940. IOL.

2   *IAR*, 1940, ii, 243-5.

3   Azad, *India Wins Freedom*, p. 37.

4   R.C. Majumdar, *History of the Freedom Movement* (Calcutta, 1962), iv, 606-9.

5   Munshi, *Pilgrimage to Freedom*, i, 59.

Congress policy, was reinstated with supreme authority – a position he had really never abandoned – and in deference to his wishes it was resolved that non-violence should apply not only to the struggle of independence but also to the defence of 'free India'.[1]

Gandhi had no immediate plans. He was reluctant to launch a mass movement. His hesitation seems to have been due to the fact that such a movement at this time might not have secured popular support. There was no immediate issue on which he could possibly arouse the masses. Congress leaders may have been concerned with the question of independence, and some of them with the desire to fight fascism, but these were essentially matters which did not interest the ordinary people. Though there had been shortages of consumer goods since the outbreak of the war and a rise in the cost of living, this primarily affected the urban population which was a small minority. The Indian peasants, more than eighty-five per cent of the population, constantly at war with poverty and starvation, showed little interest in the constitutional debates. There is thus good reason to believe that if Gandhi had given the call to start civil disobedience, the masses might not have responded.[2] What is perhaps less appreciated is the fact that the public, realistically conscious of the rapidly changing economic situation in war-time conditions, moved away from the impracticalities of the Congress leaders. War brought wider opportunities for employment. Industrial developments were stimulated, businessmen made money through war contracts. Congress, which had been previously demanding rapid Indianization of the defence services, now began to urge the people not to enlist for a war with which the Congress had refused to cooperate. The people, wiser than the Congress, in a country like India where bread was more important than politics, did not listen.[3] At the end of the war there were two million Indians in uniform.

Gandhi, shortly after he had been authorized by the Congress to launch civil disobedience, met Linlithgow. In an endeavour to escape from the trap of ineffectiveness, Gandhi now demanded freedom of speech to criticize the war. Free speech, maintained Gandhi, was the test of Britain's professed devotion to democracy. Linlithgow was prepared to grant the liberty allowed to conscientious objectors in Britain. They were absolved from the duty of fighting and allowed to profess their faith in public, but they were not permitted to persuade others to abandon their allegiance or discontinue their efforts. Gandhi

---

1   *IAR*, 1940, ii, 212-13.

2   Mss. Eur. F.125/124, C.P. Ramaswamy Aiyar to Linlithgow, 6 Aug. 1942. IOL.

3   J. Srivastava, 'India and the World Order', *Modern Review* (Jan. 1942), p. 28.

was not satisfied with this, and Linlithgow was unwilling to concede anything further.[1] Having failed to secure a face-saving device from Linlithgow, Gandhi had no alternative but to start civil disobedience. Gandhi had an amazing knack for giving a moral aspect to political problems. It was a political issue – the refusal of the government to give an assurance of India's freedom after the war. But it was not only on a political, but also on a pacifist, plank that Gandhi initiated his campaign. The question of freedom of India was relegated to the background and freedom of speech became the main issue of national agitation.

While Gandhi had no clear-cut programme, the government for almost a year, since the outbreak of the war, had been making elaborate arrangements to deal with a Congress threat of civil disobedience. In a series of letters exchanged with the provincial governments, and in various discussions at Delhi and Simla, views had been gathered, anxieties assessed, and reactions to the proposed remedies collected. The result of these efforts was the Revolutionary Movement Ordinance (RMO) which was finalized in the summer of 1940.[2] The Revolutionary Movement Ordinance was to be issued together with a manifesto laying down the policies and intentions of the government which accused the Congress of a determination to overthrow the government through its campaign of civil disobedience. The manifesto went on to say that the government had never accepted the pretence of the Congress to speak for the whole of India and held it to be their duty to respect the views and interests of other communities and parties which did not agree with the Congress. It further claimed: 'There must be countless Indians, who will condemn or disown the decision of the leaders of the Congress and who will feel that, whatever the future may hold in store, India can now best fulfill her destiny and her due place among the nations of world only after the total extinction of the political party which, at this vital juncture, has seen fit to betray them'. The supporters of constituted authority had nothing to fear: they were not only guaranteed protection so long as the movement lasted, but were also assured of due recognition for their loyalty when the movement was defeated.[3]

Reginald Maxwell, the Home Member responsible for drafting these documents, was anxious to strike at the Congress 'before the public have too far forgotten' their grievances against the Congress ministry. He proposed 'nor merely to reduce the Congress to a condition in which

---

1 Mss. Eur. F.125/19/458, telegram from Linlithgow to Amery, 27 Sept. 1940. IOL.

2 For details of the RMO see L/P&J/8/585, ff. 118-27. IOR.

3 *Ibid.*

they will be prepared to make terms but to crush the Congress finally as a political organization'.[1]

If the purpose of the Revolutionary Movement Ordinance was merely to deal with the Congress as a 'war menace', it was unnecessary. The government was already armed with the Defence of India Rules which enabled it to take arbitary action against any person or group in the name of the war effort. The desire to adopt an explicitly political Revolutionary Movement Ordinance suggests that Linlithgow's thinking with reference to the Congress stretched beyond the military necessity. Indeed, this measure had been first mooted in 1937 when it was feared that the Congress might refuse to cooperate with the reforms inaugurated under the 1935 Act.[2] The resignation of the Congress ministries in 1939 reinvigorated the demand for strong legislation to 'crush the Congress'. In a personal letter to the governors, Linlithgow admitted that despite the vagueness of the phrase 'Revolutionary Movement', 'the situation primarily envisaged is still a clash with the Congress'. He also drew their attention to the significance of the decision reflected in the wording of the Revolutionary Movement Ordinance which declared Congress as a whole an unlawful association. More importantly, wrote Linlithgow, 'I feel very strongly that the only possible answer to a "declaration of war" by any section of Congress in present circumstances must be declared determination to crush the organization as a whole.'[3]

It is thus clear that the government preferred a separate Revolutionary Movement Ordinance for two reasons: first, the possibility that the Congress might not be fully suppressed until sometime after the end of the war, in which case the Defence of India Rules would have lapsed; and second, it was considered desirable to make known the government's long range intentions to those who might otherwise be inclined to sit on the fence and waver in anticipation to an eventual Congress return to power. It would also allay the fears of government officials that actions taken in pursuance of British orders might lead to future victimization.

The updated package plan envisaged the arrest of the Congress leadership, the dismissal of officials considered disloyal, the closing of educational institutions and the seizure of bank accounts and party

---

1 L/P&J/8/585, Maxwell to Laithwaite, 25 Apr. 1940. IOR.

2 Mss. Eur. F.125/4/29, Linlithgow to Zetland, 17 May 1940, IOR; see also Glendevon, *The Viceroy at Bay,* p. 159.

3 L/P&J/8/507, Linlithgow to all Governors, 8 Aug. 1940. IOR. It is interesting that on the very day on which Linlithgow appended his signature to this letter decreeing the 'extinction' of the Congress, he had publicly announced the August offer seeking the cooperation of the Congress in the war effort.

premises, and the imposition of collective fines on troublesome areas. The comprehensiveness of the Revolutionary Movement Ordinance is indicated by the fact that the important legal question as to what constituted 'a revolutionary movement' was resolved simply by the statement that any movement declared to be revolutionary by the Viceroy was legally to be considered such.[1]

Confident of Churchill's support, Linlithgow had carefully finalized his plans for a pre-emptive attack upon the Congress without any reference to the India Office. He had been under the impression that Churchill would give him a blanket approval of his scheme. Linlithgow had perhaps not realized that for questions relating to India the approval of the entire War Cabinet would be required. The War Cabinet could not prevent Churchill from making speeches,[2] but felt that Indian policy was too important to be left to him alone.[3] Viewing the Indian situation from a greater distance and with an eye on the reaction in Britain and the USA, it could not openly decree the extinction of the Congress.

The first difficulty arose when Amery was suddenly presented with a request for a stand-by approval of the Revolutionary Movement Ordinance on 11 September 1940, in a telegram explaining that 'you may not have received' the full text of the Government of India's plan, sent by air mail a few days earlier.[4] In a subsequent telegram Linlithgow said:

> I and my advisers are now clear that we are rapidly moving towards the moment when we shall have to proclaim [the declaration of an organization as an unlawful association under the Criminal Amendment Act] Congress, arrest Working Committee, including Gandhi and leaders of Congress in all Provinces. I trust that you and Cabinet will feel that we shall take no action stronger than the situation requires, and that we must be free to take decisions and to act from day to day without reference home.[5]

Amery, however, refused to be panicked into action. He found it difficult to understand how the situation could have suddenly deteriorated. There was nothing in the recent telegrams received from India which gave the impression of an impending crisis there. Reports had shown only that Gandhi was gradually developing his policy of

1 L/P&J/8/585, draft of the RMO. IOR.
2 War Cabinet Paper W.P. (42) 334. PRO.
3 Mss. Eur. F.125/11, Amery to Linlithgow, 1 Sept. 1942. IOL.
4 Mss. Eur. F.125/19, telegram from Linlithgow to Amery, 11 Sept. 1942. IOL.
5 Mss. Eur. F.125/19/558; telegram from Linlithgow to Amery, 21 Nov. 1940. IOL.

discouraging Indians from participating in the war effort. On the other hand, the conviction of Nehru and other *satyagrahis* for seditious speeches had been quietly received.[1] After much deliberation the Cabinet decided to send the following reply:

> We should make it clear that we were prepared to support him [the Viceroy] in whatever steps were necessary to maintain peace in India and India's effective part in the war. Before, however, we could agreed to Congress being proclaimed we must know exactly what his programme involved. *Prima facie,* we thought it would give rise to an infinity of trouble if it was intended to make membership of the Congress party a criminal offence, and we found it difficult to see why it should be necessary to go further than proclaim the Working Committee. The War Cabinet would be glad to receive any new facts explaining how the situation was developing and which had bearing on the need for taking immediate action.[2]

Amery began a protracted correspondence with Linlithgow over the implications of his policy. The point at issue was whether, if a situation arose in which action had to be taken against Congress, the Congress party as a whole should be declared an unlawful association, or whether it would suffice to proclaim as illegal the All India Congress Committee, the Congress Working Committee and the Provincial Congress Communities where necessary.[3] Amery argued that to make membership of the Congress party a criminal offence might cause embarrassment and provoke reactions. While it might be less convenient administratively to proceed by way of proclaiming particular committees and bodies which formed a part of the Congress organization, the object in view could be achieved by these means. The attention of the Cabinet was also drawn to the views expressed by the ministers of the three ministerial provinces, in August 1940, urging that a party which was responsible for a revolutionary movement ought not to be later allowed to return to power. The ministries in those three provinces were representative in general of the Moslem point of view and the Congress was their political opponent. If the government were to authorize those ministries to suppress the Congress parties altogether, they would, in fact, be authorizing them to eliminate their parliamentary opposition. The War Cabinet therefore rejected the proposal for declaring Congress an illegal organization.[4]

Linlithgow's scheme was considerably watered down. To begin with,

---

1   See below pp. 166-7.

2   Minute of the War Cabinet, 293 (40) 7, Cab. 65/10 dated 21 Nov. 1940. PRO.

3   Mss. Eur. F.125/19/495, telegram from Amery to Linlithgow, 16 Sept. 1940. IOL.

4   Minutes of the War Cabinet 303 (40) 2, Cab. 65/10 dated 10 Dec. 1940. PRO.

he was refused blanket stand-by approval for his scheme and was required to seek Cabinet approval prior to issuing the Revolutionary Movement Ordinance. Amery further insisted that, if action against Congress should become inevitable, it would be desirable 'for public confidence both here and abroad to represent reasons for our action against Congress movement as their programme of obstruction of war effort and their political aspiration'. He pointed out that the Revolutionary Movement Ordinance was 'primarily directed against a movement which however extreme is ostensibly political in character . . . . I am only concerned that you should take into consideration at all stages my preference from a publicity point of view that if a conflict with Congress should arise, it should appear as an outcome of war necessity rather than a political quarrel unrelated to the war'.

Amery carefully removed from the draft Revolutionary Movement Ordinance references to the 'total extinction' of the Congress, and to rewards for loyal service. The phrase declaring Congress 'as a whole' illegal was replaced with phrases which had the effect of 'proclaiming' only specified governing bodies of the Congress. He emphasized that 'the question of actual machinery to be used is largely a matter of convenience'. He agreed that the Revolutionary Movement Ordinance 'would be a most suitable instrument for dealing with a sustained emergency as soon as initial excitement has subsided and could appropriately be promulgated at that stage'. He felt strongly, however, that 'our initial action' should be 'justified in terms of war requirements, keeping public opinion in mind'.[1]

The government's strategy for cracking down on the Congress had one disadvantage: it depended upon the Congress striking the first blow by doing something 'revolutionary' to which the government could react by unleashing its planned offensive. The government concluded that the moment had arrived in September 1940 when the Congress authorized Gandhi to start a campaign against the government. But Gandhi had then launched a *satyagraha* campaign in which select individuals were asked to deliver anti-war speeches. The government could hardly label the individual *satyagraha* campaign 'revolutionary', and was thus unable to clamp down on the Congress at this stage.

The *satyagraha* campaign was opened by Vinoba Bhave on 17 October. Bhave made an anti-war speech for which he was arrested and imprisoned for three months.[2] Nehru was next arrested and sentenced to prison

1 See L/P&J/8/585, telegrams from Amery to Linlithgow, dated 18, 17 and 13 Sept. 1940. IOR.
2 *IAR,* 1940, ii, 201.

for four years.[1] The campaign consisted of three phases. The first phase was confined to individual leaders, the second involved the more prominent Congress members, while in the third phase the movement was broadened to embrace the rank and file. The technique in all cases was a ceremonial recitation of anti-war slogans: 'It is wrong to help the British war effort with men or money. The only worthy effort is to resist all war with non-violent resistance.'[2] By the end of November the campaign had been initiated in all the provinces. Thirty-two ex-ministers including seven ex-premiers were arrested.[3] The campaign achieved moderate success during the first half of 1941.

Deadlock remained complete throughout 1941. The only attempts to reach an agreement were made by the non-party leaders. In March 1941 about forty of these met under the chairmanship of Sapru.[4] Most of the members present were Indian Liberals. No one attended from the Congress or the Moslem League, and other parties were sparsely represented. A resolution was passed which proposed the supersession of the Executive Council by 'non-official Indians drawn from important elements in the public life of the country'. The decisions of the Council were intended to be final, nothing being said about a veto. But the Council was not to be responsible to the electorate, the legislature or the British Parliament. It was to be responsible directly to the Crown with no intermediaries. Finance and defence would be in charge of non-official Indians, although the position of the C-in-C as the head of the armed forces was not to be prejudiced. The members were apparently to be selected by the Viceroy.[5]

The 'non-party' resolution did not, however, suggest any direct method of ending the impasse, which was the professed objective of the conference. No approach was made either to the Congress or the Moslem League. It was suggested that if the proposals in the resolution were accepted, an atmosphere would be created in which it would be impossible for either party to remain aloof or maintain objections. That was all. In support of the resolution it was maintained that the Government of India, as then constituted, did not command confidence and therefore was unable to maximize India's war effort. Acceptance of the proposals, it was claimed, would not only provide the best

1   Menon, *The Transfer of Power*, p. 101.
2   Dorothy Norman, *Nehru: The First Sixty Years* (London, 1965), ii, 41.
3   *Asiatic Review* (1941), p. 251.
4   *Leader*, 11 Mar. 1941.
5   *IAR*, 1941, i, 307-8; see also L/P&J/8/507, Non-party Conference, 17 Mar. 1941; Hindu, 15 Mar. 1941.

possible administration, but it would also be sincere proof of Britain's genuine intention to part with power.

If the British Government had accepted these proposals and left out the Congress and the Moslem League in the reconstructed centre, what would have been the position of the Government of India? It would not have secured a united front for the prosecution of the war - which was its main objective. In the absence of support from the two major parties, the executive would have been weak in the sense that it would be afraid to face up to the Congress and the League agitation and might have hesitated to take the strong action necessary for the prosecution of the war. The principal argument in favour of the Bombay scheme was that it would mobilize the moderate Indians in support of the war effort. Members of such a government, though not representing anybody but themselves, would have to be persons who would be able to make their acts acceptable to the public without looking for support from any of the main parties. Apart from the difficulty of getting together such a set of men and inducing them to act as a team, what would be their position if their policy was repudiated by the legislature and the general public? If in deference to popular opinion they resigned their offices, they would embarrass the Government of India; and if they clung to office, they would bring no more popular support to the government than the existing Indian members of the Council. In short, the government by accepting the Bombay proposals would be exchanging a strong executive for a weak one; it would not have gained Congress support, and might possibly have further estranged Moslem opinion.

Effective prosecution of the war was the only justification for a reconstruction of the Executive Council. For that the government required maximum efficiency in the executive. At the same time it was necessary that the executive should have popular support. In other words, for securing efficiency and stability it was necessary to have official elements in the executive; and in order to get popular support it was essential to have a representative element. This was the basis of the August declaration. On the other hand reconstruction along the lines of the Bombay proposal would completely eliminate the official elements and replace them by party leaders who would be responsible neither to the legislature nor, in any real sense, to the Viceroy; and if the cabinet resigned, the position of the Viceroy would become difficult. The presence of an official element would prevent the complete break-down of the executive and would enable the Viceroy to carry on the administration in any eventuality. The difference between the August offer and the Bombay scheme, in essence, was that under the former the existing government with the cooperation of the parties would run the war; whereas under the latter, the party leaders would run the war. Put in that way the objection to the reconstruction of the central executive along the Bombay lines is obvious. Both Linlithgow and Amery rejected the proposals because the scheme was not a modification of the existing government but its supersession. Such a change was out of the question given the urgencies of the war.[1]

In June 1941, after waiting for nearly eleven months since the August offer, and in view of the refusal of the Congress to cooperate, Linlithgow felt that the time had come to go ahead with the expansion of the Executive Council 'with those who are prepared to cooperate and work with us'. Simultaneously the creation of the National Defence Council was announced.[2]

In the expanded Executive Council there were eight Indian and four British members. The British members held the important portfolios of defence, finance, home and communications. Nevertheless there was an important constitutional advance. For the first time the Executive Council had a non-official Indian majority. Amery described the change in the constitution of the Council as a 'change in the spirit, if not in the letter of the constitution'.[3] But the Congress contemptuously dismissed this change as a mere facade, the adding to government of a few 'yes men' under the thumb of the Viceroy, and dictated to in every detail by a 'meddlesome' Secretary of State in Whitehall.[4] Facts, however, pointed in another direction. Linlithgow worked in close harmony with his Indian colleagues.[5] What was more, the views of the Government of India were not once overridden from Whitehall. Whatever may have been the internal structure of the Indian Government, or its theoretical position *vis-à-vis* the government and Parliament in Britain, its relation to the British Government was in

1 *Parliamentary Debates,* House of Commons, vol. 371, cols. 47-60, 22 Apr. 1941; Mss. Eur. F.125/10/13, Linlithgow to Amery, 29 Mar. 1941. IOL.

2 War Cabinet Conclusion 58(41)6, Cab. 65/6 dated 9 June 1941. PRO. For a list of the names of the members and their portfolios see Mss Eur. F.125/21/372-4, Linlithgow to Amery, 12 July 1941. An official summary of the political situation in India may be found in 117/A/17, 'Review of all-India Constitutional Development since the outbreak of the War', (n.d.), IOR; see also Mss. Eur. F.125/19/27, telegram from Linlithgow to Amery, 1 July 1941, IOL.

3 *Parliamentary Debates,* House of Commons, vol. 373, cols. 1680-90, 1 Aug. 1941.

4 L.S. Amery, 'Indian Constitutional Development: The War Years', *Asian Review* (Oct. 1953), p. 257.

5 Two members of the Executive Council, Sir Firoz Khan Noon and Sir J.P. Srivastava, have testified that they were not once overruled by the Viceroy. See *Statesman,* 26 Aug. 1942 and *Council of State Debates,* ii, no. 3, 149.

practice substantially the same as that of one of the self-governing dominions. The duties of the Secretary of State were to act as the agent and representative of India's views and interests in the Cabinet, and as liaison officer between the two governments. There was no question of interfering with the decisions of the Viceroy and his Council on behalf of any purely British interest.

Despite non-cooperation by the Congress, India made a substantial contribution to the Allied war effort. Following the entrance of Italy into the war, the Mediterranean was closed to British shipping. As a result war production had to be stimulated east of Suez so that North Africa together with other parts of the Empire ringed around the Indian Ocean could be made self-sufficient. It was largely due to Linlithgow's initiative that the Eastern Groups Conference met at Delhi in October 1940. Delegates arrived from New Zealand, South Africa, Burma, Ceylon, Southern Rhodesia, East Africa, Hong Kong, Malaya and Palestine. As a result the Eastern Group Supply Council was established to coordinate supply and plan production in the vast area represented by these countries.[1] The South East Asia Command was based in Delhi before it moved to Ceylon. India made considerable progress in terms of war production. The supply of war materials stimulated the Indian industries. She was producing all her small-arms ammunition, field guns and machine guns. The strength of the Indian army was increased from 175,000 to over two millions. Both the navy and the air force were built up into efficient modern units, and a Women's Auxiliary Force was created. The Indian army had a distinguished fighting record: it shared in the defeat of the Italians in North Africa, and later took part in the campaigns in Iraq, Syria and Persia, as well as in Southeast Asia.[2]

The expansion of the Executive Council and the creation of the National Defence Council did not, however, ease the political situation. The hope of ending the impasse remained as remote as ever. Linlithgow and Gandhi met many times to bridge the gulf between the British and the Congress points of view. These 'free and frank' discussions always ended in cordial handshakes but without resolving the problem.

But by early summer there was a progressive decline in the number of new entrants into the *satyagraha* campaign and it rapidly became moribund. Few of the released *satyagrahis* were willing to undergo re-arrest. In Madras, out of 2,093 *satyagrahis* who were freed, only 59

1 Glendevon, *The Viceroy at Bay,* pp. 191-3; Wallbank, *India in the New Era,* p. 150.

2 Percival Spear, *A History of India* (Harmonssworth, reprint, 1970), ii, 214-7.

repeated their offence. In Orissa, of the 16 members of legislative assembly released, only two went back to prison. According to government figures, on 15 June the total number of convictions numbered 21,018; four months later this figure had advanced only to 22,182.[1]

Politically India seemed to be in the doldrums. Yet events were moving. The minority parties were still active. The Moslem ministries which were still in power were cooperating in the war effort. The Congress leaders could not ignore the growing influence of the Moslem League. Suggestions began to be heard that the *satyagraha* campaign be called off. Congress policy had left the political field to 'every kind of reactionary forces'.[2] Towards the end of August, with the release of some of the Congress leaders who had served their sentences, more protests were raised against Gandhi's handling of the campaign. Satyamurti urged the recapture of political power by the Congress in order to regain the initiative which it had relinquished by resigning from office.

The mildness of the campaign was due to Gandhi's desire not to embarrass the British during the war. Nevertheless, the imprisonment of a large number of persons, who were not criminals, was a constant source of embarrassment to the government. When Raghavendra Rao and Nalini Sarkar, members of the Executive Council, urged Linlithgow to release the *satyagrahis,* he found it difficult to refuse as this might have precipitated their resignation. He therefore referred the matter to Amery who was also under pressure from the American press to review the policy towards the detainees.[3] By releasing the *satyagrahis* the government would not only display clemency, but in view of the failure of the campaign, and as both the Hindu and Moslem members of the Council were unanimous in their support of release, it would also enhance the position of the Council. On 3 December, the government released all the *satyagrahis.*[4]

Shortly after the release of the Congress leaders, the Congress Working Committee met at Bardoli to chart its next course. Most of the time was spent in deliberating the exact meaning of the resolution passed in September 1940 which had authorized Gandhi to launch the civil disobedience campaign.[5] Gandhi wrote to Azad

1 *Quarterly Survey,* no. 17.
2 *Hindu,* 15 Apr. 1941.
3 Mss. Eur. F.125/21/581, telegram from Amery to Linlithgow, 9 Nov. 1941. IOL.
4 Mss. Eur. F.125/21/752, telegram from Linlithgow to Amery, 2 Dec. 1941. IOL.
5 See above pp. 160-1.

explaining that in the course of the Working Committee's discussion he had discovered that he had misinterpreted the September resolution: he had understood that Congress would refuse participation in the war on the grounds of non-violence, but he now found that the resolution contemplated association with the war effort as a price for a guarantee of India's independence. He therefore asked to be released from the responsibility of conducting the civil disobedience campaign.[1] The Congress Working Committee granted his wish. In another resolution, the Congress refused to cooperate in the war effort unless the government conceded its demands. 'A subject India cannot offer voluntary or willing help to an arrogant imperialism which is indistinguishable from Fascist authoritarianism'.[2]

The resolution showed that there was no change in the attitude of the Congress. The Congress leaders took little cognizance of the war situation. They perhaps failed to understand that both the Government of India and the British Government were now fully preoccupied with the war and were hardly in a position to concentrate their attention on demands which they considered to be essentially peace time questions.

Linlithgow, on the other hand, was extremely legalistic and would not move away from the letter of the constitution. His offer to include representatives of the political parties in the Executive Council was a move in the right direction, but it proved unacceptable to the Congress as Linlithgow, by continuously emphasizing its advisory character, gave the impression that it would be a decorative appendage without any real authority. With a little imagination Linlithgow might have handed over most of the departments to representative Indians, retaining for himself defence and external affairs.[3] Even Nehru at this stage was willing to leave these two subjects for the duration of the war in the hands of the Viceroy. Possibly the War Cabinet might have been reluctant to go so far as to hand over most of the departments to the Indian politicians, but it may be argued that if Linlithgow had taken the initiative and suggested a definite course to end the deadlock, the War Cabinet would have been unlikely to reject it. But Linlithgow was unable to get out of the constitutional morass, and he lost the opportunity of securing the cooperation of the main political parties.

1 *The Times*, 31 Dec. 1941.

2 *IAR*, 1941, ii, 45.

3 Mss. Eur. F.125/134/160, Laithwaite to Clauson, 7 Dec. 1939 (enclosure), 'The Crisis in India' by Guy Wint. IOL.

6
THE CRIPPS MISSION:
STILL NO WAY OUT OF THE IMPASSE

During the autumn of 1941 the Allied prospects appeared much brighter than the year before. The Axis threat to Britain had been thwarted; imperial communications in North Africa had been successfully defended against Fascist attack; and, most important, Britain was no longer fighting alone. The Soviet Union, erstwhile ally of Germany, had joined the Allied Powers.

During the last month of 1941, however, the prospect changed. The rapid conquests by Japan reversed the balance of power in the Pacific and in southeast Asia. On 7 December, 1941 the Japanese attacked Pearl Harbour, Hong Kong and Malaya. The following day the United States and Britain declared war against Japan, but a catastrophic blow was dealt to the defence of Malaya and Singapore when the British battleships *Prince of Wales* and *Repulse* were sunk off the coast of Malaya. The end came in the middle of February 1942 with the surrender of Singapore. The tide of Japanese conquest now lapped over into Burma.[1]

By May 1942 Burma was in Japanese hands. Valuable oil fields had to be destroyed, and the Burma road to China had been cut. Burma could now be used as a shield along the west to protect the new Japanese empire in southeast Asia. Burma was also a wedge, for its conquest had isolated China and made it less defensible against Japanese aggression. Most important, Burma could be a spring board for Japanese union with German forces in Iran.

India in March 1942 thus appeared to be the focus of a giant pincer movement by the armed forces of Germany and Japan.[2] If the Axis could succeed in closing the pincer, they would control a wide belt stretching from the Pacific Ocean to the Mediterranean and the Atlantic.

---

1 B. H. Liddell Hart, *History of the Second World War* (London, reprint, 1973), ch. 17, pp. 212-38.

2 It is now known that the Axis Powers never agreed to concentrate on a drive towards a link up. The conquest of Burma completed Japanese pre-war planning. For months the Japanese had contemplated whether to advance to the West or to expand further into the Central Pacific. On 15 May, the Japanese informed the Germans that their next offensive would be against Midway and Hawaii. The Japanese Fifteenth Army was, however, ordered to stabilize the position in Burma and while it might carry out air raids, no specific operations into China or India were authorized. The British and Americans were perhaps unaware of these decisions. See Garry Hess, *America Encounters India, 1941-47* (Baltimore, 1971), p. 61.

The only contact between the United States and mainland Europe and Asia would then be via the Arctic route to Soviet Russia.

The need for India's cooperation in the war was imperative. Apart from 'preserving lines of air and sea communications to Australia, [the Allies] had to hold the Indian bastion at all costs'.[1] In a few weeks' time the war status of India had been changed from that of a somewhat unwilling ally of Britain, remote from the enemy, to one that was on the front line directly in the path of the Japanese. India's strategic importance was summed up by Linlithgow when he wrote on the day after the fall of Singapore:

> I am carrying here, almost single-handed, an immense responsibility. Indeed, I do not think I exaggerate to affirm that the key to success in this war is very largely in my hands.[2]

In those critical months of early 1942, Linlithgow saw himself as the Churchill of the East, standing at the head of the Indian empire, the sole obstacle preventing a juncture of the Japanese and the German forces in India or the Middle East.

Indeed, the importance of India to the Allied war effort was also recognized by leaders in China and the USA. After the outbreak of the Japanese war they became increasingly concerned with the political situation in India which might hinder the war efforts of the Allies. Chiang Kai-shek, the President of the Chinese Republic, was particularly perturbed as China's sea route was blocked by the Japanese. India as the main base of supply was therefore of crucial importance to China's defence. Chiang was afraid that political unrest in India might encourage Japan to invade India, in which case China would be isolated in its fight against the Japanese. In these circumstances Chiang came to India in April and appealed to the people to 'exert themselves to the utmost in the cause of freedom for all mankind', for only in a free world could the Chinese and Indian people obtain their freedom.[3] At the same time he publicly urged Britain to concede real political power to the Indians 'as speedily as possible'.[4]

On his return to China, Chiang instructed his ambassadors in London and Washington to convey to Churchill and Roosevelt his reactions after the visit to India.

1 Dwight D. Eisenhower, *Crusade in Europe*, p. 28, cited in Tara Chand, *History of the Freedom Movement in India* (Delhi, 1961-72), iv, p. 339, see also Mss Eur. F. 125/130, Halifax to Linlithgow 3, 22 June 1942. IOL.

2 Mss. Eur. F.125/22, telegram from Linlithgow to Amery, 16 Feb. 1942. IOL.

3 *IAR*, 1942, ii, 121.

4 *Ibid.* pp. 121-2; See also L/P&J/12/2315, Linlithgow to Amery, 23 Feb. 1942. IOR.

I feel strongly that if the Indian political problem is not immediately solved, the danger will be daily increasing. . . . If the Japanese should know of the real situation and attack India, they would be virtually unopposed.[1]

His message to Roosevelt said: 'If the British Government does not fundamentally change their policy towards India, it would be like presenting India to the enemy'.[2]

Chiang's forebodings seem to have left Churchill cold. But pressure was also building up in the United States State Department. The US Foreign Relations Committee was concerned with the situation in India and there was 'a serious under-current of anti-British feeling'. The man-power of China and India as sources of military strength were of vital importance to the Allied war effort. It was argued that the Indians would hardly wish to fight just in order to prolong Britain's mastery over them. 'The only way to get the people of India to fight was to get them to fight for India'.[3] Members argued that the USA had done much for Britain through Lend-Lease and that she should demand that India be given the status of a dominion.[4]

The discussions in the Foreign Relations Committee seem to have impressed President Roosevelt. Roosevelt, who had previously refused to comment on the Indian problem, now stated that the Atlantic Charter applied to the whole world, including the people of Asia living under European domination.[5] This was the first public statement by the American President on the Indian problem. It was particularly significant because Churchill had earlier denied that the Atlantic Charter applied to India.[6] Roosevelt had hesitated to send a direct message to the British Government, but he could not keep quiet altogether because 'of the great interest to us from the point of view of the war'. He therefore asked his Ambassador in London to let him have 'a slant on what the Prime Minister thinks about the new relationship between Britain and India'.[7]

1 *Foreign Relations of the United States of America* (Washington D.C., 1959), 1942, i, p. 605-6, telegram from Chiang Kai-shek to Dr. T. V. Soong, 24 Feb. 1942 (henceforth *For. Rel.)*

2 *Ibid.*

3 *For. Rel.,* 1942, i, 606-7, Memorandum by the Asst. Secy of State (Long), 25 Feb. 1942.

4 *Ibid.*

5 W. H. McNeill, *America, Britain and Russia, Their Cooperation and Conflict, 1941-6* (London, 1953) p. 41.

6 *Parliamentary Debates,* House of Commons, vol. 374, cols. 68-69, 8 Sept. 1941.

7 *For. Rel.,* 1942, i, 604, telegram from Secretary of State to the Ambassador in the UK 25 Feb. 1942.

The American Embassy in London informed Roosevelt that Churchill was anxious to keep him posted of the British Government's plans
in regard to India. While expressing a desire to produce a solution to
the Indian problem, Churchill argued that the Congress was very
unpopular with the Moslems who, he claimed, constituted the majority
of the Indian army, for which reason he was afraid of taking any steps
which might alienate them. Churchill passed on the following points
'for the President's information':

1. Approximately seventy-five per cent of the Indian troops and
volunteers were Moslems.

2. The fighting people of India were from the northern provinces
and largely antagonistic to the Congress. The huge population of the
low-lying centre and south were not vigorous and were incapable of
fighting.

3. There was ample man power in India willing to fight. The problem concerned training and equipment.[1]

The facts of army composition, however, as given by Major
General Rob MacGregor McDonald Lockhart, military adviser to the
Secretary of State for India, revealed a different picture. He stated:

> The latest available figures for the class composition of the Indian
> army are for 1 January 1941. These show that out of a total of
> 418,000 Indian Army personnel at that date, 155,000 (approxi-
> mately 37%) were Mohammedans and 263,000 were Hindus and
> other religions (including 51,000 Sikhs).[2]

Linlithgow himself supplied the following estimate of the proportion
of the components of the Army for the year 1942:[3]

Hindus:	41 per cent
Moslems:	35 per cent
Sikhs:	10 per cent
Gurkhas:	8½ per cent
Others:	5½ per cent.

Roosevelt, however, accepted Churchill's figures without verification
and carefully avoided any reference to India which would offend
British sentiments.[4]

In India, too, the new threat from the Japanese had already dawned

---

1 *For. Rel.*, 1942, i, 608, telegram from the Charge in the UK to the Secretary
of State, 28 Feb. 1942.

2 L/PO/6/106b, Note by Major General Lockhart, The Indian Army in Relation
to Constitutional Policy, 25 Feb. 1942. IOL.

3 Mss. Eur. F.125/22, Linlithgow to Amery, 6 Mar. 1942. IOL.

4 Robert Sherwood, *Roosevelt and Hopkins* (New York, 1952), pp. 211-2.

on the Indian leaders. On 2 January 1942, Sapru with several other leaders had cabled to Churchill their suggestions for ending the constitutional deadlock.[1] Admitting that 'detailed discussion of the question of the permanent constitution may well wait until after the victory is achieved', they appealed for some immediate 'bold stroke of far sighted statesmanship . . . to enlist India's whole hearted active cooperation in intensifying the war effort'. This, they urged, should be in the nature of a declaration: 'India is no longer to be treated as a dependency to be ruled from Whitehall', and henceforth her constitutional position and power should be identical with those of the other units of the British Commonwealth.[2]

At the same time in Britain the Labour members of the War Cabinet were becoming increasingly concerned over the continued constitutional impasse in India.[3] On 19 December 1941, at a meeting of the War Cabinet, Ernest Bevin, Minister of Labour and National Service, questioned whether British policy was 'calculated to get the fullest war effort from India' and proposed an early discussion of the position.[4] Churchill's previous history made him, of course, the deafest in his response to these proposals. He warned his colleagues 'of the danger of raising constitutional issues, still more of making constitutional changes, in India at a moment when the enemy is upon the frontier'.[5] The Labour members, Bevin and Attlee, argued that the critical position in India might give rise to a demand for a discussion in Parliament at short notice. Thus the dual pressure of the Labour Party and the Americans ensured that a fresh attempt would be launched to bring the Indian parties together and into full cooperation with the war effort. While Roosevelt tackled Churchill, the Labour Ministers prepared for battle in the War Cabinet.[6]

Linlithgow was consulted. His advice was to pay no heed to 'left wing pressure and pressure from academic theorists or sentimentalists, reflected in a paper so important as *The Times*'.[7] Linlithgow believed that in their existing state of social and political organization a *levée*

1 *The Times*, 5 Jan. 1942.

2 For a full text of the telegram see Mss. Eur. F.125/124, Sir Tej Bahadur Sapru to Laithwaite, 2 Jan. 1942. IOL.

3 H. V. Hodson, *The Great Divide* (London, 1969), p. 91.

4 War Cabinet W. M. (41) 131st conclusions, Minute 4, 19 Dec. 1941, PRO.

5 L/PO/6/106a, telegram from Churchill to Amery, 7 Jan, 1942. IOR.

6 B. Shiva Rao, 'The Cripps Mission', in *Modern Asian Studies*, vol. 5, no. 3 (July 1941), pp. 274-5; V. B. Kulkarni, *India and Pakistan*, (Bombay, 1973), p. 350.

7 Mss. Eur. F.125/22/19, Linlithgow to Amery, 21 Jan. 1942. IOL.

en masse of the Indian peoples was out of the question and that Indian political leaders were powerless to call one forth, whether directed against the British Government or against the Japanese invader. Only the Government was capable of meeting the military crisis; moreover, the surviving strength and prestige of the *Raj* was perfectly equal to the task of expanding the Indian army on the requisite scale. Political concessions in such circumstances, he thought, were gratuitous and dangerous, and would imperil both the present and the future.[1] There was no possibility of giving satisfaction to the Congress leaders who, in his opinion, were 'entirely ruthless politicians'. Any concessions to the Congress would alienate the Princes and the League. They would not enhance the war effort nor put a united India behind the British. 'India is hopelessly, and I suspect irremediably, split by racial and religious divisions which we cannot bridge, and which become more and more acute as any real transfer of power by us draws nearer'. And then, in language which Attlee was to describe as 'crude imperialism' and 'an astonishing statement to be made by a Viceroy',[2] Linlithgow put the substance of his political belief:

> India and Burma have no natural association with the Empire, from which they are alien by race, history and religion, and for which as such neither of them have any natural affection, and both are in the Empire because they are conquered countries which had been brought there by force, kept there by our controls, and which hitherto it has suited to remain under our protection. I suspect that the moment we lose the war or take a bad knock, their leaders would be much more concerned to make terms with the victor at our expense than to fight for the ideals to which so much lip service is given.[3]

Linlithgow therefore concluded that, since India was so vital to the success of the Allied arms, he would rather face such troubles as might arise from a continuation of the status quo than those that might arise as 'a result of making concessions which are ill advised and dangerous and on which we might have to go back for reasons of imperial security at a later stage in the war'. In order to assuage popular feeling in Britain and in Parliament, the Viceroy's advice was to 'harp' on the Indian differences: to insist that in no circumstances would HMG go back on its pledges to the Moslems; to bring out the incompatibility of the League's demands with those of the Congress.[4]

Attlee was disturbed by Linlithgow's suggestion for dealing with the

1 *Ibid.*

2 See below p. 179.

3 Mss. Eur. F.125/22/19 telegram from Linlithgow to Amery, 21 Jan. 1942. IOL.

4 *Ibid.,*

Indian problem. He made no secret of his disappointment. 'I must confess', he wrote to Amery, 'that the general effect of the despatch does not increase my confidence in the Viceroy's judgement'. Attlee suggested sending someone with a 'mission to bring the political leaders together'. He warned that there was a 'lot of opinion here which we cannot ignore which is not satisfied that there is nothing to be done, but sit tight on the declaration of August 1940'.[1] Referring to the Viceroy's telegram in which he said India was being 'kept there by our controls', Attlee commented: 'If it were true it would form the greatest possible condemnation of our rule in India and would amply justify the action of every extremist in India'. He called for a renewal of effort to get the leaders of Indian political parties to unite and was convinced that Linlithgow was unfit for the job. The task should either be entrusted to some person of high standing already in India or sent from Britain with wide powers to negotiate a settlement in India; or, alternatively, that some Indian leaders be brought to Britain to discuss a settlement. He concluded: 'Lord Durham saved Canada to the British Empire. We need a man to do in India what Durham did in Canada'.[2]

It was a powerful memorandum which could not be ignored by Churchill, specially since it was put forward by an influential member of his Cabinet.[3] Attlee's hand had been strengthened by the inclusion of Cripps in the ministry as Lord Privy Seal and Leader of the House of Commons, and by his own appointment as Deputy Prime Minister.

Churchill, who had previously refused even to discuss the Indian question, now suddenly drew up a policy statement which he would broadcast in the form of an appeal to the Indian people:[4] India, he proposed to say, was in grave danger and there was no time to make changes in the constitution. The Indians should cooperate wholeheartedly to save India from invasion and to lay down the foundations for a new future. The basis of that future would be India's complete freedom to control her own destiny. For this purpose he invited the Indian leaders to come together in a representative Defence Council.

1 L/PO/6/106a, Attlee to Amery, 24 Jan. 1942. IOR.

2 L/PO/6/106a, War Cabinet Paper W.P. (42), Memorandum by Attlee, 2 Feb. 1942. IOL. Shortly afterwards, Sir Percy Harris, the Liberal Whip, spoke in the House of Commons in almost identical terms. He said, 'We solved the problem in Canada by the discovery of Lord Durham. Can we not find another Lord Durham and send him to India with full powers to try with good will to solve the urgent and vital problem of India'. Cited in Tahmankar, *Sardar Patel*, p. 171.

3 Paul Addison, *The Road to 1945; British Politics and the Second World War* (London, 1975), pp. 200-5.

4 L/PO/6/106b, telegram from Amery to Linlithgow, 11 Feb. 1942; L/P&J/ 10/2, Amery to Linlithgow, 13 Feb. 1942. IOR.

The main duty of the Council during the war would be to serve India by consultation with the government on the progress of the war and to help in the recruitment of men, the production of munitions, the organization of air raid precautions and other aspects of the war effort. The Council would nominate for inclusion in the Viceroy's Council representatives who would attend the meetings of the British War Cabinet and the Pacific War Council. Similarly, at the end of the war, it would nominate Indian representatives to the Peace Conference. After the war, the Council would work as the constituent assembly to frame India's future constitution. The British Government would accept any constitution agreed upon by the Council.[1]

Churchill's proposed statement, it may be pointed out, had left the executive and legislative position untouched. It proposed a popularly elected Defence Council with representation on the War Cabinet in London, the Pacific Council and the Peace Conference, while it purported to fulfil the British Government's pledge of bringing Indian parties together on the constitutional issue by offering to accept this Council as the future constituent body. Such a plan might have provided an instrument for the eventual solution of the constitutional problem on lines which the Congress could not denounce as undemocratic and which the British government could put before the Moslems and the Princes as being in keeping with its declaration.

Linlithgow raised several objections to Churchill's scheme. He pointed out that the proposed Council would cause resentment in the existing National Defence Council. The new body would not be content to sit occasionally, but would insist upon a continuity session which would stamp it as a parallel executive body. Secondly, the existing Legislature would be by-passed, and so far as conducting the war or planning the postwar world was concerned, it would have to be content with ratifying of the decisions of an extra-constitutional body. Thirdly, communal rivalries inseparable from the constitutional problem would be imported into the conduct of the war. Summing up the defects of Churchill's proposal, Linlithgow said that it 'precipitates the whole constitutional controversy, which is so largely communal and on a present view irreconcilable, into the conduct of war and day to day government'.[2]

Linlithgow's criticism of the draft statement showed that in some ways he had a better grasp of the situation than his superiors in White-

---

1   L/PO/1066, telegrams from Amery to Linlithgow, 11 Feb. and 13 Feb. 1942. IOR.

2   Mss. Eur. F.125/22, telegram from Linlithgow to Amery, 13 Feb 1942. IOL.

hall. In an atmosphere charged with communal tension, it was hardly likely that the main political parties would accept the offer, and Linlithgow had some justification for claiming that the imminence of any far reaching change in the governmental structure was likely to inject communal venom into the army which had so far remained free from that malaise. Yet his implicit suggestion that the Government should wait till the time was more opportune also revealed his dislike for taking an initiative. Even since the outbreak of the war he had been advocating a policy of 'lying back', with the result that when he had made the 'August offer' it was too late and the political parties had raised their price for cooperation. He was going to commit the same mistake again in 1942. There was no certainty that Churchill's scheme would be accepted, but in order to escape from the impasse it might have been worth taking a risk.

On 25 February Linlithgow sent an alternative 'constructive' suggestion: at the outset the British Government would make it clear that it had no intention of impeding India's freedom in order to preserve British interests. The government would not insist on provisions to safeguard British concerns in the postwar constitution of India: these would be the subject of diplomatic negotiations. Second, His Majesty's Government would ensure that full power was transferred to a government under which the interests of the different communities were protected. Third, in the middle of a war it was not possible to make profound changes in the government. The leaders of all the parties would be called to take up responsibility at the centre and in the provinces. Because of the war the official members of the Executive Council could not be dropped immediately, but the Viceroy would be prepared to discuss the matter with his prospective colleagues. The position of the C-in-C would remain unimpaired but a non-official member would be associated with the coordination of defence. Fourth, the British government desired to see the establishment of an autonomous government in India as soon as possible after the war, and to recognize without delay the *de facto* status of India under a national government. During the interim period the control of the India Office over Indian affairs would be exercised with an increasingly lighter hand, and its relations with the British Government would become progressively more diplomatic and less departmental in character. Finally, the British government would set up an autonomous government in India immediately after the war, and would undertake to accept in advance any constitution framed as contemplated in the declaration.[1]

The most obvious change in Linlithgow's draft from Churchill's

1   Mss. Eur. F.125/22, telegram from Linlithgow to Amery, 25 Feb. 1942.

was that it eliminated the combination in the same body of the postwar function of constitution-making and the wartime functions of an extra-constitutional body of political representatives who would inevitably press for more power and responsibility. Linlithgow also sought to retain the official members of his Executive Council. This was necessary from a purely practical point of view. The Viceroy already had enormous responsibilities under the constitution as Governor General and the Crown Representative. The outbreak of hostilities in the Far East presented Linlithgow with the additional problems of defence. Now Churchill proposed that he should cooperate with a Council of active and possibly obstructive politicians. It was a triple burden, difficult if not impossible for one man to shoulder without support — a point which the War Cabinet had overlooked.

The fall of Singapore on 15 February compelled Churchill to put off the broadcast.[1] In view of Linlithgow's objections, the proposal for setting up an advisory body which would also serve as a future 'constituent assembly' was abandoned.[2] It was now decided to make a declaration which would both outline the procedure for arriving at the new constitution and India's future status, and invite Indian leaders to join the Executive Council. An India Committee of the War Cabinet was set up to prepare the statement.[3] Attlee was the chairman, and its members included Churchill, Amery, Cripps, Anderson, Simon and Grigg.[4] Churchill was so occupied with the war that he never found time to attend. Nor was he interested.[5] 'Do let us have a proper talk', Amery complained to Churchill; in the whole of this business I have not had ten minutes alone with you'.[6] The various stages through which the draft declaration went make fascinating reading. The Viceroy

1 Mss. Eur. F.125/22, telegram from Amery to Linlithgow, 21 Feb. 1942.

2 Mss. Eur. F.125/11, Amery to Linlithgow, 21 Feb. 1942. IOL. For details of Linlithgow's objections see Mss. Eur. F.125/22, Linlithgow to Amery, 8 March 1942, IOL. The governors of Bombay and Madras were also critical of the proposals. See Mss. Eur. F. 125/22, Linlithgow to Amery, 21 Feb. 1942. IOL.

3 L/PO/6/106b, telegram from Amery to Linlithgow, 28 Feb. 1942. IOR.

4 All the members of this committee were well versed in the problems of India. Attlee, who presided, and Simon had both been members of the 'Simon' Commission in 1930. Cripps had direct personal knowledge of India and had close relations with the Congress leaders. Anderson had been for five years the governor of Bengal. Grigg had been the finance member of the Viceroy's council under both Willingdon and Linlithgow.

5 Churchill, however, gives a different reason for not attending the meetings of the India Committee. He claims that 'the views of the Committee were so much in accordance with my own convictions that I never found occasion to do so'. Churchill, *The Hinge of Fate,* p. 178.

6 L/PO/6/106b, Amery to Churchill, 5 March 1942. IOR.

remained opposed to any specific declaration of independence and wished to commit the British Government only to a vague assurance that it would accept a scheme which was acceptable to the people of India as a whole.

The India Committee drew up another draft declaration which Sir Stafford Cripps carried with him to India. The main features of the declaration were as follows:[1]

(a) Immediately upon cessation of hostilities, steps shall be taken to set up in India, in the manner described hereafter, an elected body charged with the task of framing a new constitution for India.

(b) Provision shall be made, as set out below, for the participation of Indian States in the constitution-making body.

(c) His Majesty's Government undertake to accept and implement forthwith the constitution so framed subject only to:

(i) the right of any Province of British India that is not prepared to accept the new constitution to retain its present constitutional position, provision being made for its subsequent accession if it so decides. With such non-acceding Provinces, should they so desire, His Majesty's Government will be prepared to agree upon a new constitution giving them the same full status as the Indian Union and arrived at by a procedure analogous to that here laid down.

(ii) the signing of a treaty which shall be negotiated between His Majesty's Government and the constitution-making body. This treaty will cover all necessary matters arising out of the complete transfer of responsibility from British to Indian hands; it will make provision, in accordance with the undertakings given by His Majesty's Government, for the protection of racial and religious minorities, but will not impose any restriction on the power of the Indian Union to decide in future its relationship to other member States of the British Commonwealth. Whether or not an Indian State elects to adhere to the constitution, it will be necessary to negotiate a revision of its treaty arrangements so far as this may be required in the new situation.

(d) The constitution-making body shall be composed as follows, unless the leaders of Indian opinion in the principal communities agree upon some other form before the end of hostilities:

(i) Immediately upon the result being known of the provincial elections which will be necessary at the end of hostilities, the entire membership of the Lower Houses of provincial legislatures shall, as a single electoral college, proceed to the election of the constitution-making body by the system of proportional representation. This new body shall be in

[1] Cmd. 6350 of 1942.

number about one-tenth of the number of the electoral college. Indian States shall be invited to appoint representatives in the same proportion to their total population as in the case of representatives of British India as a whole and with the same powers as British-Indian members.

(e) During the critical period which now faces India and until the new constitution can be framed, His Majesty's Government must inevitably bear the responsibility for, and retain the control and direction of, the defence of India as part of their world war effort; but the task of organising the military, moral and material resources of India must be the responsibility of the Government of India with the cooperation of the peoples of India. His Majesty's Government desire, and invite, the immediate and effective participation of the leaders of the principal sections of the Indian people in the counsels of their country, of the Commonwealth and of the United Nations. Thus they will be enabled to give their active and constructive help to the discharge of a task which is vital and essential for the future freedom of India.

This declaration was in no sense a sudden death-bed repentance involving a complete change of policy. Full Dominion Status, as defined by the 1931 Statute of Westminster, had already been promised as the British goal in India by the Viceroy at the beginning of 1940. The August 1940 offer had not only confirmed this, but declared the willingness of the British Government that it should come into being at the earliest possible moment after the war, provided that the Indians had agreed upon a constitution. But the August offer was vague, and the main object of this new declaration was to remove vague generalities. The full meaning of Dominion Status was set out in the language of the Balfour Declaration and even the possibility of secession was recognized. The treaty provision was inserted in order to emphasize the notion that Britain and India were on a footing of equality.

Furthermore, these proposals had the advantage of leaving intact the pledges in the August offer without making it necessary to repeat them; it contained clear promises without any specific commitments, such as the replacement during the war of an Executive Council of selected and representative individuals by one of purely political complexion. The Viceroy at first thought that this declaration was a great improvement on the previous one but, after consultation with the Commander-in-Chief, he changed his mind and sent in a barrage of fresh criticism. His special target was the 'option clause'.[1]

In London, however, the 'package deal' was no longer negotiable

[1] Mss. Eur. F.125/22, Linlithgow to Amery, 8 March 1942. IOL. see also Hodson, *Great Dividie*, pp. 94-5.

for it represented armistice terms in a ministerial dispute which threatened to split the War Cabinet. Linlithgow could use persuasion with Churchill and Amery: with the India Committee there was no such chance. Linlithgow's criticism and even his threat to resign[1] had little effect on the final proposals. This was a fatal mistake on the part of the India Committee and was bound to affect the progress of the subsequent negotiations. [2] An atmosphere charged with so much uncertainty did not augur well for the success of the mission.

At the last moment Amery pointed out that the Declaration was not self-explanatory. He revived Attlee's idea of sending an emissary to India 'charged with the task of getting the Indians to agree to cooperate now on the basis of a general understanding as to the future'.[3] Churchill also agreed that immediate issue of the declaration without preliminary sounding of Indian political opinion would be unwise. It would probably lead to the rejection of the Declaration by the Congress and would give rise to a division of opinion in Britain.[4] It was necessary to send someone to India to discuss and negotiate in order to find out how far the Indian leaders would accept the proposals, and he therefore accepted Sir Stafford Cripps's offer to undertake the mission. The draft declaration was finally approved by the War Cabinet on 9 March.[5]

Cripps arrived in New Delhi on 22 March. After preliminary talks with the Viceroy and the Executive Council, he proceeded to interview the leaders of the various political parties and communities. Apart from Gandhi, who attended in his personal capacity, the political leaders included Azad and Nehru on behalf of the Congress; Jinnah from the Moslem League; Sir Sikander Hyat Khan and Fazlul Huq; V. D. Savarkar of the Hindu Mahasabha; Dr. B. R. Ambedkar and M.C. Rajah from the Depressed Classes; Sir Tej Bahadur Sapru and M. R. Jayakar of the Indian Liberal Federation; representatives of the Sikhs, Indian Christians, Anglo-Indians and Europeans; and representatives of the Indian States.[6]

---

1 Mss. Eur. F.125/158, telegram from Linlithgow to Amery, 10 March 1942; The Advisers to the Secretary of State for India had also criticised the proposed offer. See L/PO/6/106, note by the Advisers to Secretary of State, 6 March 1942.

2 Hodson, *Great Divide*, pp. 91-2.

3 L/PO/6/106b, Amery to Churchill, 5 March 1942; L/PO/6/106b, telegram from Amery to Linlithgow, 10 March 1942.

4 War Cabinet (W.M.) 31st conclusions, Minute 1, 9 March 1942, PRO. At first Amery had contemplated flying out to India himself, as sending anyone else 'would be a slap in the face to Linlithgow'. L/PO/6/106b, Amery to Churchill, 5 March 1942. IOR.

5 *Ibid.*

6 For details of these interviews see L/P&J/10/4, Note of interviews by Cripps.

The Cripps proposals were favourably received in India. The offer was more specific than the previous vague pledges regarding India's self-government at some future and unspecified date; a definite date for India's transition to full Dominion Status had been set. The offer also provided for a constitution to be drafted by the representatives of the Indian people, rather than by the British Government as in the past. These proposals could not fail to please the Indians. But there were other points in the plan which did not appeal to the various groups. Apart from the possibility of partition which the long term proposals might have involved, they were open to another objection, namely that the rulers and not the people of the states would determine their future.[1] Cripps offered a reasonable defence for both. As regards the objections to the nomination by the states, Cripps claimed that the British had no control over the states. It was, he said, a question of fact which could not be disputed. The 'option clause' was justified on the grounds that it would leave the people free to settle communal differences in any constitutional way they chose, and that no minority group would be compelled to accept a constitution of which it did not approve.[2] No scheme could be successful which did not obtain the approval of the main parties in India. It was also arguable that any scheme which placed the 90 million Moslems under a predominantly 'Hindu' rule would not be acceptable to them,[3] hence the 'option clause'.

The 'option clause' was necessary to prove British *bona fides.* To deal with the charge of deliberate delay, two new features were introduced. First, the British Government indicated its own idea of what might be a suitable constitution-making body and its intention to give effect to it if the Indians could not by then agree on a better alternative. The other feature was that the need for agreement among the various communities need not hold back those parts of India which wished to go ahead. This was put the other way round in the form of non-accession of provinces that feared oppression from the constitution agreed by the majority. In this respect individual provinces were simply put in the same position as that in which the Indian States had always been. It is worth noting that the declaration implicitly waived the stipulation made by the Act of 1935 that the federation could

IOR. For an account of Cripps meeting with the Executive Council see Mss. Eur. F.125/141, note by Mr Pinnel, 23 March 1942; John Glendevon, *The Viceroy at Bay* (London, 1971), pp. 228-9.

1 See L/P&J/8/510, telegram from Linlithgow to Amery, 27 April 1942. IOR.

2 L/P&J/10/4, press conference by Cripps, 29 March 1942. IOR.

3 Mss. Eng. Hist. C.628, Typescript article on the Cripps Mission by Sir Louis Stuart. Bodleian Library, Oxford.

come into effect only if a certain number of states joined.[1] It was not even stipulated that a majority of provinces were required to set up the Dominion of India, though presumably, if a constitution was framed by the majority of the kind of convention suggested, a majority of the provinces would probably adhere. There was nothing mandatory in the option given to the provinces to remain aloof from the union. Many nationalist leaders had all along contested Jinnah's right to speak for Moslem India, and the draft declaration merely provided the means of testing whether their contention was accurate or not. The draft declaration created nothing more than the means whereby India's freedom might be consummated.[2] It did not declare, 'there shall be a Pakistan' it simply provided for the non-accession of unwilling provinces — on conditions which the most ardent supporters of Pakistan regarded as fatal to their chances of success. In any case the object of the provision was not to break up India, but merely to get rid of the charge that constitutional progress was held up by the insistence on prior agreement among the communities; and to compel the Congress to face the necessity of finding a constitutional solution which would persuade the Moslems to come in, instead of asking the British to coerce the Moslems into acceptance of the scheme.

Nor was there anything particularly new about the option clause. The British Government was merely following the precedent set in the case of other Dominions, where unity had come about by the initiative of certain colonies for closer association, others coming in later, and in some instances not at all. In the case of Canada the original Dominion of 1867 consisted only of Ontario, Quebec, New Brunswick and Nova Scotia. Manitoba came in 1870, British Columbia in 1871, and Prince Edward Island in 1873. Newfoundland, which was included in the original constitution, did not join until 1949. In Australia, New South Wales stipulated that it would enter the Australian Commonwealth after a referendum in which it decided itself the size of the majority which was to count for adhesion. In 1898 the referendum gave a clear majority of several thousands, but not enough to meet the arbitrary figure laid down by New South Wales. Adherence was secured by a second referendum in 1899. Western Australia also came in after a referendum in 1900. New Zealand decided to stay out altogether and became a separate Dominion. Similarly, in the case of South Africa, Natal had insisted on having a special plebiscite.[3]

1   1935 Act. Section 5.

2   *Civil and Military Gazette*, 3 April 1942.

3   W. David McIntyre, *Colonies into Commonwealth* (London, revised edition, 1974), chs. 2-4.

The elegance of the Cripps offer lay in balancing the forces for Indian unity against those for division.[1] The 'option clause' did not imply that the British Government did not desire the maintenance of the unity of India.[2] But it believed that this union was more likely to come about if the different elements were free to decide for themselves and to weigh the economic, social and strategic disadvantages of a failure to achieve union. It is significant that the Congress resolution which rejected the proposals itself contained the following passage:

> Nevertheless the Committee cannot think in terms of compelling the people in any territorial unit to remain in an Indian Union against their declared and established will.[3]

In retrospect it appears that the Congress acceptance of the 'option clause' was not such a sudden change of heart as it may at first seem. It was the culmination of a process which had begun immediately after the passage of the 'Pakistan' resolution of March 1940. Gandhi had opposed the two-nation theory as 'vivisection'; nevertheless, he had admitted: 'Muslims must have the right of self-determination that the rest of India has. We are at present a joint family. Any member may claim division'.[4]

The Hindu Mahasabha,[5] the Sikhs,[6] the Scheduled Castes[7] and the National Federation of Liberals rejected the Cripps offer, because they feared that the 'option clause' might involve the partition of India.

The proposals which alienated the other important parties because of the implicit recognition of 'Pakistan' also failed to satisfy the Moslem League — the very organization which they were intended to conciliate, although Jinnah was agreeably surprised at the 'distance it went to meet the Pakistan case'.[8] But he was quick to realize that the secession of the predominantly Moslem provinces would depend upon the League's obtaining a majority in the provincial legislatures, which was a very different thing from a guarantee that 'Pakistan' would be definitely

---

1 R. J. Moore 'The Stop Gap Viceroy', *South Asia Review* (Oct. 1971) p. 57. But it is worth noting that Sir Alfred Watson criticized the 'option clause' as a disastrously wrong step, jeopardizing all chances of making India a nation and containing the seed of most dangerous differences for the future'. 'The Rejected Plan for India', *The Asiatic Review* (July 1942) pp. 246-52.

2 L/PO/423. part iv, 'Note on Declaration of Policy' by Amery (undated). IOR.

3 *Cmd.* 6350, Congress Resolution of 2 April 1942.

4 D. G. Tendulkar, *Mahatma* (Bombay, 1951-4), v, 333-34.

5 *Cmd.* 6350, Resolution of the Hindu Mahasabha, 3 April 1942.

6 *Ibid.* the Sikh All Parties Committee to Cripps, 31 March 1942.

7 Cmd. 6350, p.

8 L/P&J/10/4, note by Cripps of an interview with Jinnah, 25 March 1942.

established. The League therefore rejected the offer because the creation of 'Pakistan' was conceded by 'implication' only, its actual creation being relegated to the 'realm of remote possibility'.[1]

An examination of the actual operation of the 'option clause' will show why Jinnah refused so favourable an offer. The two major provinces where the Moslems were in a majority were the Punjab and Bengal. In the Punjab the legislative assembly was 172 strong, and of this number, 89 were Moslems and 83 non-Moslems. Even if a quarter of the Moslem members favoured union, the secession of the province would be nullified. Should the sixty per cent majority for federation be unavailable, then the issue would be thrown open to a plebiscite of the entire population of the province. In the Punjab the population of about 28 million was divided between Moslems and non-Moslems in a ratio of 4:3 Moslems in the Punjab would have to vote overwhelmingly for a partition to scrape a bare majority. In Bengal the Moslems constituted fifty-five per cent and non-Moslems forty-five per cent of the population, and here again eighty per cent of the Moslems would have to poll in favour of secession to bring about a break from the rest of India. Thus while Cripps's proposal did concede the possibility of a division of India, the actual method of constitution-making made the possibility extremely remote indeed.

The proposal Cripps brought with him in 1942 might well have been acceptable to the Congress in 1939 when the war was remote from India. But in March 1942, with the Japanese on the eastern frontiers, the Congress was more keen on securing immediate power in order to organize popular resistance.[2] Post-war arrangements could wait until the risk of immediate attack had been overcome. Cripps realized that the 'defence clause' of the proposals would be the crucial issue. Churchill had stated that the aim of the plan was to 'rally all forces of Indian life to guard their land from the menace of the invader'.[3] Yet the plan made no definite proposals for Indian responsibility for defence, or for organizing and arming the Indian people, or for the rapid expansion of key Indian war industries.[4] The War Cabinet had concentrated on spelling out the post-war arrangements and gave little attention to the immediate political changes. It believed that until

---

1 Resolution of All India Moslem League, 11 April 1942 Cmd. 6350, pp. 10-20.

2 Hodson, *Great Divide*, p. 104.

3 Churchill's statement in the House of Commons, 11 March 1942, cmd. 6350 3-5.

4 K. L. Mitchell, 'Some Comments on British Plans', *Amerasia* (May 1942) pp. 118-20.

there was agreement upon the future, all discussions of the interim changes would be governed by the desire of the different parties to manoeuvre for position with reference to the future, and they would put forward extreme demands both against each other and against the British government in the hope of pre-empting the situation, or at any rate of not giving it away from their point of view. The War Cabinet had hoped that once there was agreement on the future, Indian leaders would consider participation in the wartime government from a practical point of view. Yet the neglect of the immediate future was to prove to be a fatal omission.[1]

Cripps was convinced that unless the British Government agreed to meet the Congress view on the defence question, there was little prospect of success.[2] In February Linlithgow had written that 'it may well be found possible to associate a non-official member much more closely with the problem of coordination of the defence'.[3] Cripps accordingly proposed, with the concurrence of the Viceroy and the Commander-in-Chief, a modification of the defence clause.[4] To this the Prime Minister agreed.[5] At the same time Cripps informed the Cabinet of the deteriorating situation in India. 'The anti-British feeling is running very strong and our prestige is lower than it has ever been owing to the events in Burma and more particularly in Singapore'.[6] In view of the grave situation, he reported, 'if we cannot persuade Indian leaders to come in now and help us we shall have to resort to suppression which may . . . get out of hand'. He accordingly asked for permission, subject to the agreement of the Viceroy, to designate an Indian to some office connected with defence, without impairing the position of the C-in-C.[7] Amery supported Cripps. He argued that the inclusion of an Indian Defence member working closely with the C-in-C (Wavell) 'might prove an effective supporter for Wavell in dealing with his colleagues'.[8] But Churchill refused to compromise on defence without submitting the issue to the Cabinet.[9] When the Cabinet met, it

1 L/PO/423, Part III, in a memorandum Sir David Monteath had pointed out this 'fatal flaw' in the draft proposals, 6 March 1942. IOR.

2 'Report on Mission to India', a memorandum by Cripps dated 6 July 1942 circulated to the War Cabinet. (Cripps Papers).

3 Mss. Eur. F.125/22, telegram from Linlithgow to Amery, 25 Feb. 1942. IOL.

4 Colin Cooke, *Life of Richard Stafford Cripps* (London, 1957), p. 290.

5 Mss. Eur. F.125/22, telegram from Cripps to Churchill, 29 March 1942.

6 L/PO/43, telegram from Cripps to Churchill, 1 April 1942. IOR.

7 Mss. Eur. F.125/22, telegram Cripps to Churchill, 1 April 1942. IOL.

8 L/PO/423, Secretary of State, minute serial no. P30/42, 2 April 1942. IOR.

9 L/PO/6/106c, telegram from Churchill to Cripps, 2 April 1942. IOR.

approved the discussion with the Congress leaders but was 'disinclined to depart from the published text of the Declaration' and insisted on being informed of any new proposal before committing itself.

Meanwhile in Delhi a rift between Cripps and the Viceroy was beginning to show. On 2 April, the Viceroy telegraphed his fear and asked that he and the Commander-in-Chief be allowed to cable their views separately from Cripps's telegram.[1] The latter's hands were now tied and the way opened for the undermining of his influence. No progress could be made without the concurrence of the Viceregal Lodge.

On the same day (2 April) the Congress had adopted a resolution rejecting the Cripps offer, but agreed not to publish it and instead to proceed with their negotiations on the interim proposals. Despite its opposition to the long term proposals, the Congress had apparently decided to put aside its objections and concentrate on the immediate issues. Thus the discussions centred around clause (e) of the Declaration, with special emphasis on defence. From them it emerged that there would be an Indian defence member, in addition to the British C-in-C who would continue to be the Supreme Commander of the Armed Forces in India. But the point on which the Congress leaders were anxious was to secure effective powers for the Indian Defence Member.

On 3 April when the talks were at an extremely critical stage, there arrived in New Delhi a Colonel Louis Johnson who was to be the 'personal representative of the President of the United States of America'. Although he lacked knowledge of Indian politics, he knew Roosevelt's interest in India and was aware of the President's message to Churchill. With Cripps's permission he took park in the negotiations on the defence formula. On the following day (4 April) he met Cripps and Wavell. The two Englishmen told Johnson that 'the appointment of an Indian Defence Minister would lead to chaos and loss of all army morale', but Cripps himself admitted that the demands of the Congress should not be rejected out of hand.

Cripps reported to the Cabinet that the Congress was split into two groups. The 'Gandhi wing of non-violence' was against the proposals altogether and unwilling to cooperate in the war effort. But this group was in a minority. The remainder, Cripps said, were in favour of participating in the war provided the organization of defence was in the hands of an Indian Member.[2] Cripps did not indicate the source

1 Mss. Eur. F.125/22, telegram from Linlithgow to Amery, 2 April 1942. IOL.
2 Mss. Eur. F.125/22, telegram from Cripps to Churchill, 4 April 1942. IOL.

of his information, but apparently he was voicing what was essentially Nehru's point of view. Cripps believed that if, with a suitable alteration of clause (e), the Congress could be persuaded to accept the proposals, they would then work to maximize the Indian war effort; and he had been assured (probably by Nehru) that there was no question of the Indians making a separate peace with Japan. Cripps warned the War Cabinet that if the Congress did not accept the offer 'the situation will in my view become very difficult and we shall be attempting to carry on the war in at best a neutral atmosphere and at worst a hostile one'.[1]

He felt that it would be a mistake to allow a breakdown to come on the issue of defence alone, and he turned his mind to a search for a compromise that would cover the over-all direction of military operations by the British War Cabinet with the organization of an Indian Defence Ministry put in Indian hands. Therefore he requested the War Cabinet to concede some specific responsibilities to an Indian Minister of Defence. In moving in this direction Cripps had kept himself in close touch with the views of the Viceroy and the Commander-in-Chief. He now put forward three alternatives.

i. To stand firm upon the existing position.

ii. To hand over the Defence Ministry to an Indian, subject to a written convention that the Defence Minister would not in any matter affecting the prosecution of the war act contrary to the policy laid down by His Majesty's Government and communicated through the Commander-in-Chief.

iii. To create a new office for an Indian Minister connected with Defence and to hand over to him any function of the Defence Ministry which the Commander-in-Chief considered could be handed over.

Cripps ruled out the first proposal as it would make failure inevitable. He would personally have preferred the second proposal, but did not recommend this since the Commander-in-Chief was opposed to it. He therefore recommended the third proposal, although he felt there was little chance of its acceptance.

At Delhi the situation was hardening. Linlithgow and Wavell would have nothing to do with Cripps's effort to evolve a new defence formula. At this moment Johnson called on Wavell and explained to him the set-up of the United States defence establishment.[2] Wavell seemed con-

---

1   *Ibid.*

2   The British organization of the War Office differed from the military organization in the USA and many other countries of Europe. The American and Continental arrangement provided that the Minister of War would only be con-

vinced that he had noting to lose by accepting the third proposal suggested by Cripps.[1] Wavell and Johnson then secured the Viceroy's approval.[2]

The War Cabinet agreed to the third alternative, provided detailed arrangements were agreed with the Viceroy and the Comander-in-Chief.[3] On the basis of this reply Cripps informed Azad and Jinnah of the revised defence formula. The proposal was rejected by the Congress, which regarded the subjects listed for transfer of so little importance as to make the position of the Indian Defence Member almost ludicrous.[4]

At this juncture Johnson suggested that the defence formula be put in a modified form: a representative Indian would take over the existing Defence Department but transfer to the War Department (of which the Commander-in-Chief would be in charge) any function that Her Majesty's Government might desire the Commander-in-Chief to retain.[5] The snag in the formula appeared to be that anything which was not specified in the list transferred to the War Member would be automatically taken over by the Indian Defence Member and could not be taken back by the War Member if required. The formula, therefore, required a departmental examination. After a careful scrutiny a formula was evolved which was acceptable to the Viceroy. It provided for the Defence Department to be placed in charge of a representative Indian Member, with the exception of the functions to be exercised by the Commander-in-Chief or War Member. The new Defence Department would take over such functions of the existing Defence Department as were not specifically retained by the War Member.

It was decided that this formula would be taken by Johnson to Nehru as his own suggestion. The advantage would be that if the Congress decided to accept the formula, it would come as a suggestion from the Congress for the approval of the British government; and if the Congress turned it down, the previous formula sent to Azad by Cripps would remain as the only official offer.[6]

cerned with providing men, material, barracks, transport etc., but had no say in matters of military policy, executive command and promotion. All these were under the Commander-in-Chief. This system had the advantage of freeing the Commander-in-Chief from all administrative responsibilities, leaving him with purely executive and policy responsibilities.

1   See above. p. 192.
2   *For. Rel.*, 1942, i, 630, telegram from Johnson to Hull, 9 April 1942.
3   L/PO/6/106c, telegram from Amery to Cripps, 6 April 1942. IOR.
4   *Cmd.* 6350.
5   Mss. Eur. F.125/141, note by Pinnel, 7 April 1942. IOL.
6   Mss. Eur. F.125/11, note by Pinnel, 7 April 1942. IOL.

The new defence proposal was considered by the Congress Working Committee which amended it on the lines of the formula drawn up by Johnson, but it differed materially from the earlier approach to the problem by the British government: instead of reserving defence as the responsibility of the British Government and asking the Indian member to accept certain unimportant functions, the Congress Working Committee's proposal was to consider the National Government responsible for the whole field of administration, including defence, but to reserve to the Commander-in-Chief for the duration of the war certain functions essential for the discharge of his responsibilities and the carrying out of military operations.

In the days that followed, Johnson worked with passionate enthusiasm to keep the negotiations alive. There were many difficult and intricate negotiations and finally on 8 April the 'Cripps-Johnson' formula was finalized:[1]

(a) The Defence Department would be placed in charge of a representative member, but certain functions relating to the conduct of the war would be excercised, until the new constitution came into operation, by the Commander-in-Chief, who would be in control of the War activities of the armed forces in India, and who would be a Member of the Executive Council for that purpose.

(b) A War Department would be constituted under the Commander-in-Chief. This Department would take over such functions as were to be exercised by the Commander-in-Chief.

(c) The Defence Member would be in charge of all other matters relating to the Defence Coordination Department in addition to other important matters closely related to defence.

(d) In the event of any functions failing to be discharged in relation to Defence or any dispute arising as to the allocation of any function, the decision would rest with Her Majesty's Government.

Cripps pressed Churchill to accept the new proposal: 'Without it there is no prospect of success but on this basis there is now considerable chance'. He also assured Churchill that his proposal contained the alterations desired by the Viceroy and the Commander-in-Chief.[2] In spite of this claim, the Viceroy reserved his position in regard to this new formula pending discussion with the Commander-in-Chief. On the other hand, Cripps maintained that he did not regard the new formula as anything alarming, indeed, he claimed that it was based on the Viceroy's own draft formula of 7 April.[3]

Johnson's manoeuvres had produced hopes of a settlement. Church-

1 Mss. Eur. F.125/22, telegram from Linlithgow to Amery, 9 April 1942. IOL.
2 Mss. Eur. F.125/22, telegram from Cripps to Churchill, 10 April 1942. IOL.
3 Mss. Eur. F.125/22, Cripps to War Cabinet, 22 April 1942. IOL, see also L/P&J/8/510, memorandum by Lord Privy Seal, 6 July 1942. IOR.

ill could not reject the defence proposal drawn up by Johnson and Cripps. But at this fateful moment Roosevelt's adviser, Harry Hopkins, arrived in London on 8 April to discuss military plans. The next morning he met Churchill who questioned Johnson's authority to mediate. Hopkins assured Churchill that Johnson had nothing to do with the Cripps Mission and that, indeed, Cripps was probably seeking to use Johnson, and indirectly Roosevelt's name, to work out a settlement.[1] When Hopkins finished, Churchill cabled Cripps and Linlithgow that Johnson was not acting as Roosevelt's representative.[2]

When the Cabinet met to discuss the new defence formula, it was not convinced by Cripps's arguments. They urged a return to an amplified version of the Cabinet's orginal plan. The War Cabinet also demanded an assurance that if an agreement on defence arrangements were reached, the scheme in all other respect would be accepted.[3] Its attitude had hardened.

Linlithgow felt compromised and insulted when he learned that a draft of the proposed formula for an Indian Defence Minister had been 'concocted' by Johnson and shown to Nehru with Cripps's approval. On 8 April, Linlithgow complained to Cripps 'about the manner in which I and the Commander-in-Chief had been passed over'.[4] He then cabled Amery, expressing a 'strong feeling of grievance' and warning that 'the latest Congress manoeuvres might well be designed to drive a wedge between His Majesty's Government and the USA'.[5]

Next day Linlithgow wrote to Cripps advising him to make the constitutional position of the Executive clear at the meeting which Cripps was to have with Azad and Nehru that afternoon.[6] That evening he asked Cripps whether he had done so. Cripps replied that he had talked to the Congress leaders of 'National', not 'Cabinet' Government, and had told them that 'the Viceroy would doubtless do all he could by means of appropriate conventions'. Linlithgow objected.[7] He now repudiated the idea of 'conventions' as impracticable under a written constitution. He endeavoured to secure his position by forcing Cripps

---

1 Sherwood, *Roosevelt and Hopkins,* ii, 92.

2 L/PO/106, telegram from Churchill to Cripps, 9 April 1942. IOR.

3 L/PO/106c, telegram from War Cabinet to Cripps, 9 April 1942, IOR. See also War Cabinet Conclusions 40 (42), 2 April 1942, PRO.

4 Mss. Eur. F.125/141, Note by Linlithgow, 8 April 1942. IOL.

5 Mss. Eur. F.125/22, Linlithgow to Amery, 9 April 1942. IOL.

6 Mss. Eur. F.125/22, Linlithgow to Cripps, 9 April 1942.

7 Mss. Eur. F.125/142, Note by Pinnel, 9 April 1942. IOL.

to withdraw his promise of National Government. This he did by asking the Cabinet for clear instruction on the point:

> I must know with precision what are the instructions of His Majesty's Government to which I am to work . . . Whether the Governor-General must continue to have the right to differ from his colleagues . . . or he must promise that in no circumstances will he refuse to act on their advice.[1]

The Cabinet's reply virtually sealed the fate of the Mission. 'There can be no question of any convention limiting in any way your powers under the existing constitution. . . . If the Congress Leaders have gathered the impression that such a new constitution is possible, this impression should definitely be removed'. As to the defence question, the Cabinet was prepared to accept the Johnson-Cripps formula if accepted by the Viceroy and the Commander-in-Chief.[2]

Linlithgow was taking an excessively literal view of the situation. Cripps had never suggested that the constitutional rights of the Viceroy should be modified. Indeed he denied such a possibility publicly[3] His cable of 4 April had merely referred to 'the new arrangement whereby the Executive Council will approximate to a Cabinet'. When Churchill asked him to explain the point he had promptly cabled his agreement with Linlithgow that there was no question of the Executive overriding the responsibility of the Viceroy to His Majesty's Government.[4] As a negotiator Cripps was seeking a middle position between the letter of an imperial constitution and the spirit of a National Government.

On 10 April, Churchill himself took the chair at the India Committee. He declared that a convention limiting the Viceroy's authority had never been contemplated in the discussions prior to Cripps's departure to India. On the same day Cripps received the crucial telegram from the War Cabinet which dealt the Mission its *coup de grace*. Cripps was asked 'to bring the whole matter back to the Cabinet's plan' with which he had been sent out.[5] By now Cripps was being bombarded from Whitehall with telegrams of disapproval, and, nettled by what appeared his colleagues' distrust, he offered to hand over to someone else.[6] Churchill cabled sympathetically, but firmly, that Cripps's desire to reach a settlement with the Congress had drawn him into a

1 Mss. Eur. F.125/22, telegram from Linlithgow to Amery, 10 April 1942. IOL.
2 L/PO/6/106c, telegram from War Cabinet to Linlithgow, 10 April 1942. IOR.
3 See below p. 199.
4 Mss. Eur. F.125/22, telegram from Cripps to Churchill, 6 April 1942. IOL.
5 L/PO/6/106c, telegram from War Cabinet to Cripps, 9 April 1942. IOL.
6 Mss. Eur. F.125/22, telegram from Cripps to War Cabinet, 10 April 1942.

position away from that approved by the Cabinet. He also made it clear that he did not approve of the negotiations.

> It was certainly agreed between us that there were not to be negotiations but that you were to try to gain acceptance with possible minor variation or elaborations of our great offer which has made so powerful an impression here and throughout the United States.[1]

The Congress Working Committee met to consider the Cripps-Johnson formula on the morning of 9 April. An atmosphere of tense expectation prevailed in Delhi. Rajagopalachari was reported to have said that agreement was certain.[2] Nehru and Azad called on Cripps later in the afternoon. So far as 'defence' was concerned the Congress leaders accepted the revised formula. The conversation then turned to the position of the Executive Council and the Viceroy's powers under the proposed interim government. Cripps informed them that he could not deviate from the draft proposals.[3] It was now clear that Cripps had been sent to India with his hands bound to the declaration. He could not go beyond its terms and was denied the role of a negotiator. Suddenly the perspective of the Congress suffered a radical change.

At this stage it is necessary to pause to examine how far Cripps during the negotiations had foreshadowed the conversion of the Executive Council into a Cabinet. At the very outset Cripps had shown to Linlithgow a list of a new Executive, wholly Indian except for the Commander-in-Chief. 'That's my affair', snapped Linlithgow, claiming that 'the implementation of paragraph (e) [of the proposal] should be done by him as Governor General'.[4] Cripps pointed out that 'the ultimate responsibility lay with the War Cabinet but if it was merely a question of collecting the right personnel in India that was obviously a matter for him [Linlithgow]'.[5]

On 24 March Cripps told the existing Executive Council that the participation of the Indians in the Council would, save defence, 'be welcome to any extent that his Excellency [the Viceroy] desired'.[6] Linlithgow had cabled to check the point with Amery, who replied:

1 L/PO/6/106c, telegram from Churchill to Cripps, 10 April 1942. IOR.

2 B.Shiva Rao, 'India, 1935-47' in C.H.Philips and M.D.Wainwright (eds.) *The Partition of India; Policies and Perspectives 1935-47 (London, 1970)*, pp. 434-5; Humayun Kabir, *Muslim Politics 1906-42*, pp. 56-7; *The Times* 8 and 9 April 1942.

3 For an account of this meeting see Nehru's Press Conference on 12 April. *IAR*, 1942, i, 238-9.

4 Hodson, *Great Divide*, p.98.

5 L/P&J/10/4, Note by Cripps, 23 March 1942. IOR.

6 Mss. Eur. F.125/141, Executive Council meeting, 24 March 1942. IOL.

> War Cabinet are uncommitted on this issue, though it was clear
> from discussions that they would be prepared for positions on
> Executive to be offered to political leaders provided this did not
> embarrass the defence and good government of the war during the
> present critical time.[1]

He could not say that the War Cabinet 'would not be prepared to
reduce or abolish official members'. It is worth noting that on 6 March
the Advisers to the Secretary of State had recommended that 'the
Viceroy's Executive Council should be forthwith Indianized'.[2]

On 25 March Linlithgow drew Cripps's attention to his telegrams of
February and early March in which he had set forth his view that while
he was prepared to invite party leaders to join his Executive he would
not promise the removal of all official members as a 'pre-requisite of a
political truce'.[3] He had in mind the heavy administrative burden that
the Viceroy would incur if he lost the official advice offered in the
Home and Finance Departments. Still, his cable had expressed a desire
'to recognize without delay the *de facto* status of India under a National
Government'.[4] He now said that if Cripps secured the assent of the
Indian parties to the declaration he 'was prepared to take big risks because the situation would call for them. . . if Sir Stafford could do big
things he would not find His Excellency falling short"[5] Linlithgow
imposed two conditions: first, both Congress and the League must
agree to cooperate; secondly Cripps must not 'steal His Excellency's
cheese to bait his own trap'.[6] Cripps accepted the reasonableness of
both of Linlithgow's conditions.

Linlithgow's somewhat magnanimous language gave Cripps confidence in the Viceroy's support concerning the general reconstitution
of the Executive:

> Under the new arrangement whereby the Executive Council will
> *approximate to a cabinet* presumably any question coming within
> the competence of the Government of India . . . will be for decision
> by the Government of India as a whole and not by any particular
> Minister.[7]

It should be noted that Linlithgow did not demur at 'the new arrange-

---

1 L/PO/6/106b, telegram from Amery to Linlithgow, 25 March 1942. IOR.

2 *Ibid.* Note by the Advisers to the Secretary of State. 6 March 1942.

3 Mss. Eur. F.125/22, Linlithgow to Amery, 25 Feb. 1942. IOL.

4 *Ibid.*

5 Mss. Eur. F.125/141, memorandum of a conversation between Linlithgow and
Cripps on 25 March 1942. IOL.

6 *Ibid.*

7 Mss. Eur. F.125/22, telegram from Cripps to Churchill, 4 April 1942. IOL.

ment', but merely observed that such an arrangement would preclude the Moslem League's cooperation unless it was assured of a majority in the Cabinet, or a substantial number of members reinforced by the clear maintenance of the Governor General's control.[1] In short, Linlithgow foreshadowed a League objection to introducing the conventions of a cabinet government but he did not at that stage express any objections of his own. Nor did Churchill's reply to Cripps's cable object to 'the new arrangement'.[2]

As for the manner of Indian participation in the counsels of government, the question does not seem to have been discussed. However, Linlithgow had mentioned cables in which he had expressed a wish 'to recognise without delay the *de facto* status of India under a National Government'. Two days previously Cripps had listened to Shiva Rao's exposition of the term 'National Government':

> . . . even within the framework of the existing consitituion, a great deal could be done to convert in practice the executive council into a cabinet, to enlarge the powers and even the size of the legislature and to make the viceroy the normal constitutional head of the government.[3]

Cripps's mind was 'working on the same lines'. After the meeting of 25 March Cripps assumed that Linlithgow's desire for National Government would carry him in the same direction. On 28 March, at a press conference, he told the whole world:

> 'The object of the scheme is to give the fullest measure of government to the Indian people at the present time consistent with the possibilities of a constitution which cannot be changed until the end of the war. . . . All you can do is to change the conventions of the constitution. You can turn the Executive into a Cabinet'.[4]

Azad understood this to mean that Cripps was holding out the prospect of an Indianized Executive Council functioning as a Cabinet. In his memoirs, Azad claims that Cripps had promised 'categorically that the Executive Council would function exactly like a Cabinet' whose advice would be binding on the Viceroy.[5] However, in his official letter rejecting the draft declaration he was less precise:

> . . . You had referred both privately and in the course of public statements to a National Government and a Cabinet consisting of Ministers. These words have certain significance and we had imagined

1 Mss. Eur. F.125/22, telegram from Linlithgow to Amery, 5 April 1942. IOL.

2 L/PO/6/106c, telegram from Churchill to Cripps, 5 April 1942. IOR.

3 B. Shiva Rao, *India 1935-47*, in Philips and Wainwright (eds.), *Partition of India*, pp. 413-67, see p. 428.

4 L/P&J/10/333, Press conference by Cripps, 29 March 1942. IOR.

5 Azad, *India Wins Freedom*, p. 51.

that *the new government would function with full powers as a Cabinet with the Viceroy acting as a constitutional head.*[1]

Whether Cripps was as categorical in his first interview with Azad as the latter maintained is not clear from the official documents; Cripps makes no mention of such matters in his interview notes.[2] But it appears that there was more than a grain of substance in Azad's grievance over the way in which Cripps appeared to go back on his earlier assurances. H V Hodson has already revealed something of the inside story;[3] and while his analysis of the general triangular relationship between Cripps, Linlithgow and the War Cabinet is correct, his account does not quite give the full picture, nor does he seem to have seen all the telegrams that passed between Cripps and the War Cabinet.

Since 6 April Churchill and Linlithgow appear to have recoiled from their earlier commitments. Churchill told the War Cabinet on 9 April that he had in no way signified to Cripps his assent to the complete Indianization of the Executive Council;[4] yet Amery had told the Viceroy that the War Cabinet would accept complete Indianization of the Executive Council if necessary.[5] As to the convention limiting the Viceroy's power to override it, it was specifically minuted at the War Cabinet meeting on 10 April that 'no such proposal had ever been made, or indeed contemplated, in the discussions before the Lord Privy Seal had left this country';[6] Linlithgow had approvingly used the term 'National Government' in February and early March, and also he and Wavell were party to the memorandum to Azad in which Cripps had used it.[7] Nor had anyone protested when shortly after his arrival in Delhi Cripps had told Hodson: 'You realize that the Cabinet has quite made up its mind that India shall have everything in the way of *de facto* Dominion Status and complete Indianization of the Executive Council'.[8] Finally Churchill denied Cripps the status of a negotiator,[9]

1 Cmd. 6350. Azad to Cripps, 10 April, 1942. Italics mine.

2 L/P&J/10/4, note of interviews by Cripps. IOR. Linlithgow has, however, claimed that 'Cripps had talked very freely of a "National Government" presided over by the Viceroy who would stand in much the same relation to it as the King does at home'. Mss. Eur. F.125/11, Linlithgow to Amery, 14 April 1942. IOL.

3 Hodson, *The Great Divide,* pp. 90-105.

4 L/PO/6/106c, War Cabinet W. M. (42) 45th Conclusions, 9 April 1942; See also Mss. Eur. F.125/23/44a, telegram from Linlithgow to Amery, 7 August 1942. IOL.

5 L/PO/6/106b, telegram from Amery to Linlithgow, 25 March 1942. IOR.

6 L/PO/6/106c, War Cabinet to Linlithgow, 10 April 1942. IOR.

7 See above p.190.

8 Hodson, *The Great Divide,* p. 103; see also Mss. Eur. F.125/14, note by Pinnel, 6 April 1942. IOL.

9 L/PO/6/106c, telegram from Churchill to Cripps, 10 April 1942. IOR.

though his instructions implicitly required him to negotiate some scheme whereby Indian political leaders might be brought into full cooperation with the war effort.

In his most specific written reference to the question Cripps assumed that the Executive Council would *approximate to a Cabinet*.[1] In his cables he had denied any intention to bind the Viceroy to his Council's advice, yet expressed confidence that the Congress would accept the sort of convention that he envisaged. His early conversation with Shiva Rao[2] suggests a conception of government in which the Viceroy would normally act as a constitutional head. But the vital test of Cabinet Government − responsibility to an Indian legislature − did not or could not exist during the war. Ministers would have the weapon of resignation, but, if differences arose over issues like the scorched earth policy or a separate armistice against the wishes of the British Government, the Viceroy would have the power to override the majority view. Despite Azad's claim, it seems unlikely that Cripps spoke of the Viceroy's abdicating his responsibility to His Majesty's Government except for defence.

Though Cripps was never explicit about the intended Cabinet convention, a member of his team, Professor Coupland,[3] referred to the precedent of the ministries in the provinces which had operated not as 'cabinets with full power' but as 'quasi-cabinets'. 'The Governor . . . had acted on the advice of his ministers on all save certain matters on which he retained and occasionally exercised his power to dissent and override'.[4] However, whereas the provincial governors had normally to accept the advice of their Minister, the Viceroy was entitled by the statute to dissent from the majority of his Council over any measure 'whereby the safety, tranquillity, or interest of British India . . . may be in his opinion essentially affected'. Cripps accepted that a convention whereby the Viceroy set such power aside would be in breach of law and he did not contemplate it. Yet, in other cases, the Viceroy might still work his Council as if it were a Cabinet. Since the expansion of the Viceroy's Council in July 1941, Linlithgow had in fact been doing just that.[5] This is not to say that the Viceroy would have worked a reconstituted council without exercising a veto but merely to conclude

1 Mss. Eur. F.125/22, telegram from Cripps to Churchill, 2 April, 1942. IOL.
2 See above p. 199.
3 Sir Reginal Coupland, Beit Professor of Colonial History at Oxford, was in India studying the constitutional problem of India for a report which he wrote on his return to Oxford. He joined Cripps as an Adviser at the request of the India Office.
4 Reginald Coupland, *The Cripps Mission,* (London 1942), pp. 54-55.
5 See chapter 5.

that within the existing constitution Cripps might well have envisaged the Council normally operating as a cabinet.

Coupland confirmed that the conventions that Cripps contemplated could confer the realities of power upon the Indian parties. Furthermore, he claimed, as India and Britain had a common interest in winning the war, the political leaders were unlikely to press advice which was contrary to 'the safety, tranquillity, or interest of British India'.

The working of the 'conventions' as envisaged by Cripps or the possibility of Government-Congress collaboration during the war was, however, made difficult by a distrust of the Congress among a section of the officials.[1] The distrust was made worse by fears of Gandhi's pacifism. In his memoirs Churchill records his naive belief that Nehru alone was in favour of fighting the Japanese and that the rest were pacifists.[2]

It was such attitudes that lay behind the tacit Churchill-Linlithgow hostility to the Cripps Mission. Neither of them trusted the Congress or wanted Congress members in the Executive. After 6 April, Churchill and Linlithgow so hardened their position that Cripps had to inform the Congress leaders on 9 April 'that nothing could be said . . . even vaguely and generally about the conventions that should govern the new government and the Viceroy. This was a matter in the Viceroy's sole discretion and at a later stage it could be discussed directly with the Viceroy'.[3] It is not surprising therefore that Azad and Nehru believed that Cripps had betrayed them. After this Cripps had little choice. There were two options open to him.

Cripps could announce that he had offered Congress a substantial concession which the opposition of Churchill and Linlithgow had forced him to retract. He could justify his negotiations by reference to his instructions, reveal that he had consulted the Viceroy, and argue the practicability of the convention he was contemplating. The effects of such action would have been to redeem his reputation with the Congress and substantiate the Congress imputation of betrayal by the Churchill administration. Alternatively, Cripps could keep the inside story of the mission to himself, present a loyal defence of the British policy and blame the Congress for the failure. The first course of action seemed hazardous particularly at a moment when Britain was engaged in a life and death struggle. Moreover he would be damning

1 Churchill, *The Hinge of Fate*, p. 181.
2 *Ibid.* pp. 187-8.
3 Cmd. 6350, Azad to Cripps, 10 April 1942. See also B. Shiva Rao, 'The Cripps Mission' review article in *Modern Asian Studies*, vol. v, no. 3, (July 1971) p. 276.

his Cabinet Colleagues and precipitating his own and probably other Labour Ministers' resignation. He therefore decided upon the latter course.

Cripps blamed the Congress for the failure[1]. The Congress, he said, had demanded the immediate amendment of the constitution and had asked for a 'National Government' untramelled by the control of the Viceroy or the British Government. He interpreted the second demand as a system of government 'responsible to no legislature or electorate, incapable of being changed and the majority of whom would be in a position to dominate large minorities'.[2] On his return to Britain, Cripps carried his criticism even further, raising the communal issue for the first time.[3] He alleged that the Congress wanted a 'nominated cabinet . . . responsible to no one but itself', which would 'constitute an absolute dictatorship of the majority' over 'all minorities in India'. The problem of how to safeguard the rights of the religious and racial minorities was a real one but it had not been a major issue in the negotiations.[4] Hence Cripps's claim that communal disagreement prevented a settlement is hardly justified.

Although the Congress had demanded the immediate formation of a National Government, they had at no stage demanded that the Congress alone should control the Government. In fact the Congress claimed to be willing to take in members of all communities and groups in the National Government.[5] Moreover, it may be argued that when a Cabinet was formed on an all-party basis, the members of the minority communities could have withdrawn from the Cabinet if they had thought that the interest of their communities were not being safeguarded, and might thus have brought about a dissolution of the Cabinet.[6] How-

1 Professor Benjamin H. Kizer also blamed the Congress for the failure of the Cripps Mission, 'Another View of The Cripps Mission', *Amerasia* (July 1942), pp. 233-5.

2 L/P&J/8/510, broadcast by Cripps, 11 April 1942. IOL.

3 *Parliamentary Debates,* House of Commons, Vols. 379, cols. 826-43, 28 April 1942.

4 R. P. Dutt, *A Guide to the Problem of India,* (London, 1942), p. 180. It is quite possible that once the proposals were accepted in principle by the various parties and concrete discussions as to the formation of Government started, the communal problem might have emerged. See Frank Moraes, *Witness to an Era, India 1920 to the Present Day* (London, 1973) p. 102.

5 Azad had stated: 'We are not interested in the Congress as such gaining power, but we are interested in the Indian people as a whole having freedom and power'. Cmd. Paper 6350; see also *Discovery,* p. 472; *Harijan,* 2 Aug. 1942.

6 A more fundamental question which may be raised is whether the Westminster type of cabinet government could function at all in a plural society. Dr Madden has argued that the Westminster Model is neither suitable nor intended for any society other than the British: it was not intended for export but was strictly 'to

ever, Jinnah was suspicious of Congress's sincerity and it is very doubtful whether he would have allowed his party to cooperate with the Congress in the National Government. But that is quite different from a 'tyranny of the majority over the minority'.

The Cripps mission was successful from certain points of view. The draft declaration was a compromise which had been accepted to avert a Cabinet crisis, but not all ministers hoped with equal sincerity that it would succeed: to some it was primarily an exercise in public relations to appease American opinion, a section of British opinion and moderate Indian opinion, rather than an all-out attempt to bring the Congress and other parties into the Indian Government.[1] Doubts were expressed in the British left-wing newspapers, even before Cripps left for India, that the proposals were a 'right-wing fraud', endeavouring to put forward a Churchill-Amery policy under the cover of Cripps.[2] The utterances of Churchill and his previous attitude towards India encouraged scepticism. Churchill had all along been opposed to political advance in India and his opposition to the Government of India bill of 1934 was on record.[3] He had argued that India was unfit for self-government and any advance in that direction was a step towards catastrophe — abdication, dissolution and chaos.[4]

Left to himself, Churchill would not have thought of raising the Indian question and particularly not during the war. But, as Amery put it, 'the pressures outside upon Winston [Churchill] from Roosevelt, and upon Attlee and Co [sic] from their own party, plus the admission of Cripps to the War Cabinet suddenly opened the sluice gates'.[5] In these circumstances Churchill had been persuaded to send Cripps in an apparent attempt to end the deadlock. The ambivalence of his intention in making the Cripps offer is revealed in a telegram to Linlithgow;

> It would be impossible owing to the unfortunate rumours and publicity, and the general American outlook, to stand on purely negative attitudes and the Cripps Mission is indispensable to prove our honesty of purpose and to gain time for necessary consultations.[6]

be consumed only on the premises'. See A. F. M. C. Madden, 'Not for Export: Some Evidence and Consideration of the Westminster Model Overseas from the Twelfth to the Twentieth Centuries'. (Forthcoming).

1 Hodson, *Great Divide*, p. 103, see also L/PO/42/15, note of an interview between Graham Spry and Lauchlan Currie, 9 May 1942. IOR.

2 Mss. Eur. F.125/22, Amery to Linlithgow, 9 March 1942. IOL.

3 See chapter 3.

4 Tara Chand, *History of the Freedom Movement*, iv, 209.

5 Mss. Eur. F.125/11, Amery to Linlithgow, 10 March 1942. IOL.

6 L/PO/106b, Churchill to Linlithgow, 10 March 1942. IOR.

Churchill viewed Cripps' mission more as an exhibition of the British government's intentions than as a sincere contribution to the solution of the Indian problem. This is more or less explicit: 'For him [Churchill] ', wrote Amery to Linlithgow, 'the main thing about it [the Cripps mission] has been the good effect in America; for the rest he isn't interested, really disliking the whole problem as much as before.'[1] It has to be added that Amery himself, on hearing of the failure of the mission, 'heaved a sigh . . . of relief now that it is over'.[2]

In so far as the purpose of the mission was to gain favourable publicity in the USA, it was quite successful. Churchill was satisfied. 'The effect throughout Britain and in the United States', wrote Churchill, 'has been wholly beneficial'.[3] The Cripps offer was hailed in the United States as proof of Britain's sincerity and as an offer of reasonable compromise which the Congress should accept.[4] The dominant mood was expressed in a *New York Times* editorial:

> But we can see that simple things that make for human brotherhood are good and true in India as in our own country; and we can say to the Indian leaders that if they refuse this gift of freedom for petty, or personal, or spiteful reasons, they will lose the American comradeship that is now theirs for the asking.[5]

The Mission was equally successful in making the Americans aware of the complications of the Indian problem. 'How can one find a solution that will satisfy at once the Provinces under representative rule and the States under local princes; the upper castes and untouchables; the Hindus and the Moslems', asked the *New York Times*.[6] 'India is such a maze of vertical and horizontal divisions'. 'The land of contrasts in cultures, peoples, religions, is not one but many Indias', discovered the *American Mercury*.[7] Lord Halifax also filled in the gaps[8] with a version that did 'much good', as Amery explained, by showing the United States 'the complexities of the Indian political structure and inherent difficulties of any easy off-hand solution'.[9] As the possibility

1 Mss. Eur. F.125/11, Amery to Linlithgow, 10 June 1942, IOL.

2 Mss. Eur. F.125/11, Amery to Linlithgow, 11 April 1942. IOL.

3 L/PO/106c, Churchill to Cripps, 11 April 1942. IOR.

4 *The New Republic*, 6 April 1942; see also *The Nation*, 4 April, the *Christian Science Monitor*, 31 March, the *Loss Angeles Times*, 31 March and the *New York Times*, 31 March 1942.

5 *New York Times*, 31 March 1942.

6 *Ibid.*, 13 April 1942.

7 *American Mercury*, June 1942.

8 Lecture in the New York town hall on 7 April 1942.

9 *Parliamentary Debates*, House of Commons, vol. 379, cols. 905-917, 28 April 1942.

of success in the Cripps talks appeared to recede, most newspapers began to be critical of the uncompromising attitude of the Congress party: 'If it [rejection of the proposals] means that the Indians at the bottom prefer invasion, enslavement and probably civil war, American disappointment will, of course, be deep and bitter'.[1]

In Britain most of the Press and political leaders accepted the official explanation that responsibility for failure rested with the Congress. In a Parliamentary debate on 28 and 29 April, some members of the Labour Party challenged the Government and called for the re-opening of negotiations. Amery and Cripps argued that the maximum concessions possible had been offered and that they could not yield on Britain's obligations to defend India and to protect the minorities against Hindu domination.[2]

The failure of the Cripps Mission left a scar on British relations with the Congress, limiting if not entirely precluding for the time being chances of a reconciliation. A frustrated Congress gravitated towards the leadership of Gandhi and in desperation to non-cooperation.[3]

Gandhi had taken little interest in the Cripps Mission, but he was disappointed by its failure to resolve the Indian deadlock. He understood this to mean that there was no prospect of a political settlement so long as the war lasted. Linlithgow, after the departure of Cripps, was more than ever reluctant to seek Congress cooperation. He argued that since the Congress had rejected the British government's offer there was nothing more to be done during the war.[4] Everything in India was 'now subordinate to getting ahead with the war', and the Cripps Mission had receded into the background.[5]

Nonetheless it was recognized by both Linlithgow and Amery that the situation was not, and could not be, as though Cripps had never been to India. Ways and means would have to be found to deal with the situation, though not necessarily with reference to the Congress. Linlithgow sought to enlist the support of non-Congress leaders who were willing to cooperate. He proposed to reorganize the Executive Council to include more representative Indians who would be capable

1 *New York Herald Tribune,* 3 April, see also *New York Times,* 1 April, *Christian Science Monitor,* 13 April and *The Washington Post,* 13 April 1942.

2 No. 158 above.

3 Eric Stokes, 'Cripps in India', review article in *Historical Journal,* vol. XIV, (1971) no.2 pp. 427-34, see especially p. 434.

4 Mss. Eur. F.125/105, Linlithgow to Sir S. M. Hallet, 5 May 1942. IOL.

5 Mss. Eur. F. 125/11, Amery to Linlithgow, 10 June 1942, IOL. *TOP* ii, 197-200.

of mobilizing popular support for the war.[1] The Executive Council was enlarged from twelve to fifteen members, as many as eleven non-official Indians being included in the fifteen. While the Commander-in-Chief took over as the new War Member, the Defence portfolio was handed over to Sir Firoz Khan Noon. Two Indians, Sir Ramaswami Mudaliar and Maharaja Jam Saheb of Nawangar were also appointed to sit in the British War Cabinet along with other representatives of the Dominions.[2] By so reorganizing the Government of India, Linlithgow demonstrated so far as it was possible that there was an alternative to the concept of a 'National Government'; he also showed his determination to manage India's defence without the cooperation of the Congress.

By refusing to accept the Cripps offer the Congress seems to have suffered some loss of popularity.[3] Linlithgow's attempt to secure the support of the non-Congress groups showed his rejection of the Congress claim to indispensability in Indian politics. 'The more the Government of India . . . can publicise itself and put itself across', [wrote Amery], the better. It is ridiculous the way the press has got itself into the habit of making much of the least utterance or even [sic] movement of those Congress politicians and tends to ignore the doings and sayings of those who have the real responsibility and much greater ability as well.[4]

Gandhi realized that the unity of the Congress would be threatened unless the party quickly regained the political initiative. He took stock of the political situation in India and noticed the falling morale of the people who, fearing a Japanese invasion, had begun to lose confidence in the British capacity to defend India.[5] Reports from various parts

1 A scheme somewhat on these lines had been approved by the War Cabinet on 5 February, but had been held in abeyance during the Cripps Mission. See War Cabinet Paper W.P. (42) 53, 'Indian Constitutional Question', Memorandum by Secretary of State for India, 1 Feb, 1942, for Cabinet's approval see War Cabinet W.M. (42) 16th Conclusions, Minute 1, 5 Feb. 1942. PRO.

2 L/P&J/'/537, 'Proposed Reconstruction of the Governor-General's Executive Council', 5 May 1942; L/P&J/8/544, telegram from Amery to Linlithgow, 30 June 1942. IOR. For a discussion on the reconstitution of the Executive Council see also, L/P&J/8/544, Minutes of the War Cabinet's Committee on India (42) 15th meeting on 11 May 1942, IOR; War Cabinet W.M. (42) 68th Conclusions, Minute 5, 26 May 1942 PRO.

3 *Pioneer* (Allahabad) 12 April 1942, Coupland, *Indian Politics 1936-42*, pp. 278-8.

4 Mss. Eur. F.125/11, Amery to Linlithgow, 27 May 1942. IOL.

5 L/P&J/5, fortnightly reports from the Government of Bihar for the first half of April 1942, and from the Government of Bengal for the first half of April and May 1942, IOR; The *Statesman*, 18 April 1942. See also letter from Nehru to Lampton Berry, 23 June 1942 in Jawaharlal Nehru, *A Bunch of Old Letters*, (London 1958) pp. 491-3.

of India and Burma depicted a bleak picture. In the coastal districts of Orissa, which were threatened with invasion, the people panicked and were generally distrustful of the government.[1] In Bengal the resentment was heightened by a 'scorched earth' policy under which many homes had been destroyed and boats sunk.[2] To many Indians, the situation seemed desperate. 'The majority of the people', Azad asserts, 'were now convinced that the British would lose the war and some seemed to welcome a Japanese victory. There was great bitterness against the British which at times was so intense that they did not think of the consequences of a Japanese conquest of India'.[3] Indian confidence was further undermined by reports of the suffering caused by the British evacuation of Burma and Malaya.[4] The British did little to allay these fears. General Molesworth, the Deputy Chief of Staff in India, had at this time indicated that the Indian Army might have to abandon some parts of India if the need arose.[5]

In this situation Gandhi concluded that even if the Allies ultimately 'won' the war, it was probable that a part of India might come under Japanese occupation. Many Indians might react to the invasion by collaborating with the conquerors. Such instances were not unknown. In spite of the growing resistance movement in Belgium, France, Holland and Norway, many people had collaborated with the Germans. This could be repeated in India where foreign rule had encouraged the collaborator's mentality.[6] Indeed the fear of collaboration was heightened by the activities of Subhas Bose, the Bengali firebrand, who, having escaped to Germany and then moved on to Japan, had organized the Indian National Army from among Indian troops who had been taken prisoners of war by the Japanese.[7] Bose was immensely popular among the educated Bengali youths, the traditional reservoir of terrorists. His speeches over the clandestine *Jai Hind* Radio made the more

1 Miss Madeleine Slade's report to Gandhi *Harijan* 12 July 1942.

2 *Discovery*, p.464.

3 Azad, *India Wins Freedom*, pp. 71-2.

4 The evacuation of Burma presented a dismal picture of racial discrimination under stress. The market-place was full of harrowing tales of division of refugees between those permitted to take the 'white' road and those forced to take the 'black' road on which they were allegedly robbed by the police and exploited by opportunists along the route supplying cartage, food and water for exorbitant prices with police connivance. B. Shiva Rao, *India's Freedom Movement*, (New Delhi, 1972), p. 155; see also Congress resolution in *IAR*, 1942, i, 292-3.

5 Azad, *India Wins Freedom*, p. 72.

6 Nehru, *Discovery*, pp. 469-70.

7 For a detailed account of Bose and the INA see Hugh Toye, *Subhash Chandra Bose The Springing Tiger* (Bombay, fifth Impression: 1974); Sisir K. Bose, *A Beacon Across Asia* (Delhi, 1973), and Tara Chand, *History of the Freedom Movement in India*, iv, 414-23, give a brief but authentic account of the INA.

extreme elements in the Congress impatient for action; their hands could be forced.[1] There were speculations that a Japanese-sponsored government might be set up in Eastern India.[2] It would seem that the kind of independence for which Gandhi had been working for so long might be forestalled by liberation under different auspices. Gandhi therefore endeavoured to prevent Bose from turning the frustration of the Indian nationalists into support for the Japanese.[3]

Gandhi felt that he must try to unite the Indians around the Congress banner. He was unwilling to see India conquered by the Japanese and then reconquered by the Allies, nor was he willing to defer his hopes for Indian independence until the 'two foreign mad bulls' had settled their scores on Indian soil.[4] In his effort to arouse the masses, Gandhi began to equate the British with the Japanese. Both, he argued, were aliens, one ruling the country and the other aspiring to rule, whereas he held that India should govern herself. Nehru, while sharing Gandhi's indignation against British policy, was sceptical of his suggestion that the British were on a par with the Japanese.[5]

Gandhi's solution to the problem came as a bombshell: only an immediate declaration of Indian independence by the British could prevent the invasion of the country by the Japanese; if still invaded, India would be able to defend herself by non-violence.[6] Week after week Gandhi developed his ideas through the columns of the *Harijan* and tried to arouse the masses. Shortly after the abortive Cripps Mission he wrote:

> If the British left India to her fate as they had to leave Singapore, non-violent India would not lose anything. Probably the Japanese would leave India alone . . . Whatever the consequences, therefore, to India, her real safety, and Britain's too, lie in orderly and timely withdrawal from India.[7]

Gandhi was 'convinced that the British presence in India is the incentive for Japanese attack', and if the British 'wisely decided to withdraw and leave India to manage her affairs in the best way she could, the Japanese would be bound to reconsider the plan'.[8] Gandhi claimed that

1 B. N. Pandey, *The Break-up of British India,* (London 1969), p. 165.

2 Azad, *India Wins Freedom,* pp. 71-5.

3 L/P&J/8/596, note by D. Pilditch, 26 May 1942. IOR.

4 *Harijan,* 5 July 1942.

5 Brecher, *Nehru: A Political Biography,* pp. 285-6; Nehru, *Discovery,* pp. 464-7.

6 *Harijan,* 26 April 1942.

7 *Ibid.*

8 *Ibid.,* 3 May 1942.

'the time has come during the war, not after it, for the British and the Indians to be reconciled to complete separation from each other'.[1] The following week he issued a call 'to Every Briton' in which he argued that the British were the 'bait' that tempted Japan: let that 'bait' be removed and all would be well, within and without.[2] Gandhi's rhetoric revealed an ignorance of the international military situation: he did not realize that the invasion of India, if it took place at all, would be a part of the giant pincer movement necessary for the link up in the Middle East of the German and the Japanese armies.[3] This would have come about whether the British troops were present in India or not. It may only be surmised that the Japanese might have been more tempted to invade India if the Allied troops had been withdrawn, leaving India's sole defence to Gandhi's non-violent non-cooperation. The dangers were recognized by Azad and Nehru who attempted to convince Gandhi that the problem was not as simple as he imagined.[4] But Gandhi was impervious to arguments: 'Leave India to God', he wrote, 'If that is too much, then leave her to anarchy'.[5] British rule, he wrote, was 'ordered anarchy'; he was prepared to risk complete lawlessness in India as a result of the disappearance of the 'ordered anarchy' so that the people might evolve a popular order out of the chaos.[6]

Gandhi had not perhaps thought out the implications of his demand that the British should leave India: he was certainly no military strategist. Furthermore his insulting comments on American policy towards coloured people and in the treatment of the American Negroes led to some exasperation on the part of the United States.[7] Adverse reactions to some of his statements caused Gandhi to shift the ground of his attack upon the British.[8] The demand for the British withdrawal was originally put forward on the argument that it would reduce the temptation to the Japanese to invade India, and if they came nonetheless it would enable India to resist them non-violently. All these notions were now forgotten and the withdrawal of the British was called for on two quite different grounds. First it was claimed that India in bondage could not play an effective part in the fight against Fascism; and secondly that

1   *Ibid.*, 10 May 1942.
2   *Ibid.*, 17 May 1942.
3   See above p. 173.
4   Azad, *India Wins Freedom*, pp. 73-5; *Discovery*, pp. 468.
5   *Harijan*, 24 May 1942.
6   *Ibid.*
7   *Ibid.*, 14 June 1942.
8   *Ibid.*, 21, 28 June and 5 July 1942; Tendulkar, *Mahatma*, vi, 116-7, 141-3; *Hindu*, 29 June 1942.

the Allies have no moral cause for which they are fighting, so long as they are carrying the double sin on their shoulders, the sin of India's subjection and the subjection of the Negroes and the African races.[1]

Gandhi admitted that there was 'obviously a gap' in his writings: he could not be asking the Allies to take steps which might lead to their defeat. Abrupt withdrawal of the Allied troops might result in Japan's occupying India and thereby imperil the defence of China. Confessing, that 'I had not the remotest idea of any such catastrophe resulting from my action', Gandhi now conceded that American and British troops might remain in India 'by virtue of compact with free India' if this was deemed necessary for Allied success.[2]

Gandhi had considerably modified his position. But at the same time his intention to launch a civil disobedience campaign became manifest and more than offset any goodwill achieved by his conciliatory statements. Gandhi's plan was to take a stand which would automatically be obstructive, and which, he hoped, would compel the government to respond to the Congress demands. His scheme caught the imagination of the Congress rank and file; their mood was changed and their expectations raised to a high pitch. There was a desperation in it, an emotional urge which gave second place to logic, reason or any calm consideration of the consequences of such action. Few paused to question Gandhi's judgement.[3] Nor had Gandhi himself considered the international consequences of his campaign. The idea of starting a mass agitation was based on a narrow view of nationalism. In the conflict between the two, nationalism triumphed over internationalism. The dangers of war were basically ignored.

Let us now retrace our steps and see the reaction of the Congress to Gandhi's plans. Following the departure of Cripps, the Congress Working Committee met at Allahabad on 27 April. Gandhi did not attend the meeting but sent a note embodying his views: Britain had not only dragged India into a war against her will but had also shown itself incapable of defending India. India bore no emnity to Japan, and if Britain left India, India would be able to defend herself better.[4] Gandhi's note came in for severe criticism. With a clearer grasp of the international situation, Nehru pointed out that 'the whole background of the draft is one which will inevitably make the whole world think we are passively linking up with the Axis Powers'.[5]

1 *Harijan*, 14 June 1942.
2 *Ibid.*, 14 and 28 June 1942.
3 *Discovery*, p. 475.
4 *IAR*, 1942, ii, 200-4.
5 Cited in S. C. Bose, *The Indian Struggle* (London, 1964), p. 348.

In the note Gandhi had said *inter alia*

> Britain is incapable of defending India . . . Japan's quarrel is not with India. She is warring against the British Empire. If India were freed her first step would be to negotiate with Japan. The Congress is of the opinion that if the British withdrew from India, India would be able to defend herself in the event of Japanese or any other aggressors attacking India.[1]

Nehru drew up another draft resolution which considerably modified the language of the Gandhi version and expunged some of the passages that were likely to create misunderstanding. However, the central issue, namely the call to Britain to relinquish its hold on India, was retained in the new draft.[2]   Congress adherence to non-violence was also re-stated, but in terms of the special circumstances prevailing. The most significant change was that Nehru's draft contained no reference to Japan or to Britain's incapacity to defend India.[3]

The Congress Working Committee met again at Wardha on 6 July, with Gandhi in attendance. For the first time Gandhi spoke about a 'Quit India' movement, but did not touch the question of non-violence.[4] The Congress Working Committee was faced with a dilemma. Azad was particularly unhappy about the proposed campaign. He had no doubts that if the Japanese invaded India they must be opposed. 'I felt', wrote Azad, 'that it would be intolerable to change an old master for a new one'.[5] He says that he also warned Gandhi not to lull himself into the belief that the authorities would permit him to remain at large and direct a movement against themselves. Nehru agreed with Azad, but other members of the Congress Working Committee, including Sardar Patel, Rajendra Prasad and Acharya Kripalani, subordinated their judgement to Gandhi's. Characteristically, they argued that Gandhi would certainly find a way out.[6] A strange logic. After eight days of incessant discussion Nehru and Azad reluctantly accepted Gandhi's resolution proposing a mass movement.[7] Gandhi later admitted that his resolution was opposed by Nehru with 'a passion which I have no words to describe'.[8]

Gandhi's opponents had two major reservations about the 'quit India' campaign: firstly they feared that non-violent non-cooperation would sap the people's will to resist the Japanese; furthermore, they

1 *Cmd. 6430*, p. 38.
2 *IAR*, 1942, i, 204-6.
3 *Ibid.*
4 Azad, *India Wins Freedom*, p. 73.
5 *Ibid.* p. 65.
6 *Ibid.* p. 75.
7 *Ibid.* pp. 76-7; S. Gopal, *Jawaharlal Nehru*, pp. 291-3.
8 Mss. Eur. F.125/124, Gandhi to Linlithgow, 14 Aug. 1942. IOL.

doubted that such tactics would succeed in driving out the British. The 1940-1 *Satyagraha* campaign made very little difference to the war effort and had been cheerfully ignored by the government. Would the people respond to a fresh call for non-cooperation in 1942? The Congress Working Committee could not be sure. But despite the uncertainty the Congress accepted the scheme, feeling that if it sat idle at the critical moment it might lose its claim to the leadership of the nationalist movement. To justify that claim it would have to do something, even if it meant treading the barren path of non-cooperation[1]

The Congress Working Committee adopted a resolution of 14 July which made it clear that, though Gandhi had changed his mind on the immediate withdrawal of the Allied troops from India, he still insisted on the immediate transfer of power to Indian hands as the only way to resolve the deadlock. The resolution argued for the immediate recognition of Indian freedom and the ending of British rule in India 'both for the sake of India and for the success of the cause of the United Nations. The continuation of that rule is degrading and enfeebling India and making her progressively less capable of defending herself and of contributing to the cause of world freedom'. 'The possession of empire', the resolution continued, 'instead of adding to the strength of the ruling power, has become a burden and a curse'. It went on to suggest the formation of a composite provisional government, which would represent all important sections of the people and whose 'primary functions must be to defend India and resist aggression with all the armed as well as the non-violent forces at its command, together with its Allied Powers'.

It was claimed that the Congress was 'anxious not to embarrass in any way the defence of China and Russia, whose freedom is precious and must be preserved, or to jeopardize the defensive capacity of the United Nations'. But, and here was the sting of the resolution, 'the Committee is no longer justified in holding the nation back from endeavouring to assert its will against an imperialist and authoritarian government which dominates over it and prevents it from functioning in its own interest and in the interest of humanity'. The Congress Working Committee therefore resolved to 'sanction for the vindication of India's inalienable right to freedom and independence the starting of a mass struggle on non-violent lines . . . Such a struggle must inevitably be under the leadership of Gandhiji'[2]

1 Brecher, *Nehru: A Political Biography,* pp. 285-6.

2 Text of the CWC resolution of 14 July can be found in *The Times,* 16 July 1942. The same resolution with some minor modifications was adopted by the AICC on 8 August 1942. See M. Gwyer and A. Appadorai (eds.), *Speeches and Documents on the Indian Construction 1921-47* (London, 1957)., ii, 541-4.

It may be noted that there was a shift in emphasis in the 14 July resolution as compared with the Congress reply to the Cripps proposals. In the earlier statement the main stress had been on the organization and arming of the Indian people for defence, with the corollary that only responsible Indian government could achieve this task.[1] But now the emphasis was on complete and immediate independence, following which, it was asserted, India would willingly cooperate with the Allies.

The resolution was undoubtedly ill-judged in its effect alike within India and on world democratic opinion. It revealed a fatal contradiction which betrayed the confusion of purpose which had led to its adoption. Between the preamble and the conclusion there was a clear discord which no explanation could bridge. It was recognized that the war was not a war which was being fought between two rival powers, the outcome of which could be regarded with indifference, but a war in which India was vitally concerned in the success of the Allies, so that the aim of the resolution was declared to include 'the success of the cause of the United Nations', and acceptance of India's role as 'an ally of the United Nations'. The resolution specifically laid down the concern of the Congress 'not to weaken in any way the defence of China or Russia' or 'to jeopardize the defensive capacity of the United Nations'. But it is all too clear that the resolution contemplated a course of action which, if carried out, could only mean internal conflict and disorganization in a major country of the Alliance, such as in practice would jeopardize the defensive capacity of the Allies.

Obsessed with the desire for India's freedom, Gandhi — and many within the Congress — failed to see the wartime problems confronting the British Government. The War Cabinet had made the Cripps offer to meet the Congress demand of responsible government to organize India's defence. Now the Congress had gone one step further and demanded not only full transfer of power, but also the expulsion of the British from India. It is difficult to see how Linlithgow could have complied with their demands. The previous obstacles to meeting such demands, namely, the various pledges given by the British Government to protect the minorities and princes and the importance of retaining India to the Empire as a vital base for Allied military operations, were still present. In many ways the summer of 1942 was the most crucial and difficult period for the Allies.[2] They had suffered severe reverses in Southeast Asia and the Pacific.[3] In the midst of these crises it could

1 Compare Congress resolution of 2 April 1942. Gwyer and Appadorai, *Speeches and Documents*, ii, 524-6, see p. 526.

2 Liddell Hart, *Second World War*, pp. 343-69.

3 See above pp. 173-4.

hardly be expected that the War Cabinet would devote its attention to making another offer. Any devolution of power to Indian hands without prior agreement among the various communities would exacerbate the communal tension and dislocate India's war effort.[1]

Moreover, the extreme demands of the Congress had considerably alienated its support both in India[2] and abroad.[3] In Britain the Cripps mission had created a favourable climate of opinion, and there was no immediate pressure for further concession to the Congress.[4] The Congress demand that the British leave India was denounced as a 'scarcely veiled threat of a sell out to Japan'.[5] Even the National Executive of the British Labour Party, which had hitherto supported Congress demands, regarded the resolution as a 'proof of political irresponsibility' which 'might imperil the fate of all freedom loving peoples and thereby destroy all hopes of Indian freedom'.[6]

The Moslem League's reaction to the Congress resolution was hostile. It accused the Congress of attempting not only

> to coerce the British government into handing over power to a Hindu oligarchy and thus disabling them from carrying out their moral obligations and pledges given to the Mussalmans and other sections of the peoples of India from time to time, but also to force the Mussalmans to submit and surrender to the Congress terms and dictation.[7]

The British government could scarcely ignore the League's warning. The acceptance of the Congress demands would infuriate the League and might have led to communal riots likely to infect the Indian army

1 Mss. Eur. F.125/13, telegram from Linlithgow to G. S. Bajpai, 21 July 1942. IOL.

2 *Manchester Guardian*, 6 May 1942; The *Times of India*, the *Bombay Sentinel*, and the *Bombay Chronicle* (a Congress mouthpiece) also showed discontent with the Congress attitude. See Mss. Eur. F.125/6, Lumley to Linlithgow, 17 July 1942, IOL. For the reaction of non-Congress leaders like Sir Sikander Hyat and Dr B. R. Ambedkar see Mss. Eur. F.125/23/409, Linlithgow to Amery, 23 July 1942; for statements by Sir Chimanlal Setalvad and Sir Cowasji Jehangir see *The Times*, 20 July 1942.

3 In the USA the Congress resolution received a bad press. see *New York Times**, 5 May and 18 July 1942; *Chicago Sun*,* 21 July 1942; *Newsweek**, 13 July 1942; *The New Republic*,*27 July 1942. The attitude of the United States State Department towards India was markedly cool after the failure of the Cripps mission. See *For. Rel.*, 1942, i, 651-3., Memorandum of conversation with Graham Spry, by Chief of Near East Division (Alling), 13 May 1942, Hull, *Memoirs of Cordell Hull*, ii, 1484; *New York Times*, 24 July 1942.

4 Mss. Eur. F.125/11, Amery to Linlithgow, 6 May 1942. IOL.

5 *Amerasia*, (New York, August 1942), p. 253.

6 *The Times*, 23 July 1942. Cripps gave expression to similar feelings. *Ibid.* 6 Aug. 1942.

7 Sherwani, *Pakistan Resolution to Pakistan*, pp. 72-3.

which had so far remained free from communal bitterness. If that happened India's war effort might be seriously hampered.[1]

More temperate and yet in some ways more forceful criticism came from the Congress leaders themselves. Rajagopalacharia, who had broken away from the Congress after the Cripps mission, pointed out that the 'withdrawal of the government without simultaneous replacement by another must involve the dissolution of the State and Society itself'. He went on to assert that unless the two major political organizations, the Congress and the Moslem League, could agree on some plan for a provisional national government which could take over power, and this had so far proved impossible, only chaos could follow abdication by the British, and that the only people to gain would be the Japanese.[2]

This was plain common sense. But Gandhi was not at this time open to common sense. 'I want independence', he declared, adding in justification, but contrary to all evidence, 'that will help England win the war'.[3] He continued to harp on this untenable thesis that the demand was in the interest of the Allied Powers and that no protest would deter him from his purpose.

It may be recalled that during the 1940-1 *satyagraha*, Gandhi had withheld cooperation but stopped short of active opposition. The call for mass action, he had said, 'will not come before the close of the war. There is neither warrant nor atmosphere for mass action'.[4] He had refrained from launching a mass movement for a variety of reasons: he had feared that it might lead to communal discord since the League regarded the Congress as its prime enemy;[5] and he was not sure that the Congressmen believed in non-violence whole-heartedly. Finally, he had not wished to embarrass the British.

> Whilst by their own action the British government have made it impossible for the Congress to cooperate with them in the prosecution of the war, the Congress must not embarrass them in its prosecution. I do not desire anarchy in India.[6]

In July 1942 all these dangers were still present and the situation was further aggravated by the presence of the Japanese on the frontiers of India. Yet Gandhi was now quite explicitly willing to risk the danger

1 Mss. Eur. F.125/22, telegram from Linlithgow to Amery, 26 June 1942; Mss. Eur. F/125/13, telegram from Linlithgow to Bajpai, 21 July 1942. IOL.
2 Text of the letter is quoted in Coupland, *Indian Politics 1936-1942*, Appendix ix, p. 338.
3 *Harijan*, 28 June 1948.
4 *Dawn*, 2 Nov. 1941.
5 *Ibid*.
6 *Harijan*, 2 Sept. 1940.

of anarchy. He had not, however made any preparation for mass non-violent civil disobedience, possibly hoping that the response to his call would be so staggering that the government would be paralyzed by a spontaneous strike throughout the country.[1] This policy only emphasizes the bankruptcy of an approach which sought to meet a serious war situation with a policy of empty bluff — at best no more than a gamble.

No one except Gandhi with his child-like faith could have seriously believed that the government would sit idle while the All India Congress Committee was preaching 'open rebellion'. We have already noted above the elaborate plans of the government of India to nip the movement in the bud. As Gandhi began to unfurl his plans for rebellion, the government also moved swiftly. In the period between the meeting of the Congress Working Committee in July and the assembly of the All India Congress Committee in August, the government carried on a propaganda campaign to mobilize public opinion in favour of drastic action against the Congress. Sir Frederick Puckle, the Secretary of Information to the Government of India, stated in a strikingly forthright manner that the main objective of the propaganda was

> to mobilize public opinion against the Congress policy as detrimental to the successful conduct of the war. . . . Speeches, letters to the local press, leaflets, cartoons, posters, whispering campaigns are possible media for local publicity. Instructions to All India Radio stations will be given by the Centre.[2]

Similarly the Home Department issued instructions that 'public opinion in England and even more in America should be prepared well in advance for any strong action we may eventually take'.[3] Laithwaite, the Viceroy's Secretary, sent telegrams to the governors outlining the action to be taken in the event of the All India Congress Committee ratifying the 'Quit India' resolution.[4] The plan consisted of three stages.[5] The first stage was to be the sort of propaganda work Puckle had outlined. Ratification of the Congress Working Committee's resolution without any substantial amendment would signal the commencement of the second stage. As soon as this took place,

1 Nehru, *Discovery*, p. 476.

2 Cited in K. A. Abbas and N. G. Jog. *A Report to Gandhiji* (Bombay, 1944), p. 17. This circular was reportedly leaked and was widely quoted in the nationalist press. See *Harijan*, 23 August 1942.

3 L/P&J/8/596, telegram from the Government of India Home Department to Secretary of State, 7 June 1942. IOR.

4 Mss. Eur. F.125/110, telegram from Laithwaite to Secretaries of the Governors, 24 July 1942. IOL.

5 L/P&J/8598, telegram from the Government of India, Home Department to Secretary of State, 3 Aug. 1942. IOR.

the Bombay Government would inform the Government of India, all the Governors, Chief Commissioners and Political Residents by telegram containing a pre-arranged code word. No action would be taken, however, until the Government of India sent a further telegram containing another prearranged code word which would be the signal for action. On receipt of the telegram from the Government of India, the Bombay government would arrest Gandhi and all the members of the Working Committee present at Bombay under Defence of India Rule 26. Immediately all the provincial governments would 'proclaim' as illegal organizations under the Criminal Law Amendment Act, the Congress Working Committee, the All India Congress Committee and each Provincial Congress Community operating within its jurisdiction, but not the Indian National Congress as a whole. The provincial governments were also asked to seize relevant Congress offices and funds, and arrest all individuals whom they considered competent to organize a mass movement. The third stage would supervene if the government's attempt to abort the movement failed. At this stage it would be necessary to 'proclaim' the Indian National Congress and promulgate an Emergency Powers Ordinance.[1]

With its contingency plans prepared, the Government of India marked time and waited for the Congress to put itself in the wrong. The wisdom of the government in allowing the Congress leaders to go on preaching rebellion and making plans was questionable. There was some discussion in the Viceroy's Executive Council in which it was suggested that a general warning should be issued to caution the Congress, but the suggestion was dropped in the hope that, when the Wardha resolution came up for confirmation at Bombay on 7 August, the ultimatum contained in it might be withdrawn in view of its widespread condemnation, not only in Britain and the USA, but also in India itself. When the day of decision drew nearer, Amery, speaking in the House of Commons, warned the Congress Leaders that there would be no compromise with rebellion.[2]

The All India Congress Committee met on 7 August, and after discussion for two days it confirmed the 14 July resolution. The main arguments were repeated, but in view of the controversy of the preceding weeks two new points were added. To meet the charge that the Congress was backing out of the war and becoming 'isolationist', the resolution declared that a free India would join the Allies in fighting the Axis Powers. Secondly, to reassure the minorities it was stated that

1 *Ibid.*
2 *Parliamentary Debates,* House of Commons, vol. 382, cols. 674-75, 30 July 1940.

the provisional government would be a 'composite government representative of all the important sections of people in India'; and the constitution to be drafted later on by a constituent assembly would be a federal one with the largest measure of autonomy for the federating units and with residuary power resting in the units — an important departure from the unitarian doctrine of the Congress leaders in earlier years.

The ultimatum was not tempered. It was asserted, indeed, that developments since the Wardha meeting had confirmed the futility of all promises or guarantees for the future and the necessity for the immediate withdrawal of British rule from India. Gandhi had won the day.

The resolution provided the pretext for which the government had been waiting: it now asserted forcefully that it stood for the defence of India against the threatened invasion by Japan, in contrast to Congress attempts at disrupting that defence. It described the Congress as pro-Japanese, — and made this the political basis for keeping the Congress leaders in prison for the duration of the war and refusing further political advance. In the early morning of 9 August, only a few hours after the termination of the All India Congress Committee meeting in Bombay at which the Quit India resolution had been passed, the police began the arrest of the Congress leaders in Bombay. Elsewhere in the country, the local police officials arrested other leaders who were not to be found in Bombay. The Government reported modestly that the 'total number of arrests did not exceed a few hundreds'.[1] In a single province, however, — the United Provinces, the number of people arrested on 9 August was 547.[2]

In fact the carefully drawn plan of the Government of India to smash the Congress with a heavy hammer did not yield the desired result. The plan assumed that the Government would have to deal with a movement similar to that of the 1920s and 1930s. But to its surprise the movement of 1942 had nothing in common with the previous civil disobedience campaigns. The use of force largely suppressed the open manifestation of the trouble, but it merely sent the rebels underground, and not only the politically conscious classes but also a considerable section of the masses had become involved. In any case the Government received virtually no effective or willing help from Hindus; almost all

[1] Government of India, *Congress Responsibility for the Disturbances, 1942-3* (New Delhi, 1943), p. 21.

[2] L/P&J/5, fortnightly report from Government of UP for the Second Half of August, 1942.

Moslems remained neutral at Jinnah's bidding.[1] Linlithgow admitted in December 1942, 'uprising continues to call for utmost vigilance'.[2]

The prolonged struggle and the continuation of the acts of sabotage were disconcerting. The result was that the early confidence of the government in its power to obtain quick mastery over the situation faded. For the first time in the history of Britain's relations with India there was the appearance of a widely shared defeatist mentality. The campaign revealed that the Congress was a real mass organization and that the Hindus were in general firmly behind it. Officials began to record the opinion that this was a 'movement of the people', and that the saboteurs had the backing of the people. Reports from provincial governments indicated the growing alienation of all classes from the government. Nearly a year after Linlithgow's departure, the Governor of Bengal wrote to Wavell, the new Viceroy, in despair: '. . . great majority of educated Hindu opinion is against us, and while the terrorist parties are comparatively small there is an undercurrent of general Hindu sympathy with them, and even admiration for them'.[3] The British Chief Secretary of Bengal reported thus: 'All sections of Indian opinion may be said to be at one in support of the demand for immediate transference of power and the establishment of a national government'.[4]

Such mistrust and antipathy was bound to wear down the early self-confidence of the administration in its ability to deal effectively with the disturbances which it attributed to the Congress. But disillusionment came and permeated everyone from the lowest cadre to the highest executive. To Churchill, the Viceroy confessed: 'I am engaged here in meeting by far the most serious rebellion since that of 1857, the gravity and extent of which we have so far concealed from the world for reasons of military security'.[5]

So far as the effect of the disturbance was concerned, Linlithgow admitted that the 'Quit India' movement had considerably hampered the British war effort. In addition to the disruption of communications with the threatened Eastern region, the movement had caused a breakdown in the supply of essential commodities to the troops. 'Fortyfive per cent of India's production of *khaki* was halted by strikes, the

---

1 Mss. Eur. F.125/137, reports of a Press Conference held by Jinnah, 13 Sept. 1942. IOL.

2 Francis G. Hutchins, *Spontaneous Revolution,* p. 329.

3 L/P&J/5/260, Casey to Wavell, 22 June 1944. IOR.

4 Cited in Brecher, *Nehru: A Political Biography,* pp. 290-91.

5 Mss. Eur. F.125/158, telegram from Linlithgow to Churchill, 31 August 1942. IOL.

production of leather goods was cut by fifty per cent', cigarette production was hampered by the shortage of cigarette papers as a result of damage to the factory manufacturing them. The factories producing sewing cotton were closed down and cotton thread for sewing military clothes was unavailable.[1]

This is not to argue that the British were unable effectively to regain control. It seems clear that in this confrontation, despite the earlier reverses and some loss of morale, the government was always comfortably a move ahead of the Congress. This was partly because the intelligence services, — and the insistence by Gandhi on openness in dealings, — made it relatively easy for them to know the Congress programme and therefore made it possible for the government to be ready to meet the Congress moves. And partly, too, because the Government on this occasion changed the rules of confrontation as it had been played till then, by moving against the leadership the moment it had put forward its ultimatum. It did not, as past governments had done, treat the ultimatum merely as a first move, thus giving the Congress some time to build up its activities. Nipped in the bud, Gandhi's movement collapsed. Linlithgow thus demonstrated his firm conviction that if the Congress raised rebellion it could be contained by force.

In the period after the 'Quit India' campaign, — during Linlithgow's last months in India, — the issue of the 'transfer of power' or the initiatives to end the political deadlock receded in the background. Liberal opinion in Britain and the USA, President Roosevelt's plea for national participation, Chiang Kai-shek and his urging, were all muted. The principal figures in Britain and India were rather wearied of the whole business. Linlithgow and Churchill were in full control. There was a remarkable unanimity between the two and neither was willing to start a fresh round of negotiations so soon after the abortive Cripps Mission and the unsuccessful Congress rebellion. The failure of the Cripps mission was accepted on the British side as tantamount to the closure of an episode in Anglo-Indian relations. There had been no retrospective discussion of the Mission in the Cabinet or its India Committee: 'More extraordinarily', Amery wrote to Linlithgow, 'Winston [Churchill] decided that there was no particular point in his telling the Cabinet anything about [Cripps's] experiences and conclusions, and in fact the Cabinet had not discussed the matter at all since his return!'[2] The Viceroy delightedly commented on the margin: 'Shabash' ('well done'). He was eager to forget about the mission; the Congress leaders were out of harm's way and he was only anxious to

1 Hutchins, *Spontaneous Revolution,* p. 327.
2 Mss. Eur. F.125/11, Amery to Linlithgow, 6 May 1942. IOL.

get on with the war. Linlithgow, hanging on at the end of a Vice-royalty which had already been extended twice, was interested really in keeping the machinery ticking over, and shied away from suggestions that there should be any constructive planning for a solution of the constitutional impasse. Linlithgow's position was understandable. The Congress leaders were in prison, and he was content to maintain the *status quo*. He did not wish to reopen negotiations or take the initiative which his successor would have to grapple with and implement. He preferred to let his successor have a free hand and begin on a clean slate. In a final analysis of India's problem, he conveyed his views to Amery:

> The position is very easy here at the moment. . . . None of these people know what to do. . . . The Muslim League has no wish to do anything, the Congress are completely at a loss; the Princes, the Depressed Classes and the minorities have nothing to gain by activity. . . . Jinnah has everything to gain by letting things remain as they are . . . the longer Gandhi remains shut up and unable to take any active part in politics, the worse it is for the Congress and the more their stock goes down.[1]

He drew comfort from the reflection that 'Gandhi is out of the way of doing mischief. The Muslim League is growing stronger'.

Amery, too, was no more interested in finding a way out of the impasse. For him the main problems were finding a successor for Linlithgow, and of filling the various governorships. But he, like others, had little rationale for his work other than to hold on for the duration of the war. Cripps, fading from the scene by the end of 1942, tried to initiate an economic and social programme as a means of instilling new life into a weary government of India, but his efforts resulted only in fruitless discussions and long memoranda.[2]

The Government held on and directed its attention solely to the prosecution of the war effort, — a perfectly reasonable aim from the point of view of the British, given the exigencies of the time. But it provided no basis for a government of India, because, given such an aim, its prime requirement was that there should be no undue movement, that is, no political activity that was not directed towards British war efforts. So all issues of a national government were shelved. Linlithgow dismissed the Congress as irreconcilable. Even if there were a constitutional change, he did not believe that it would enhance the prosecution of the war. He therefore allowed things to remain as they were. The impasse which began with the outbreak of the war remained unresolved when Linlithgow left India finally in October 1943.

1   Mss. Eur. F.125/12 Linlithgow to Amery, 19 July 1943. IOL.

2   L/E/8/2527, 'A Social and Economic Policy for India', Memorandum by Cripps, 10 Dec. 1942. IOR.

7

CONCLUSION

Linlithgow turned homewards on 20 October 1943. More than half his long Viceroyalty had been in wartime. In fact, the second world war was probably the most important influence on his period of rule. It was the war which prevented the implementation of the 1935 India Act.

The first point to be made in any attempt at an overview of Linlithgow's Viceroyalty is that he went to India with a genuine desire to implement the 1935 Act. He believed that the chief aim of the Act was to maintain the unity of India by federating the princely states with the British Indian provinces, and by granting responsible government to the provinces. He sincerely hoped that the 1935 Act would pave the way to Dominion Status.[1] The provincial part of the constitution was not only successfully implemented in 1937, but Linlithgow was also able to make it acceptable to all parties. He came to India holding the view that no government which did not have the support of the Congress could function smoothly. The results of the 1936 elections confirmed him in his views: the Congress emerged as the dominant party in eight provinces.

The Congress had contested the elections with the avowed purpose of destroying the new constitution. After the landslide victory in the election, the decision on the acceptance of office which had so long been kept in abeyance could no longer be postponed. The Congress was divided on the issue but the 'moderates', backed by Gandhi, were able to carry a resolution allowing for the acceptance of office. The resolution, however, contained a rider: office would be accepted only if the governors assured the Congressmen that they would not use their 'special powers'.

The Congress demand for these assurances was unrealistic. The safeguards were for use in emergencies and could not have been used

---

1 Professor Moore's contention that the 1935 Act was designed by the British Conservatives to delay the self-government is in conflict with the opinion of Sir Cyril Philips who believes that 'since 1917 . . . successive British governments had been honestly, though slowly, working towards self-government for twenty years'. See R.J. Moore, 'The Making of India's Paper Federation', in C.H. Philips and M.D. Wainwright (eds.) *The Partition of India: Policies and Perspectives* (London, 1970) pp. 54-78; for Philips's comment see p. 11. Professor Gallagher in personal conversation has expressed the opinion that, had not the working of provincial autonomy been cut short by the war, India might have attained dominion status even before 1947.

for any other purpose in the face of a strong ministry backed by a disciplined majority. The Congress criticism arose ostensibly from its lack of understanding of the working of parliamentary government only when ministries are weak and majorities are factious would such emergencies arise. Technically the Crown in Britain had far greater legal powers than any Viceroy in India. In practice these powers were not used because there was no occasion for their use, but they lay in reserve to be used if an emergency demanded. For example, the mere threat to create peers was sufficient to dispose of the emergency which arose out of the rejection of the budget by the Lords in the early years of the century. Moreover, once the Act started functioning smoothly, the Viceroy (or the governor) would generally exercise his 'special powers' on the advice of his ministers, and this would be in spite of the words of the Act which placed them outside the ministers' sphere of the function. The importance of 'convention' was ignored by the Congress.

The Congress demand put Linlithgow in a difficult position. If he gave way he would be violating the spirit of the very Act he was trying to implement, apart from letting down the minorities for whose benefit the 'special powers' had been devised. On the other hand, if he stood firm, the Congress might refuse to accept office in those provinces in which it commanded a majority and the governors would have been compelled to take over direct administration. This would mean the virtual scrapping of the constitution even before it was tried. It was largely due to Linlithgow's very considerable negotiating skill, his patience and his good faith that Congress, which had earlier rejected the constitution and proclaimed that it would only go to the legislature to destroy the 'slave constitution' from within, was induced to accept office in the provinces without the governors' 'special powers' being compromised. Once in office the Congress ministries displayed an increasing awareness of, and readiness to shoulder, their responsibilities. For more than two years these ministries functioned smoothly. The Congress was at last experimenting in 'collaboration' with the imperial power. This surely was Linlithgow's greatest achievement: it ought not to be forgotten.

After the long and acrimonious debate, Congress did not receive the assurances it demanded. When it finally accepted office it had already lost the opportunity of securing the cooperation of moderate and non-League parties. In Bengal Fazlul Huq and his Krishak Proja Party had been anxious to form an alliance with the Congress but were pushed into the arms of the Moslem League. Perhaps if the Congress had extended its cooperation to Huq, the Moslem League might not have made much headway in Bengal. It may be recalled that in 1946 it was in Bengal that the Moslem League won over ninety-five per cent of votes in favour of 'Pakistan'. Similarly, in the Punjab, the Unionist Party deprived of Congress cooperation was persuaded to associate with the Moslem League.

These mistakes were not confined to non-Congress provinces. In the Congress majority provinces too, the Congress, perhaps unwisely, clung to the theory of homogeneous cabinets and refused to form an alliance with the Moslem League. It has been claimed by several historians that there was an electoral pact between Congress and the Moslem League by which the Congress had agreed to include nominees of the League in the United Provinces ministry. To prove this view attention has been drawn to similarities in the election manifestos of the Congress and the League. Such comparisons were superficial, and against this thesis it may be argued that the election manifestos of most parties had some general resemblances to that of the Congress. But in its details the Congress manifesto with its emphasis on socialistic principles and secularism stood apart from the rest. After a close examination of the evidence it is possible to conclude that there was no electoral agreement between Congress and the Moslem League, and consequently there was no breach of faith when Congress failed to include the League nominees in the United Provinces cabinet.

Proceeding from this mistaken belief that the Congress was guilty of a breach of promise, Azad and Khaliquzzaman among the participants, and later commentators like H.V. Hodson, Ian Stephens, K.B. Sayeed and Sir Penderel Moon have all claimed that the failure to form a Congress-Moslem League coalition in the United Provinces turned Jinnah into an implacable foe of the Congress, revitalized the Moslem League and ultimately led to partition. It is surely difficult to attribute partition to so trifling a cause. An error or a series of errors in tactical judgement cannot explain such a momentous event: there were more fundamental forces at work. In this book it has been suggested that economic considerations coupled with the exigencies of the war, gave the crucial impetus to the Moslem demand for a separate state. Exclusion from power drove the Moslem League into opposition everywhere, and the Congress governments provided the most convenient peg on which to hang all Moslem grievances - real or supposed.

There is another plausible explanation for Moslem separatism. Congress had emerged from the 1936 election as the dominant party, but its performance among Moslem electors had been dismal. It had secured only 26 out of 486 Moslem seats. The Hindu Mahasabha also fared badly; indeed communal parties generally suffered. Nehru read the election results as the deliberate rejection by the electorates of communalism and a 'massive' support for Congress's secular policy. Nehru was reading too much where too little existed. He also deceived himself into believing that Congress, which had contested only 54 Moslem seats and won 26 (50 per cent of the seats contested), might have won more Moslem seats if only it had contested more of them. From this mistaken analysis emerged the Congress policy of 'contact with the Moslem masses'. Over-conscious of its own good intentions, the Congress clung to the belief that it did, and could, represent the Moslems. The election results had shown otherwise, but still the Congress leaders continued to deceive themselves. Unaware that its campaign among the Moslems had backfired and provoked Moslem antipathy, the Congress ignored the risk it ran of alienating the Moslems. Nehru condemned the Moslem League leaders as relics of an outworn feudalism and asserted that owing to the primacy of economic motives the Moslems would disown them. This was an over-rationalized conclusion which overlooked the religious susceptibilities of the Moslem masses. The League leaders, in order to save themselves from complete annihilation, raised the cry of 'Islam in danger'. The result was phenomenal, but not unexpected. Within two years the League was able to claim the adherence of millions of new members and its organization began to permeate the countryside.

Jinnah was frustrated not merely by the exclusion of his party from the United Provinces ministry: his frustration went much deeper. The assumptions on which he had moulded his policies until 1937 were proving to be wrong. He had hoped that separate electorates and the organization of the Moslems on a separate political platform would enable him to control the governments of the Moslem majority provinces and, perhaps, act as a balancing factor in other provinces. But electoral defeats dashed his hopes to the ground. His party fared disastrously in the Moslem provinces and was excluded from any share in the government because party alignment cut across the religious line. While the Congress controlled eight provincial ministries, the Moslem League did not have a voice in a single government. It was in opposition everywhere. At the centre, the picture seemed still more dismal if the proposed federation went ahead.

The federal scheme embodied in the 1935 Act was the first effort to establish a constitutional relationship between the Indian states and British India. The disparate nature of the federating units (provinces and states), and the differences in the powers of the central authority in the executive, legislative and judicial fields with respect to states and provinces, as well as the peculiar position of the Crown, especially in its relationship with the states, gave the proposed federation a character which had little precedent anywhere in the world.

The Act, as always in a federal system, was the outcome of a compromise between many conflicting elements, and it had to be passed by a predominantly Conservative parliament in the United Kingdom. At a time when British political parties had seemed close to collision over Indian policy and any agreement with the Indians themselves appeared unlikely, federation had emerged and was seized upon. It was never fully approved in Delhi, and it was accepted in Britain for reasons which had more to do with British political problems than with the reality of Imperial power in India. Lord Reading, a former Viceroy, saw in the federation a way of avoiding the dominion issue. Hoare was persuaded to accept federation because it 'diverted the dangerous cry for Dominion Status and for immediate responsibility at an Indian centre into much safer channels'.[1] The Labour Government of 1929-30, with no specific proposals of its own, and worried likewise about the implications of Dominion Status, had been happy to endorse the federal plan. In India itself, while 'the Moslems' favoured the establishment of a loose federation with maximum powers for the provinces, 'the Hindus' looked towards a strong central government; and the princes saw in it an opportunity to escape from the autocratic control of the Political Department. A general consensus of all these elements seemed to guarantee for the moment the acceptance of federation as the formula for the future development of India.

When it came to their implementation, the federal negotiations ran into difficulties. By 1936, when Linlithgow was beginning to press ahead, the forces arrayed against him were formidable. The attitude of the various groups had hardened during the interval and were now mostly opposed to federation, though for conflicting reasons: the Congress deprecated the 'undemocratic' nature of the federation; the Moslem League feared 'a Hindu' domination at the centre; the princes while wanting a share in the federal administration were fearful of losing their sovereign rights; and the 'diehards', though they had acquiesced in the provincial part of the Act, were still hostile to the federation.

Right from the start Linlithgow had made clear his intention to push ahead with the federation. While his sincerity cannot be doubted, the approach he adopted may be open to criticism. He sent envoys to

1   Mss. Eur. E.240/52, Note by Hoare, 1934. IOL.

hasten the accession of the states to the federation. This procedure, though having obvious merits, specially for a Viceroy who wished to keep the negotiations under his own control, had also certain disadvantages. The rulers, faced with what appeared to he high level pressure, were apparently frightened. Individual approaches to the rulers by the Political Agents, whom they knew and trusted, might have been more likely to convince them on the issues about which they really cared - personal status and the sovereignty of their states. Linlithgow may indeed have erred in the tactics he deployed to achieve federation, but this is very different from the charge, made by Viscount Templewood and Sir Penderel Moon amongst others, that he deliberately foiled its inauguration. It was Linlithgow who determined the pace of the federal negotiations and constantly reminded the British Government that time was not on his side. If Linlithgow was not able to mould events in this sphere as he wished it was because his freedom of action and initiative was circumscribed by the overcautious policies of the India Office, and by the complications of Indian politics.

That the federal scheme had its defects cannot be denied, and Congress suspicion must be accepted as genuine. But by attempting to destroy the federation, the Congress was also destroying the unity of the country. Its insistence on elected representatives from the states frightened the Moslem League, which feared that Congress might exclude it from a share of power at the centre, as it had allegedly done in the provinces, by insisting on a one party cabinet. The Congress leaders perhaps did not realize that, despite their claim to be secular, practical proof would be necessary to allay the fears of the Moslems. Working together in the federal government might have dispelled some of the misapprehensions. The demand for Pakistan gathered rapid support because of the fear that the central government would be Hindu-dominated. The consequent rallying of the Moslems to the League, the alienation of the Moslem intelligentsia from the Congress, and the doubts which they began to voice against submission to the Hindu majority at the centre were plain danger signals. The Congress failed to take heed.

The Congress overreacted to the inclusion of princely representatives in the federal legislature. It suspected that the Imperial Government would use the princes to prevent it from exercising effective control at the centre. Although such considerations were certainly present in the minds of several Conservative leaders, including Sir Samuel Hoare,[1] it was essentially a bankrupt notion.

1 See above p. 59.

Even if the princes had come in, the areas of common concern would have been extremely limited, and the provinces would have exercised substantial powers of leverage against the centre.

There are, however, strong grounds for supposing that federation, as envisaged in the 1935 Act, could never have been implemented. Even if the required number of states had agreed to accede to it, and the 'diehards' had given no trouble, there would still have remained the Congress and the League to be won over. What was essential to the success of the federation was a spirit of goodwill on the part of those who were to work it; and of such goodwill there was no vestige to be perceived anywhere. The princes had virtually withdrawn their earlier acceptance of the federal scheme, the Congress were committed to 'stultifying the constitution', and the Moslem League was determined to keep out of a Hindu-dominated centre. The persistent opposition of any one of these would have been sufficient to wreck the scheme; their combined opposition was fatal to it.

The European war, remote as it may have been from India in a military sense, had a shattering impact on India's political life. As elsewhere in the dominions and colonies, the British expatriates in India immediately took the war as a call for a demonstration of their patriotism. It is essential to keep in mind this expatriate psychology if one is to understand the apparently sudden transformation in Linlithgow's attitude. As soon as war had broken out he put the federal scheme in cold storage and directed his attention solely to the problem of the war.

The procedure by which India entered the war was constitutionally unimpeachable. Had federation been inaugurated, there would have been an organ of the government at the centre capable of giving a representative response to the Fascist challenge. The problem of what steps might have been taken, in the actual circumstances of 1939, to bring India into a more spontaneous association with the declaration of war has been the subject of much controversy. It would have been difficult for the Indian parties to retract their hostility to Fascism consistently shown in the nationalist platforms or the condemnation they had meted out to the 'Munich settlement' in 1938.

Linlithgow's subsequent consultations with the Indian leaders proved to be no substitute for consultation before the event, nor could they place any responsibility on the Indian parties. Yet it would be too simple to explain the constitutional impasse as the result of Linlithgow's failure to consult the Indian leaders before declaring war. It is extremely doubtful whether consultation with Congress leaders would have made any difference. Besides, it should not be forgotten that the initial reaction of Congress leaders, including Gandhi and Nehru, was to offer unconditional support to the Allies. They, however, changed their attitudes subsequently. In these circumstances it is little wonder that Linlithgow rapidly came to the conclusion that most Indian leaders were, to say the least, inconsistent if not untrustworthy. His interview with fifty-two Indian leaders certainly showed that they were severely divided among themselves. It was not until 1940 that Linlithgow's failure to consult them was used as an explanation for Congress's intransigence.

Linlithgow's appeal for unity and cooperation was turned down by the Congress, which refused to be associated with the war except on its own terms. It demanded a declaration of British war aims with special reference to India. The Moslem League, on the other hand, demanded that no declaration on the future of India should be made without its consent. The Congress still saw the communal problem as secondary and essentially a creation of the British, rather than as a factor in the nature of Indian society; and both Gandhi and Nehru rejected Jinnah's demand for coalition ministries, declaring that all such matters could be best settled by forming a representative constituent assembly, a proposal then rejected by Jinnah. Such were the rival and conflicting claims. The unfortunate chasm between the two major political parties in India at the moment of crisis gave proof of internal dissension and a valid reason for withholding the declaration asked for by the Congress.

The withdrawal of cooperation by the Congress was yet another step towards partition. If, instead of resigning, the Congress had utilized the pretext of the war to retrace its steps and offer to form a coalition with the Moslem League, both at the centre and in the provinces, it might not only have repaired the earlier damage, but would possibly also have been able to confront the British Government with a united front. But once the Congress resigned, Linlithgow was none too keen to have its members back in office except on his own terms which involved an agreement with the League on all outstanding issues.

It is surprising that Congress after surrendering power in 1939 should have failed to restore its position and assert itself. The British Government made a number of efforts in 1939, 1940 and 1942 to come to terms with the Congress, but each time Congress rejected them. Gandhi's authority, consecrated to the propagation of pacifism in its most extreme form, was given a new scope, and by a tragic paradox the Congress in the name of liberty contracted out of the resistance which the Allied countries were offering to the Fascist challenge. The withdrawal of the Congress ministries stranded the nationalist movement, at the very moment when it might have established in the most practical and cogent way all its legitimate claims upon the future, among the fruitless irresponsibilities of a political desert. At the same time it sharply increased the communal tension.

The pattern which Indian politics thus assumed at the beginning of the war was to remain unchanged in its main lines by subsequent developments. There were two periods at which it seemed possible that Congress aloofness from the war effort might be overcome - during the Battle of Britain in 1940, and at the time of the Japanese offensive towards the end of 1941. But on both occasions the Congress fought shy of rendering active help and the ultimate outcome was an intensification of Congress hostility to the British Government. After the first the Congress started the individual *satyagraha;* the second saw the launching of the 'Quit India' campaign. But neither the prospects of a Nazi victory nor the dangers of a Nipponese invasion softened the Hindu-Moslem antagonism.

After the fall of France, the Congress declared that it would be willing to take part in the defence of India provided her independence was immediately declared and a 'National Government' commanding the confidence of the central legislature was set up. The British response was the so-called 'August offer'. The proposals were a considerable improvement on the previous vague declarations, but there were too many checks and safeguards which made its acceptance difficult. There was hardly a sentence without qualification, so that the general impression was one of taking as much with one hand as was given with the other. A note of boldness or imagination was largely absent.

The Congress rejected the 'offer' and reverted to the leadership of Gandhi. Gandhi's initial instinct had been sound: he had offered unconditional support to the Allies. But his devotion to non-violence befogged his judgement. He now launched his symbolic *satyagraha.* His ill-conceived campaign not only resulted in the imprisonment of the Congress leaders, but also ruined goodwill and support in Britain and in the USA.

In the already complicated situation, Gandhi's steadfast adherence to pacifism created more confusion. Twice during this period the Congress abandoned non-violence and with it the formal leadership of Gandhi. And on both occasions when Gandhi was recalled, non-violence was again reinstated as the guiding principle of the Congress policy. It is a meandering series of incidents, difficult to comprehend in terms of any consistent policies. The only unsnapped thread running through it seems to be that Gandhi was acting as what he was, saint and politician at the same time, and that both he and the Congress, quite apart from whatever ideological professions were made from time to time, were at heart concerned, not so much with the morality of the use of violence in national defence, as with the effectiveness of the methods adopted to bring pressure on Britain. Easy transitions were made from one to another. The Congress ceased to swear by non-violence when the chances of negotiated settlement seemed bright. When it was necessary to frighten Britain, the services of Gandhi, with his emphasis on non violence, were requisitioned, for his message could harmonize with the anti-war mood of many people.

In 1942 the British War Cabinet attempted a fresh approach to solve the Indian deadlock. But the move was opposed by Linlithgow. He remained opposed to any attempt by the British Government to solicit the support of the political parties by making concessions under war-time pressures. He did not personally believe that the cooperation of the Congress leaders would make much difference in India's war effort, and he was confident that his government was capable of providing the necessary sinews of war. But his argument did not carry conviction. Churchill was under pressure from his Labour colleagues in the cabinet, and he could not ignore the growing desire of the Americans for a political settlement in India. Under these combined pressures, coupled with the threat of a Japanese invasion of India, Churchill somewhat reluctantly sent Cripps to India with a Cabinet plan to end the impasse.

The negotiations broke down because of the British refusal to concede the Congress demand for a 'National Government' a government which would function like a cabinet. There is no reason to doubt Azad's statement that, at the very first interview Cripps had talked of a 'National Government' functioning like a cabinet, and of the Viceroy's position becoming analogous to that of the king of Great Britain[1] a statement which Cripps never contradicted. Linlithgow's telegrams of February and March reveal that he was not opposed to the idea of a 'National Government'. Cripps had admitted that the Executive Council would 'approximate' to a cabinet. And even after the War Cabinet informed him on 6 April that the character of the

---

1 *Cmd. 6350*, Azad to Cripps, 11 Apr. 1942.

Viceroy's Council could not be changed,[1] Cripps used the phrase 'National Government' while referring to the new arrangement[2] Considering that he knew by now that the War Cabinet had rejected any such change, we might conclude that he might have hoped that once Congress accepted the offer without any prior definition of 'National Government', he could perhaps use his position in the War Cabinet to permit the Executive Council to function as a cabinet.

It is not clear why, at the last minute, the War Cabinet denied Cripps the role of a negotiator and retracted the idea of a 'National Government'. No definite answer is possible from the documents examined and a final verdict must await the publication of the private papers of Churchill and Amery.

By far the most serious criticism against Linlithgow has been concerned with his role during the Cripps mission. While the comment of Shiva Rao on this matter that Linlithgow simply enjoyed unlimited power is quite bizarre,[3] the most cogent criticism has been put forward by Professor Moore who endeavours to show that, along with Amery and Churchill, Linlithgow was responsible for sabotaging the Cripps mission.[4] It is not quite clear how Linlithgow, or the trio combined, could have done so. Cripps's offer was largely the handiwork of Attlee, and it is doubtful whether Attlee, given his strong position in the War Cabinet, would have allowed the mission to be sabotaged without even a murmur. Attlee was not only aware of Linlithgow's messages to Churchill and Amery, but was also a party to Churchill's telegram of 10 April which in effect dealt the *coup de grace* to the mission by withdrawing Cripps's plenipotentiary powers.[5] Moore's explanation that Attlee was precluded from coming to the rescue of his colleague owing to the 'obscurity of Cripps's intention' and a general 'confusion' is not convincing.[6]

It would be unfair to say that Linlithgow was hostile to Cripps's mission merely because of his disapproval of constitutional changes in the middle of the war. In fact his own 'constructive scheme' of 25

---

1 See L/PO/6/106, War Cabinet, Committee on India, I(42) 11th meeting, 6 Apr. 1942. IOR.

2 Cmd. 6350, Cripps to Azad, 7 Apr. 1942.

3 B. Shiva Rao writes: 'Linlithgow, after enjoying unrestrained power for six years, was not prepared to shed it at the bidding of Indian leaders'. *Modern Asian Studies*, V, no. 3, (July 1971) p. 273.

4 R.J. Moore, 'The Mystery of the Cripps Mission', *Journal of Commonwealth Political Studies*, XI, no. 3, (Nov. 1973) pp. 195-213.

5 See L/PO/6/106c, telegram from Churchill to Cripps, 10 April 1942. IOR.

6 Moore, 'The Mystery of Cripps Mission', p. 200.

February, which he had sent as an alternative to Churchill's proposed broadcast, was much more liberal and went further than Cripps's offer to meet the nationalist demands. It is, however, possible that Linlithgow's apparent hostility might have been the result of injured pride. In the past Linlithgow had been given to dominating his superiors, both Zetland and Amery, and he may have felt insulted when the War Cabinet not only decided on the declaration without consultation with the Viceroy, but also sent to India an emissary to negotiate a settlement over the Viceroy's head. This would suggest that the War Cabinet did not have sufficient confidence in Linlithgow: indeed the Attlee memorandum of 2 February 1942 makes no secret of that. Although there is no direct evidence, it seems probable that Linlithgow, unlike Wavell during the Cabinet mission in 1946, decided to remain indifferent and took no part in the negotiations. But this is quite different from accepting the charge that he deliberately sabotaged the mission.

The success of the mission, it might be argued, had been jeopardized at the very outset. In the first place no agreement had been reached between Linlithgow and the War Cabinet on the details of the policy. Nor was there, apparently, any understanding between the War Cabinet and Cripps upon the extent to which he might go in the way of concessions to meet the possible demands of the Indian leaders. Finally, while Cripps would negotiate the settlement, it would be for Linlithgow to implement it: but there was no understanding on the details of policy between these two authorities. The War Cabinet thus erred in sending an emissary to promote a policy which had not been fully agreed to by the Viceroy.

A decade ago most historians had little hesitation in blaming Gandhi for sabotaging the mission. Now that the trend has been reversed, it has almost become fashionable to lay the blame at the feet of the makers of imperial policy. In this case the scapegoat is, of course, Linlithgow. Historians would be better employed in looking for other more basic causes rather than attempt to 'fix' responsibilities and find 'scapegoats'.

There is little doubt that, even with the Japanese fleet in the Bay of Bengal and Burma already under enemy occupation, the Congress leaders (with few exceptions like Azad, Nehru and Rajagopalachari) were more anxious to secure immediate power than to organize 'a people's war'. A promise about the future was not good enough for them. Linlithgow was reluctant to make a constitutional declaration from a position of weakness. He was not fussed about the post-war changes, and his only concern was to ensure an Allied victory.

Political concessions in such circumstances, he thought, were dangerous. Any concession to the Congress would alienate the princes and the Moslem League. It would not significantly assist the war effort nor would it put a united India behind the British.

The Congress, however, erred in rejecting the Cripps offer; in doing so it took the country yet another step towards partition. The Cripps offer had provided an opportunity for the Congress to return to power and enter into some sort of partnership with the League without in any way compromising its principles, at the same time putting an end to the government's reliance on the League. The Congress probably failed to realize that the Cripps offer was perhaps the last opportunity to secure a free and a united India. If the Congress had accepted the offer, the League would presumably have followed suit. If a composite government had been formed in 1942 and worked to defend the country against invasion, it is possible that many of the differences between the Congress and the League might have been ironed out - cooperation in a common endeavour might have forged bonds of friendship. The 'non-accession clause', while its inclusion was necessary to bring in the Moslem League, would not have in itself permitted the secession of Moslem majority provinces from the Indian Union. The process was far too complicated: the League would have needed overwhelming support from the Moslems in Bengal and the Punjab to achieve it. This support it did not seem to possess in 1942. However, 'the non-accession clause' proved fatal to India's unity when the Cripps offer was turned down. Subsequently the League was able to claim that the British Government had conceded in principle the right of the Moslems to keep aloof from the Indian Union. This the British Government could neither deny nor retract.

After the failure of the Cripps mission, Gandhi's pacifism took on a flavour of cynicism. With the Japanese threatening India, he decided to launch a movement which, he claimed, would end the deadlock and enable India to defend herself against foreign aggression. It was a miscalculation and one more deplorable perversion of that power of leadership which, rightly directed, might have set India on the forward march. Gandhi's strength lay in the fact that he was the most competent organizer of the party. The fact that he was as irreplaceable in that capacity as any man could be, compelled deference to his views But for the first time since 1920 Gandhi's leadership was coming und challenge. He had to do something tangible if he was to ward off .ne growing influence of Subhas Bose and the 'extremists': he was cornered in a *cul-de-sac.* Obsessed with a belief in his almost divine role as the saviour of India, Gandhi intended to lead India to freedom at quick march even if he had to use means which were a negation of all he had previously stood for. In a bid to maintain his position Gandhi adopted the slogans of the revolutionaries and launched the 'Quit India' rebellion.

Faced with an external threat, the government refused to put up with internal rebellion and locked up all the Congress leaders for the duration of the war. In the absence of the Congress from the political scene, Jinnah built up massive support for 'Pakistan', thus driving the last nail into the coffin of Indian unity. So great was Jinnah's success that Gandhi, after his release from detention in 1944, was compelled to discuss with him a solution to the deadlock on the explicit basis of 'Pakistan'.

It has been maintained in this study that it was during Linlithgow's Viceroyalty that the political demand for 'Pakistan' had its early developments. The period 1936-43 produced developments of great significance for the future of Moslem India. It was during this period that the Moslem League emerged as the most important party representing the communal interests of the Moslems. It was then, though there were rumblings earlier, that the political and religious themes of modern Pakistan fused together. In 1936 the Moslem League was not very important in terms either of popular support or of representative character: in the elections held that year it had polled fewer than five per cent of the Moslem votes cast. Initially the League had more adherents in the Moslem minority provinces, but by the end of the period it had captured the Moslem majority provinces of Bengal and the Punjab. It was only when these two provinces came under the sway of the Moslem League that 'Pakistan' became a possibility. The feeling of Moslem separatism had already existed before 1936. Thereafter Moslem alienation gathered strength, but more importantly it gained an organizational form. The failure in the 1936 elections and the experience of Congress rule in the provinces were instrumental in bringing about the organization of separatism. And still more important were the exigencies of the war which drove the British to treat the League as a counterweight to the Congress opposition.

With Britain under attack, Linlithgow's personal responsibility at the head of the British-Indian Empire was enormous. As long as the Congress ministries were in office, Linlithgow could not ignore them. The Congress controlled eight provinces and had the power to interfere with the war effort if it so decided. By resigning the Congress surrendered its bargaining power. With the Congress refusing to cooperate, Linlithgow sought the support of the Moslem League and discouraged any move on the part of the Congress to return to power save on his own terms. Jinnah was the natural choice for Linlithgow to turn to, as he had been aware that Jinnah would be willing to collaborate.

Jinnah was quick to recognize the advantage of collaboration with the British. Linlithgow, who prior to the war was inclined to regard the Moslem League as a minority party, now reciprocated Jinnah's gesture. He began to impress upon the War Cabinet the importance of giving added weight to the point of view of the Moslem League. In his statement of October 1939, he implicitly accepted the League's claim to speak on behalf of Moslem India while denying the representative character of the Congress. The Viceroy conveniently ignored the earlier election results.

During this period Linlithgow continued to emphasize communal discord and pleaded for according special treatment to the Moslem League. Zetland, however, felt that the refusal of the Moslems to be a party to any self-government in India was a negative approach. In order to be successful, he argued, their demands would have to indicate the terms on which they would be prepared to participate in the government. Both Linlithgow and Zetland urged the Moslem League to put forward 'concrete proposals' to counteract the Congress demand for immediate independence and a constituent assembly to frame a constitution for India. While Jinnah hesitated to commit himself on the constitutional issue, he could not procrastinate for long.

To ward off the reproach that it had no 'concrete proposal', the Moslem League put forward the demand for the partition of India in March 1940. There is no direct evidence to suggest that the demand for 'Pakistan' had been made in response to Linlithgow's persistent request for 'constructive proposals'. But in view of earlier discussions between Linlithgow and Zetland such a possibility cannot be ruled out. The Moslem League resolution, apparently brought much relief to Linlithgow as it provided an effective reply to the Congress's insistence on immediate independence.

The Moslem League had perhaps put forward the 'Pakistan' proposal, vague as it was, more as a bargaining counter than as a demand to which it was really committed. It has been claimed that if the British had made it clear at the very outset that they would not countenance the 'Pakistan' demand, it might have petered out. Apart from the uncertainty of that supposition, it is suggested here that it would have been impolitic for the British to announce such a refusal. The refusal of the Congress to cooperate in the war effort had virtually compelled Linlithgow to renounce the weapon of imperial settlement in his need to cultivate the Moslems' support: the Congress was not only non-cooperating but also threatening civil disobedience. It could hardly be expected that in the circumstances the British would alienate the support of the Moslems by rejecting their demand out of hand. Such a rejection might have also antagonized the Punjab Moslems who constituted an important element in the Indian Army. Moreover, the British were precluded from doing so by their repeated assurances to the minorities that their wishes and interests would not be lightly overridden. Thus the idea of 'Pakistan' which was rejected in 1934 as a 'students' chimera' now gained strength rapidly. In less than five months after the passing of the Lahore resolution the Moslem League had secured an indirect endorsement of its drastic demand: the Viceroy's declaration of August 1940 virtually gave the League the power to veto any constitutional advance. In less than two years the official recognition of the theoretical validity of 'Pakistan' was admitted in the 'non-accession clause' of the Cripps offer. By sheer tenacity and refusal to compromise, Jinnah made the constitutional position almost intractable. His price for settlement had progressively risen. It had begun with keeping separate electorates in 1916, risen to 'Fourteen Points' in 1929, to composite ministries in 1937, fifty per cent of the seats in the Viceroy's Council in 1939, and finally in 1940 the partition of India.

British policy during the period was largely guided by the necessities of the war. It cannot be denied that Linlithgow had, since September 1939, refused 'to make a sincere attempt to bring Congress and the League together',[1] and that it was an 'extraordinarily short-sighted' policy to have accorded Jinnah a position of equality in negotiations with the Congress leaders so soon after his dismal failure at the elections.[2] But it would only be fair to keep in mind the fact that Congress, refusing cooperation and withdrawing its provincial ministries, was forcing Linlithgow to veer towards the Moslem League. 'The Government has no love for the League', wrote a Congress leader, 'less for its leaders. For them the League and its leaders are enemy's enemy, the common enemy being the national forces represented by the Congress'.[3] The Moslem League had little sympathy for the British, but still less did it wish the British to be replaced by the

---

[1] Moore, 'The Stopgap Viceroy', *South Asian Review,* VII, no. 1 (Oct. 1973), p. 57.

[2] D.A. Low, Review of J. Glendevon, *The Viceroy at Bay, South Asian Review,* IV, no. 3, (April 1971), p. 257.

[3] J.B. Kripalini, 'League and the War Effort', *National Herald,* 5 Oct. 1941.

Congress. By using this common denominator of hostility to the Congress, Linlithgow and his advisers sought to build a British-Moslem League alliance. But from this one cannot conclude that Linlithgow pursued a premeditated policy of divide and rule. While Linlithgow was assuredly influenced by the advantages to Britain of the political divisions between the Hindus and Moslems, it would be far from correct to say, as Professor Nanda does in a study of partition, that 'the sins of Linlithgow were visited on Wavell and Mountbatten'.[1] This would imply that Linlithgow had followed a consistent policy of fostering division. Evidence, however, points in a different direction. The British were never complete masters of the circumstances in which they were placed. They occupied the apex, but the other two points of the triangle were held by the Congress and the League. Although after the outbreak of the war, some British officials were aware of the advantages to Britain of the political division between the two major communities, the interpretation which has them creating that division oversimplifies the determinants of policy and is unconvincing as an explanation of Hindu-Moslem rivalry and the subsequent partition of the country. The truth is that while Linlithgow did not want to prolong British rule by a 'divide and rule' policy, he could not for obvious reasons agree to 'Quit India' in the middle of the war. Faced with the problems of the prosecution of the war, Linlithgow could hardly be expected to take long term views or devise a policy best suited to India's future needs. It was a question of survival, and Linlithgow was not prepared to look beyond it. The measures which he adopted were more in the nature of expedients to tide over the difficulties created by the war, than definite policies tailored to India's requirements.

What Linlithgow may, however, be blamed for is his failure to bridge the chasm that had been opened between the Moslem League and the Congress. He made no effort to awaken the Congress leaders to the imperative need of early reconciliation with the Moslem League if Indian unity were to be preserved. The Moslem League had issued several intemperate reports alleging Congress oppression of Moslems. Though Linlithgow had conducted a departmental enquiry and was satisfied that the allegations were largely baseless, he yet refused to reprimand the Moslem League or allay the misgivings of the public. Linlithgow realized that as long as the two parties quarrelled among themselves, the government would be spared the danger of facing a joint demand of any sort.

The British had laboriously built the unity of India. But what they

[1] B.R. Nanda, 'Nehru, the Indian National Congress and Partition of India', in Philips and Wainwright (eds.), Partition of India, p. 185.

failed to realize was that a constructive policy was essential if a plural society were to become a single nation. Only economic and social development could produce parties that would cut across communal lines. And, indeed, only a policy of cooperative development could have made Britain's desire for Indian unity a reality. But in Britain the doctrine of laissez-faire was still prevalent and the idea of planned development came only in the last days of the Raj. Though Montagu and Chelmsford had stressed the need for industrialization and the funding of development schemes, nothing tangible was done. It was only after the abortive Cripps mission that a programme of economic development was suggested by Cripps. In May 1942 Amery developed Cripps's idea with a plan for launching a series of five year plans after the war.[1] But these schemes came too late and nothing was done about them. Meanwhile economic rivalry had combined with religious rivalry to threaten the unity of the country.

At the same time it must be admitted that the Congress leaders had failed to adopt a clearcut policy. While they had a definite nationalist goal, they were confused about the means. Their confusion of purpose was best demonstrated in their handling of the communal situation. Consequently, the Congress found itself pushed from one tight corner to another, each seemingly more disastrous than the last. The Congress were committed to the unity of India, yet through errors of judgement and impatience to hasten independence they were instrumental in bringing about partition.

Gandhi succeeded in securing for the nationalist movement the popular support which he considered essential for bringing pressure on the British to abdicate their hold on India. It may, however, be suggested that the British could perhaps have been persuaded to leave India just as quickly if the Congress had stuck to constitutional methods and had cooperated during the war instead of resorting to non-cooperation and civil disobedience. The intention of the British with regard to India's future had been made clear in August 1917: the gradual development of self-governing institutions with a view to the progressive realization of responsible government in India. After that date successive British governments had slowly taken India towards that goal. The parliamentary debate on the principle of India's early advance to independence had been settled once and for all with the 1935 Act. The provincial part of the Act, despite its numerous 'checks and balances', had shown, when it came into operation, that it had 'teeth' and was a significant advance towards self-government in the provinces. Similarly, the federal part of the Act, even after allowing

---

1   Mss. Eur. F.125/11, Amery to Linlithgow, 27 May 1942. IOL.

for its many undesirable features, might well have been a major step towards the complete transfer of power. In support of this argument it has been pointed out that it was the 1935 Act, with few amendments, which formed the basis for the transfer of power to the two dominions, India and Pakistan, in 1947. It was the same Act which continued to serve as the interim constitution of India and Pakistan up to 1950 and 1956 respectively when they adopted their own constitutions. And even these new constitutions bore remarkable similarities to the 1935 Act: no fewer than 250 Sections of the 1935 Act were retained intact in the Indian constitution of 1950. Unfortunately it was not realized at the time that, unlike the previous Government of India Acts, the 1935 Act did not provide for a periodic revision of its provisions, but it was hoped that it would have an organic growth and perhaps it could have been modified according to need. Had the federal provisions of the Act been implemented, the independence of India would most probably have come about no later than it did, but partition might have been avoided. The failure to federate was the most decisive dent in the unity of India.

Although the deadlock remained unresolved during the period of Linlithgow's Viceroyalty, there were significant constitutional changes towards an eventual transfer of power. The Executive Council was expanded from a predominantly official and European body of seven into a body of fourteen of which the majority (eleven) were Indians drawn from all the communities. For the first time in the history of Indo-British relations the Executive Council had a non-official and Indian majority. This was a significant advance. The reorganized Council's non-official majority wielded considerable influence in the formulation of policies and were not the 'yes men' of Congress's allegiance. Although the Viceroy's veto remained, Linlithgow established a convention under which the Council enjoyed, as nearly as possible in the circumstances, the *de facto* status of a cabinet. Several members of the Council have testified that Linlithgow never once overruled it.[1] He handled the Council extremely adroitly and succeeded in making it work as a united body, responsible collectively for its decisions. It is significant that during the Congress 'rebellion' of 1942 the decision to arrest the Congress leaders was unanimously approved by the Indian members of the Council - the only two absentees being the European members.

At the same time the international status of India was greatly enhanced by her representation in the War Cabinet in London and the Pacific Council. She had her representatives in Washington, Chungking

1 See above pp. 169-70.

and on the Middle East Council in Cairo. India was also one of the signatories of the United Nations Charter.

Despite Congress's refusal to cooperate, Linlithgow successfully organized India's war effort. The Moslems, the Sikhs, the other minorities and the princes contributed significantly in men, money and material. After Dunkirk it was clear that India must face East, rather than West, and must cooperate with the other Allied powers east of Suez in meeting military needs. Linlithgow rapidly expanded the Indian department of supply, and the founding of the Eastern Supply Group was largely due to his initiative. This made a major contribution to the war effort and remedied the deficiencies of a country little prepared for the perils which were to confront it. In October 1941 a National Defence Council was set up bringing together representatives of British India and the Indian states. By 1943, when Linlithgow's term finally ended, over two million volunteers had enlisted in the army alone. Linlithgow had convincingly demonstrated that India's war effort could not be withheld by Congress non-cooperation: the main constraints being supply of arms, ammunition and training facilities. It was his outstanding achievement to have maintained public morale from 1939 to 1943 in the face of Congress hostility and acute international political difficulties and of an unbroken series of military reverses approaching ever nearer to the subcontinent.

BIOGRAPHICAL NOTES

AGA KHAN III, AGA SULTAN MOHAMMAD SHAH (1877-1957): Spiritual leader of the Ismaili Moslems. He was the founder member of the Moslem League and its President from 1907 to 1914.

DR B. R. AMBEDKAR (1891-1956): Leader of the Harijans; Member of the Viceroy's Executive Council, 1942-6; Law Minister in the Government of India, 1947-51.

RT. HON. L. C. M. S. AMERY (1873-1955): First Lord of the Admiralty, 1922-3; Colonial Secretary, 1924-9; Secretary of State for India, 1940-5.

JOHN FRANCIS ASHLEY, LORD ERSKINE (1895-1953): Assistant Government Whip in House of Commons, 1932; Governor of Madras 1934-40.

MAULANA ABUL KALAM AZAD (1888-1958): Nationalist Moslem and a leader of the Congress; president of the Congress, 1923 and 1940-6; Minister of Education in the Government of India from 1947 to 1958.

VINOBA BHAVE (b. 1895): Disciple of Gandhi; in the 1950's started *Bhoodan,* a movement for the donation of land to the poor.

THE NAWAB OF *BHOPAL,* SIR HAMIDULLAH KHAN (1894-   ): Chancellor of the Chamber of Princes, 1931-2 and 1944-7.

THE MAHARAJA OF *BIKANER,* SIR GANGA SINGH (1880-1943): India's representative in the Imperial Cabinet, 1942-3.

RT. HON. R. A. BUTLER, BARON OF SAFFRON WALDEN (b. 1902): Under Secretary of State for India, 1932-7; Secretary for Foreign Affairs, 1963-64; Deputy Prime Minister, 1962-4; Master of Trinity College, Cambridge since 1965.

THE NAWAB OF CHHATARI, AHMAD SA'ID KHAN (b. 1888): Minister of Industries, UP, 1923-25; Home Member UP, 1926-33; acting Governor of UP, 1928 and 1933; Prime Minister of Hyderabad 1947; leader of the Zamindar party and the Moslem League.

SIR STAFFORD CRIPPS (1889-1952): Lawyer Q.C. and prominent member of the British Labour party. British Ambassador in Moscow, 1940-2; member of the War Cabinet, 1942; Minister of Aircraft Production, 1942-5; President of the Board of Trade, 1945-7; Chancellor of the Exchequer, 1947-50.

LIONEL CURTIS (1872-1955): Civil servant in South Africa; Fellow of All Souls College, Oxford; Adviser on Irish Affairs, Colonial Office, 1921-4.

JOHN L. DUNDAS, 2nd MARQUESS OF ZETLAND (1876-1961): Governor of Bombay, 1917-22; Secretary of State for India, 1935-40.

SIR HARRY HAIG (1881-1956): Joined ICS in 1905; Private Secretary to the Viceroy, 1925; Home Secretary 1926-30; Home Member, 1932-4; Governor of UP, 1934-9.

SIR SAMUEL HOARE, VISCOUNT TEMPLEWOOD (1880-1959): Secretary of State for Air 1922-3 and 1924-9; Secretary of State for India 1931-5 during which he piloted the Government of India Bill, 1934; Foreign Secretary, 1935; Home Secretary, 1937-9; Lord Privy Seal, 1939-40; British Ambassador in Spain, 1940-44.

A. K. FAZLUL HUQ (1873-1962): Leader of the Krishak Proja Party; President of the Moslem League, 1916-21; Chief Minister of Bengal, 1937-43; Chief Minister and Governor of East Pakistan after 1947.

SIR ABKAR HYADRI (1869-1942): President of the Hyderabad State Executive Council, 1937-41.

PHILIP KERR, 11th MARQUESS OF LOTHIAN (1882-1940): Editor of *Round Table,* 1916-21; Parliamentary Under-Secretary for India, 1931-2; Chairman, Indian Franchise Committee, 1932; Ambassador to Washington, 1939-40.

CHAUDHURI KHALIQUZZAMAN (1889-1973): At first a prominent Congress leader; moved to the Moslem League in 1937; after 1947 was the governor of East Pakistan.

SIR SIKANDER HYAT KHAN (1892-1942): Revenue Member of the Punjab Government, 1930-5; Deputy Governor of the Reserve Bank of India, 1935-7; Chief minister and leader of the Unionist Party in the Punjab, 1937-42.

SIR COURTENAY LATIMER (1911): Joined ICS in 1934 and IPS in 1939; Agent General Western Indian States.

A. C. LOTHIAN (1887-1962): Resident in Rajputana, 1937-42 and in Hyderabad, 1942-46; Author of *Kingdoms of Yesterday* (1951).

EDWIN MONTAGU (1879-1924): Secretary of State for India, 1917-22; responsible for Montagu-Chelmsford reforms, 1919.

K. M. MUNSHI (1891-1971): Bombay Congress leader; Home Minister of Bombay 1937-9; Minister of Food and Agriculture in the Government of India, 1950-2; joined the Swatantra party.

SARDAR VALLABHBHAI PATEL (1875-1950): President of the Congress, 1931; member of the Interim government, 1946-7; Minister for Home, States, Information and Broadcasting, 1947-50.

RAJENDRA PRASAD (1884-1963): President of the Congress, 1934, 1939 and 1947-8; President of the Constituent Assembly of India, 1946-50; President of India, 1950-62.

CHAKRAVARTI RAJAGOPALACHARI (1878-1972): Madras Congress leader and for many years member of the Congress Working Committee; chief minister of Madras, 1937-9; Governor of West Bengal, 1947-8; Governor General of India, 1948-50; Central Minister, 1950-1; founder of the right wing Swatantra Party.

SIR TEJ BAHADUR SAPRU (1875-1949): Lawyer and leader of the Indian Liberal Foundation. Law Member of the Viceroy's Executive Council, 1921; Member of the Nehru Committee, 1928; attended the Round Table conference, 1930.

S. SATYAMURTI (1889-1943): Madras Congress leader; Member of Madras council 1923-30; member of the Central Assembly, 1935-43.

EDWARD FREDERICK LINDLEY WOOD, LORD IRWIN, EARL OF HALIFAX (1881-1950): Under-Secretary for Colonies, 1921-2; President of the Board of Education, 1922-4; Minister for Agriculture, 1924-5; Viceroy of India, 1926-31; Foreign Secretary, 1938-40; British Ambassador in Washington, 1941-6.

SIR FRANCIS WYLIE (1891-   ): Joined ICS in 1914 and IPS 1919. Resident in Japipur; Governor of Central Provinces, 1938-40; Political adviser to the Viceroy, 1940-1 and 1943-5; Governor of the United Provinces, 1945-7.

SIR MUHAMMAD ZAFRULLAH KHAN (b. 1893): Member of the Viceroy's Council, 1935-41; Foreign minister of Pakistan, 1947-54; Judge of the International Court of Justice at the Hague, 1954-61.

LIST OF UNPUBLISHED SOURCES

OFFICIAL

Cabinet Office Papers, Cab. 23. Minutes until 1939.

Cabinet Office Papers. Cab. 24 - Memoranda.

Cabinet Office Papers. Cab. 65 - Minutes of the War Cabinet Meetings, 1939-43.

Cabinet Office Papers. Cab. 66/67 - War Cabinet Memoranda.

Prime Minister's Office, Prem 1 - correspondence.

Prime Minister's Office. Prem 4 - papers.

India Office Records, Economic and Overseas Department Files.

India Office Records, External Department Collections.

India Office Records, Financial Department Collections.

India Office Records, Governors Report.

India Office Records, Information Department Files.

India Office Records, Political and Judicial Department Files.

India Office Records, Political and Judicial Department, Transfer of Power Papers.

UNOFFICIAL

1. *COLLECTION OF PAPERS*

Baldwin Papers
Cambridge University Library.

Brabourne Papers. IOL

Arthur Jules Dash Papers. IOL

Erskine Papers. IOL

Haig Papers. IOL

Hallett Papers. IOL

Linlithgow Papers. IOL

Reid Papers. IOL

Sir Tej Bahadur Sapru Papers.
IOL (on microfilm).

Sir Louis Stuart Papers.
Bodleian Mss. Eng. Hist. C. 627.

Wilberforce - Bell Paper. IOL

Templewood Papers. IOL

Zetland Papers. IOL

2. *UNPUBLISHED DISSERTATIONS AND MANUSCRIPTS*

Gopal Krishna,
Indian National Congress, 1918-1923
(Oxford D.Phil. Thesis, 1960).

A. F. McC. Madden
'Not for Export; Some Evidence and Consideration of the
Westminster Model Overseas from the Twelfth to Twentieth Century'.
Forthcoming.

D. J. H. Page,
Prelude to Partition: All India Moslem Politics 1920-1932.
(Oxford. D.Phil. 1974).

Gyanendra Pandey,
The Indian National Congress and Political Mobilization in the
United Provinces. 1926-1934.
(Oxford, D.Phil. Thesis. 1974).

H. S. Suhrawardy, *Political Memoirs*
(Mss.). By kind permission of Dr Kamal Hossain.

Sir Louis Stuart, *A Proposed Dominion*
Bodleian. Mss. Eng. Hist. c. 627.

Professor Edward Thompson, 'Report on India'.
(Mss) December 1939. Submitted to the Trustees of the Rhodes
Trust, Oxford. (By kind permission of Sir Edgar Trevor Williams).

INDEX

formulate 'concrete' proposals, 115-6; attitude towards demand for Pakistan, 119-21, 129, 236-9; makes contingency plans for war, 132; declaration of war, 132-4; opposed to definition of war aims, 140-1; meets leaders, 141; statement of October 1939, 141-2; not anxious to have Congress back in office, 145-8; speech at Orient Club, 148-9; criticism by 'diehards', 149; meets Jinnah and Gandhi, 149-50; advocates a policy of waiting, 147, 148, 151-3; August offer (1940), 156, 158; freedom of speech, 161-2; plan for crushing Congress rejected by Cabinet, 164-6; rejects recommendations of non-party leaders, 169; expands Executive Council, 169, 206-7, 241; creates National Defence Council, 169, 241; takes a legalistic attitude, 170; convenes Eastern Groups conference, 170, 242; on India's strategic importance, 174; views on Indian situation, 177-8; critical of Churchill's plan, 180-2; submits alternative plans, 181-2; opposes Cripps's offer, 184; threatens to resign, 185; role during Cripps Mission, 197-202; makes effort to solve Indian impasse, 206-7; and 'Quit India' campaign, 220-2; end of Viceroyalty, 223; attitude changes after outbreak of war, 229-30; alleged sabotage of Cripps Mission, 233-4; reluctant to make political concessions, 234-5; other references to, 13, 14, 45-46, 50, 53, 54, 55, 57, 63, 67

Hopetoun, seventeenth Earl of, first Marquess of Linlithgow, 2

Husain, Dr. Zakir, 99

Huq, A.K. Fazlul, 35, 46; and Moslem League, 51, 96, 224; report on Moslem grievances, 97; and Pakistan resolution, 118, 123; meets Cripps, 186, 244

Hyat Khan, Sardar Sir Sikander, 23, 35; cooperates with Moslem League, 52, 96; pact with Jinnah, 96; and Linlithgow, 115; and Pakistan, 118, 122-3; death of, 128; meets Cripps, 185

Hyderabad, 61, 62; Nizam of, 83

Hydari, Sir Akbar, 63, 244

Imperial Council of Agricultural Research, 3

Independent Moslems, 35

Independent Workers Parties, 23

India Empire Society, 85

India League, 114

India Office, 16, 36, 41, 84, 105; unhelpful to federation, 57, 85, 88; meetings at, 107-8 Amery enters, 151

Indian army, Linlithgow's concern for, 152; Congress's attitude towards, 154-5

Indian Christians, 76, 98

Indian Civil Service, 5, 31

Indian Defence Advisory Committee, 153

Indian Mutiny, 95